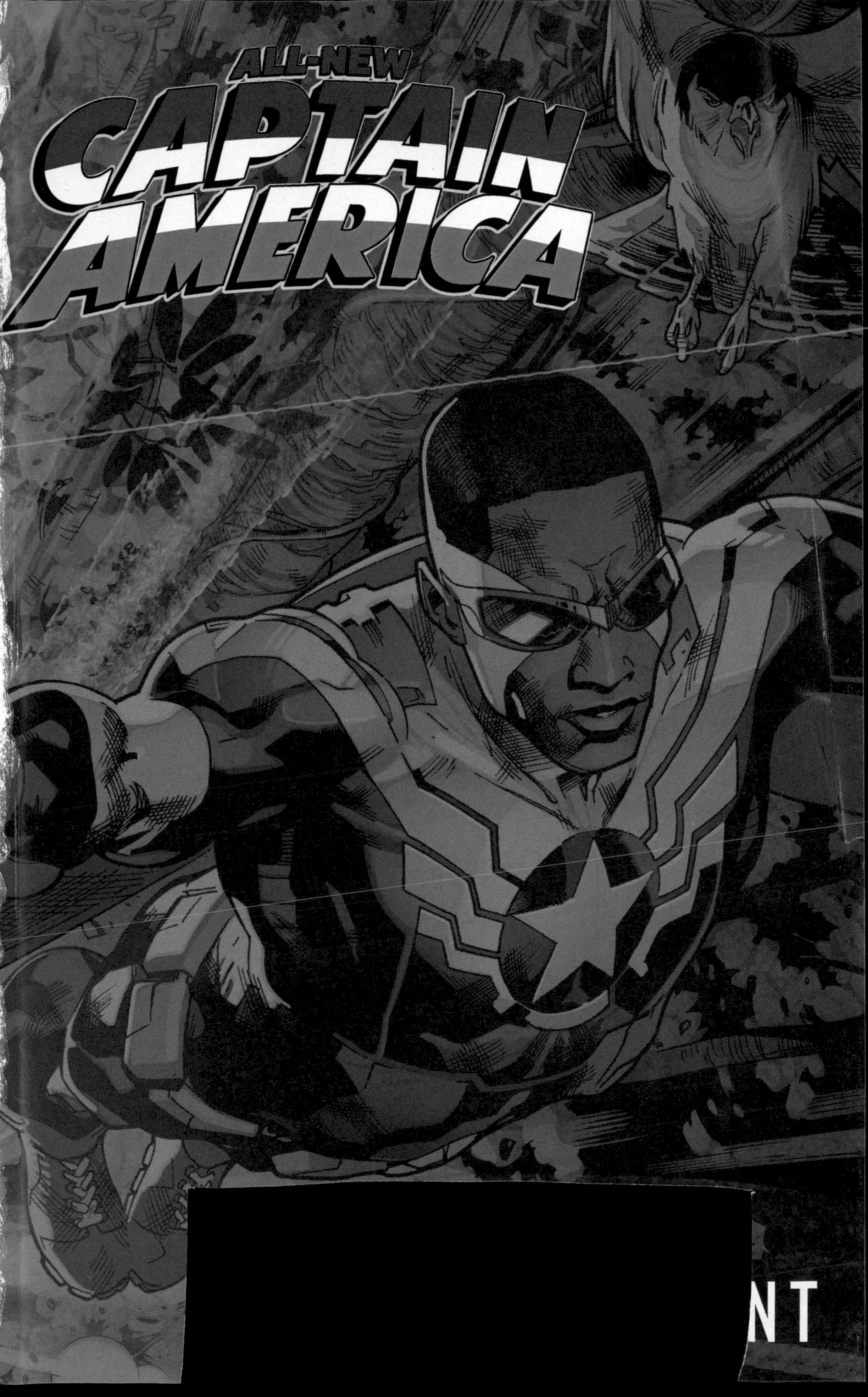
ALL-NEW
CAPTAIN AMERICA
[redacted]

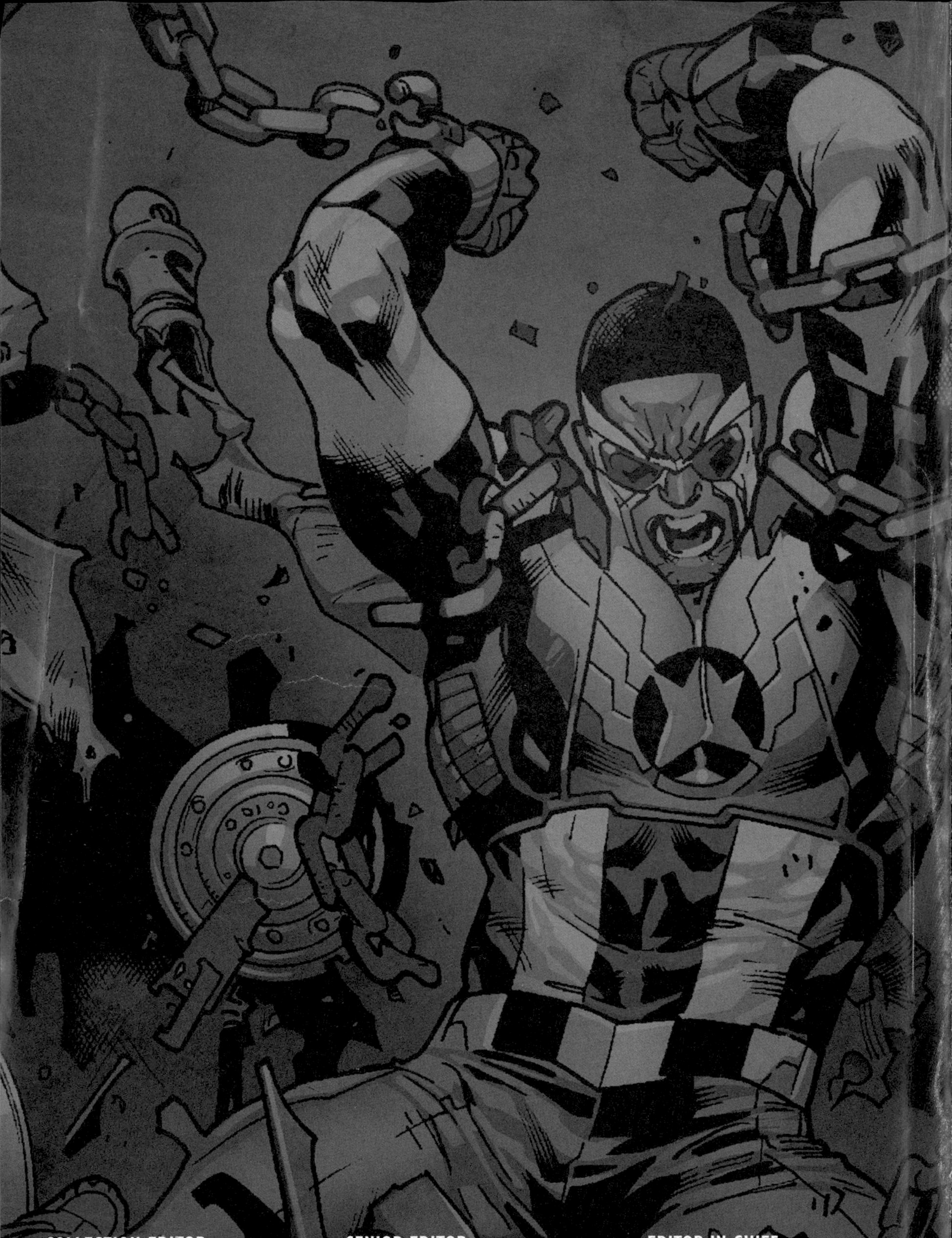

COLLECTION EDITOR
JENNIFER GRÜNWALD

SENIOR EDITOR,
SPECIAL PROJECTS

EDITOR IN CHIEF
AXEL ALONSO

ASSISTANT [redacted] ATIVE OFFICER
SARAH [redacted] **ESADA**

ASSOCIAT [redacted]
ALEX S [redacted] **CKLEY**

EDITOR, S [redacted] PRODUCER
MARK D [redacted] **NE**

NO LONGER ABLE TO WIELD THE SHIELD, STEVE ROGERS PASSED THE MANTLE OF CAPTAIN AMERICA TO HIS LONGTIME FRIEND AND COLLEAGUE, SAM WILSON, A.K.A. THE FALCON!

ALL-NEW CAPTAIN AMERICA

HYDRA ASCENDANT

WRITER
RICK REMENDER

PENCILER
STUART IMMONEN

INKER
WADE VON GRAWBADGER

COLORISTS
MARTE GRACIA
WITH EDUARDO NAVARRO (#1)
& DONO SANCHEZ ALMARA (#3)

LETTERER
VC'S JOE CARAMAGNA

COVER ART
STUART IMMONEN,
WADE VON GRAWBADGER
& MARTE GRACIA

ASSISTANT EDITORS
JAKE THOMAS
& ALANNA SMITH

EDITOR
TOM BREVOORT

CAPTAIN AMERICA CREATED BY JOE SIMON & JACK KIRBY

ALL-NEW CAPTAIN AMERICA VOL. 1: HYDRA ASCENDANT. Contains material originally published in magazine form as ALL-NEW CAPTAIN AMERICA #1-6. First printing 2015. ISBN# 978-0-7851-9376-0. Published by MARVEL WORLDWIDE, INC., a subsidiary of MARVEL ENTERTAINMENT, LLC. OFFICE OF PUBLICATION: 135 West 50th Street, New York, NY 10020. Copyright © 2015 MARVEL No similarity between any of the names, characters, persons, and/or institutions in this magazine with those of any living or dead person or institution is intended, and any such similarity which may exist is purely coincidental. Printed in the U.S.A. ALAN FINE, President, Marvel Entertainment; DAN BUCKLEY, President, TV, Publishing and Brand Management; JOE QUESADA, Chief Creative Officer; TOM BREVOORT, SVP of Publishing; DAVID BOGART, SVP of Operations & Procurement, Publishing; C.B. CEBULSKI, VP of International Development & Brand Management; DAVID GABRIEL, SVP Print, Sales & Marketing; JIM O'KEEFE, VP of Operations & Logistics; DAN CARR, Executive Director of Publishing Technology; SUSAN CRESPI, Editorial Operations Manager; ALEX MORALES, Publishing Operations Manager; STAN LEE, Chairman Emeritus. For information regarding advertising in Marvel Comics or on Marvel.com, please contact Jonathan Rheingold, VP of Custom Solutions & Ad Sales, at jrheingold@marvel.com. For Marvel subscription inquiries, please call 800-217-9158. Manufactured between 4/24/2015 and 6/8/2015 by R.R. DONNELLEY, INC., SALEM, VA, USA.

10 9 8 7 6 5 4 3 2 1

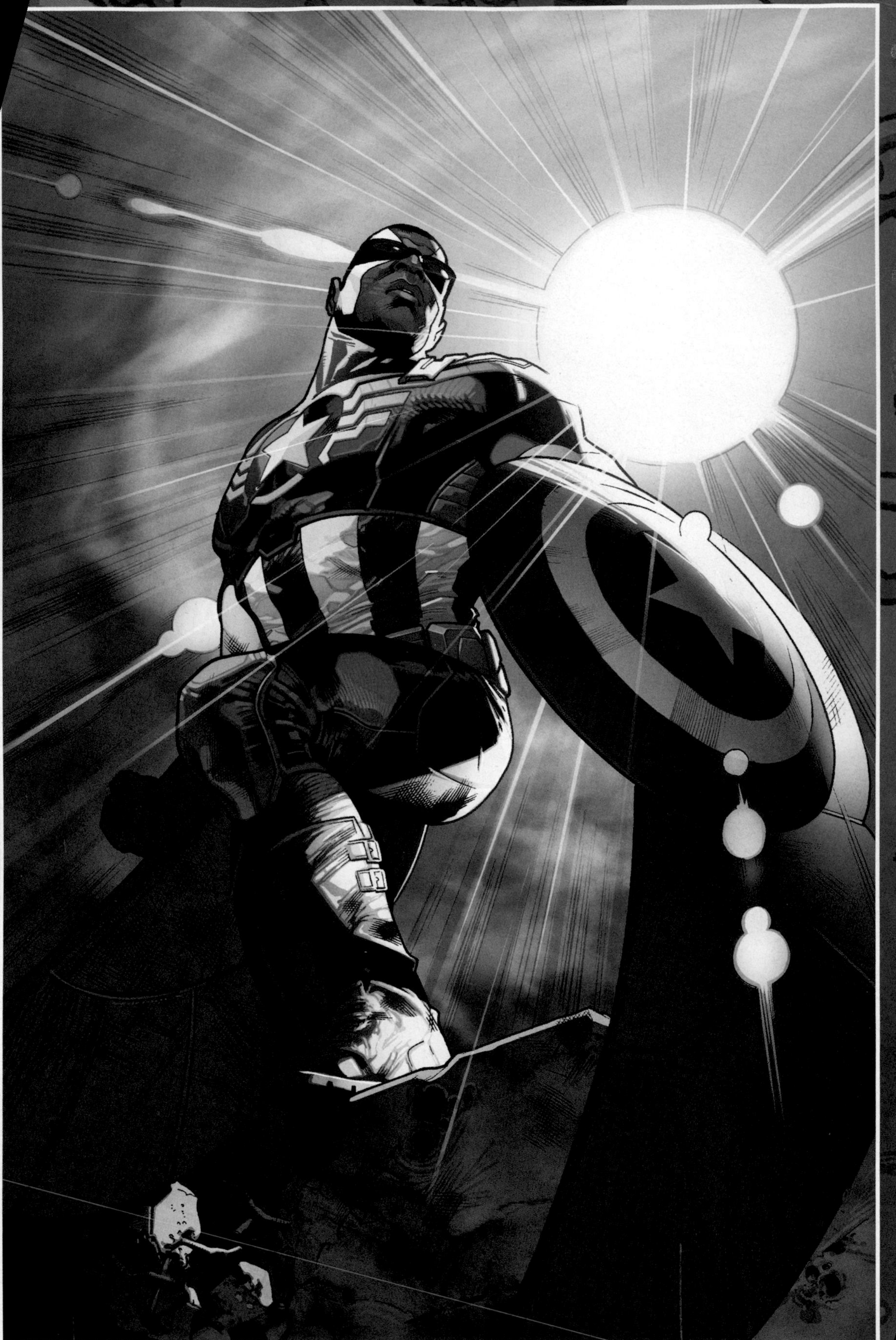

ONE

I CAN STILL HEAR MY FATHER'S SERMONS.

PEOPLE CAME FOR MILES TO LISTEN-- THE MOST RESPECTED MINISTER IN HARLEM.

I STILL HEAR HIS **UNCOMPROMISED** FAITH IN HIS FELLOW MAN...

...HIS **CERTAINTY** OF A BETTER TOMORROW.

BY THE TIME I WAS FOURTEEN, I'D SEEN ENOUGH UGLINESS IN THE WORLD, I THOUGHT HE WAS A HOPELESS DREAMER.

BUT WHILE I DIDN'T SHARE HIS FAITH IN PEOPLE...

...I **WORSHIPPED** HIM ALL THE SAME.

HE GAVE PEOPLE A REASON TO **HOPE.**

A REASON TO BE **BETTER.**

HE LIVED AS HE DIED.

GUNNED DOWN STOPPING A FIGHT.

WHEN **GOD** TOOK MOM A YEAR LATER, IT NEARLY BROKE ME.

SHOT BY A MUGGER A BLOCK FROM OUR APARTMENT.

I WANTED TO LASH OUT--PAY THE WORLD BACK FOR WHAT IT HAD TAKEN FROM US.

BUT I **COULDN'T.**

I HEARD DAD'S VOICE **TOO** CLEARLY.

HIS SERMONS LIVED ON IN ME.

A MILLION SUNDAYS WORTH OF HIS DREAMS.

DREAMS OF BRINGING HOPE TO THE HOPELESS.

DEFENDING THOSE WHO COULD NOT DEFEND THEMSELVES.

HELPING THE FORGOTTEN AND IMPOVERISHED.

FIGHTING GREED, RACISM AND HATRED.

A DREAM OF **CREATI**[...] THE KIND OF WORLD [...] **DESERVE** TO LIVE IN[...]

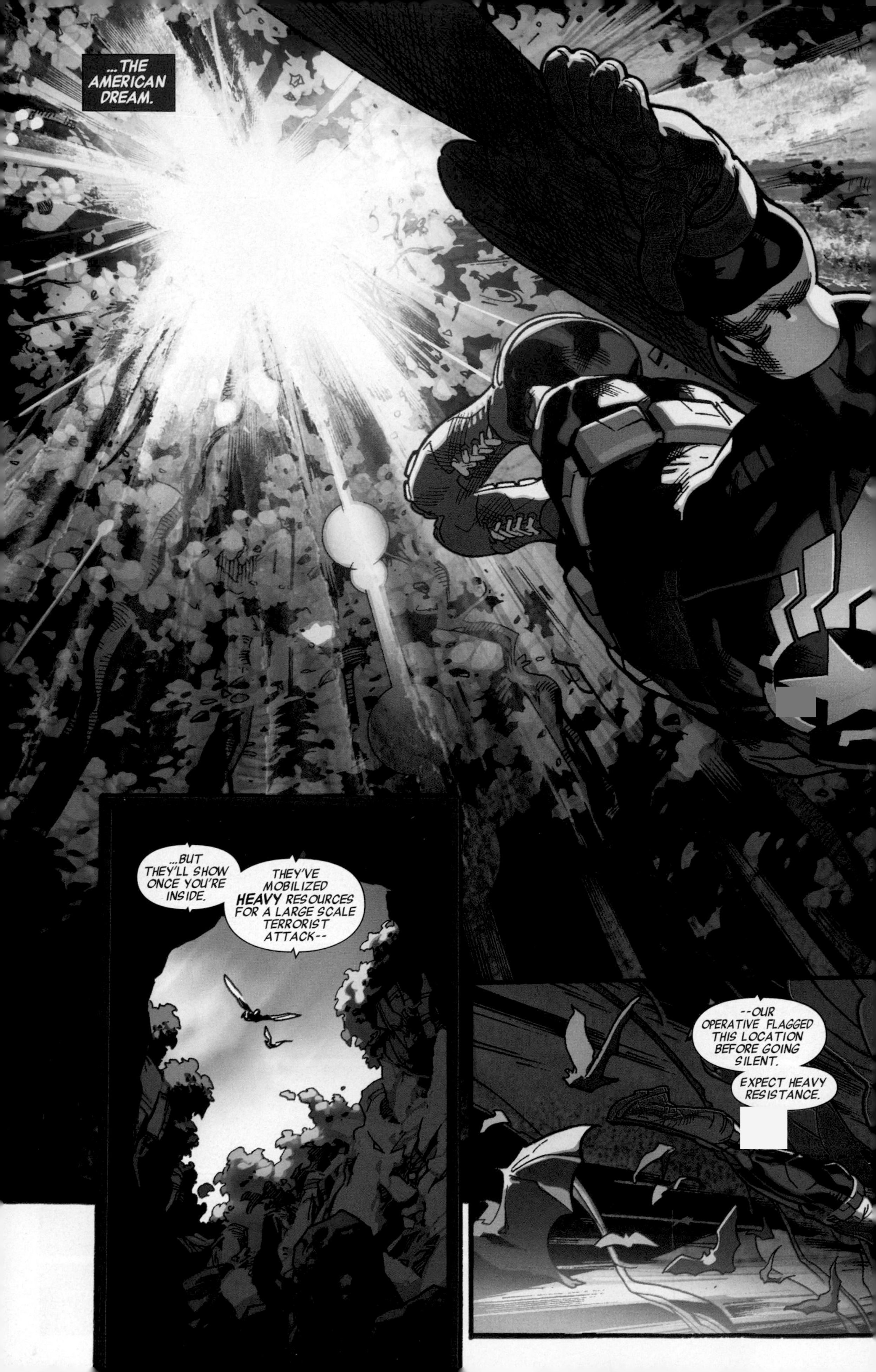
...THE AMERICAN DREAM.
...BUT THEY'LL SHOW ONCE YOU'RE INSIDE.
THEY'VE MOBILIZED HEAVY RESOURCES FOR A LARGE SCALE TERRORIST ATTACK--
--OUR OPERATIVE FLAGGED THIS LOCATION BEFORE GOING SILENT.
EXPECT HEAVY RESISTANCE.

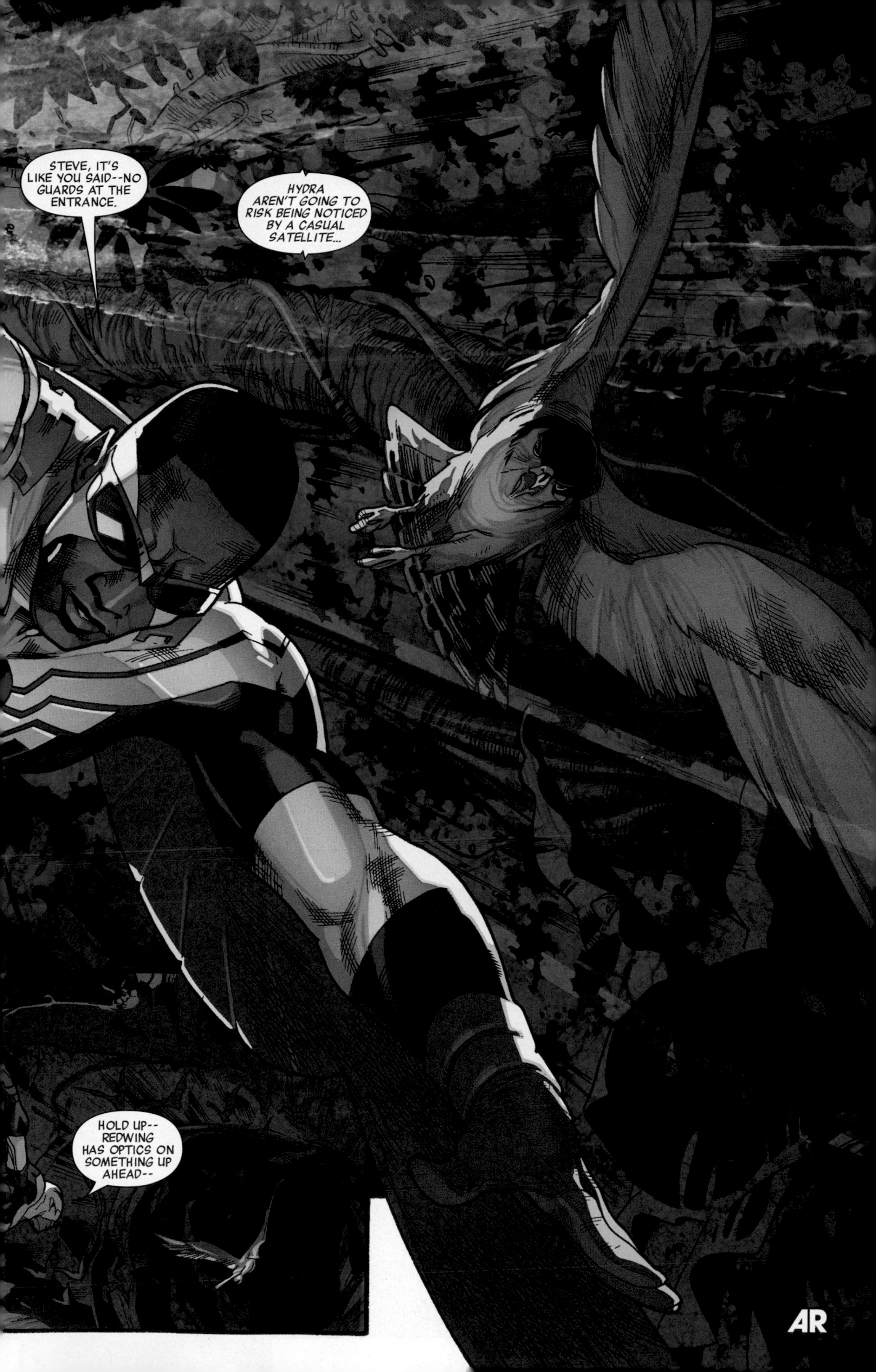
STEVE, IT'S LIKE YOU SAID--NO GUARDS AT THE ENTRANCE.
HYDRA AREN'T GOING TO RISK BEING NOTICED BY A CASUAL SATELLITE...
HOLD UP-- REDWING HAS OPTICS ON SOMETHING UP AHEAD--
AR

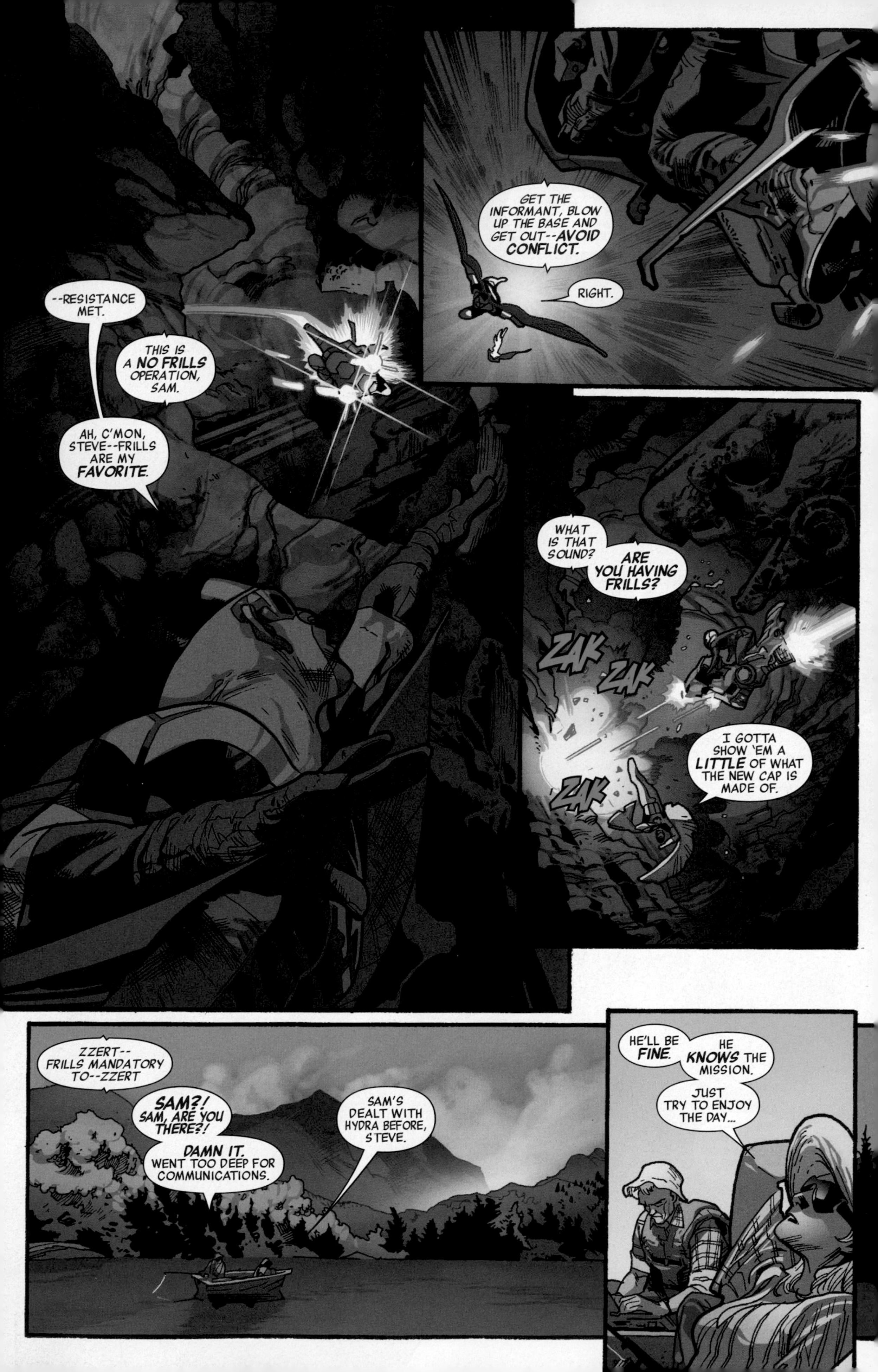

--RESISTANCE MET.
THIS IS A **NO FRILLS** OPERATION, SAM.
AH, C'MON, STEVE--FRILLS ARE MY **FAVORITE**.
GET THE INFORMANT, BLOW UP THE BASE AND GET OUT--**AVOID CONFLICT.**
RIGHT.
WHAT IS THAT SOUND?
ARE YOU HAVING FRILLS?
ZAK
ZAK
ZAK
I GOTTA SHOW 'EM A **LITTLE** OF WHAT THE NEW CAP IS MADE OF.
ZZERT--FRILLS MANDATORY TO--ZZERT
SAM?! SAM, ARE YOU THERE?!
DAMN IT. WENT TOO DEEP FOR COMMUNICATIONS.
SAM'S DEALT WITH HYDRA BEFORE, STEVE.
HE'LL BE **FINE**.
HE **KNOWS** THE MISSION.
JUST TRY TO ENJOY THE DAY...

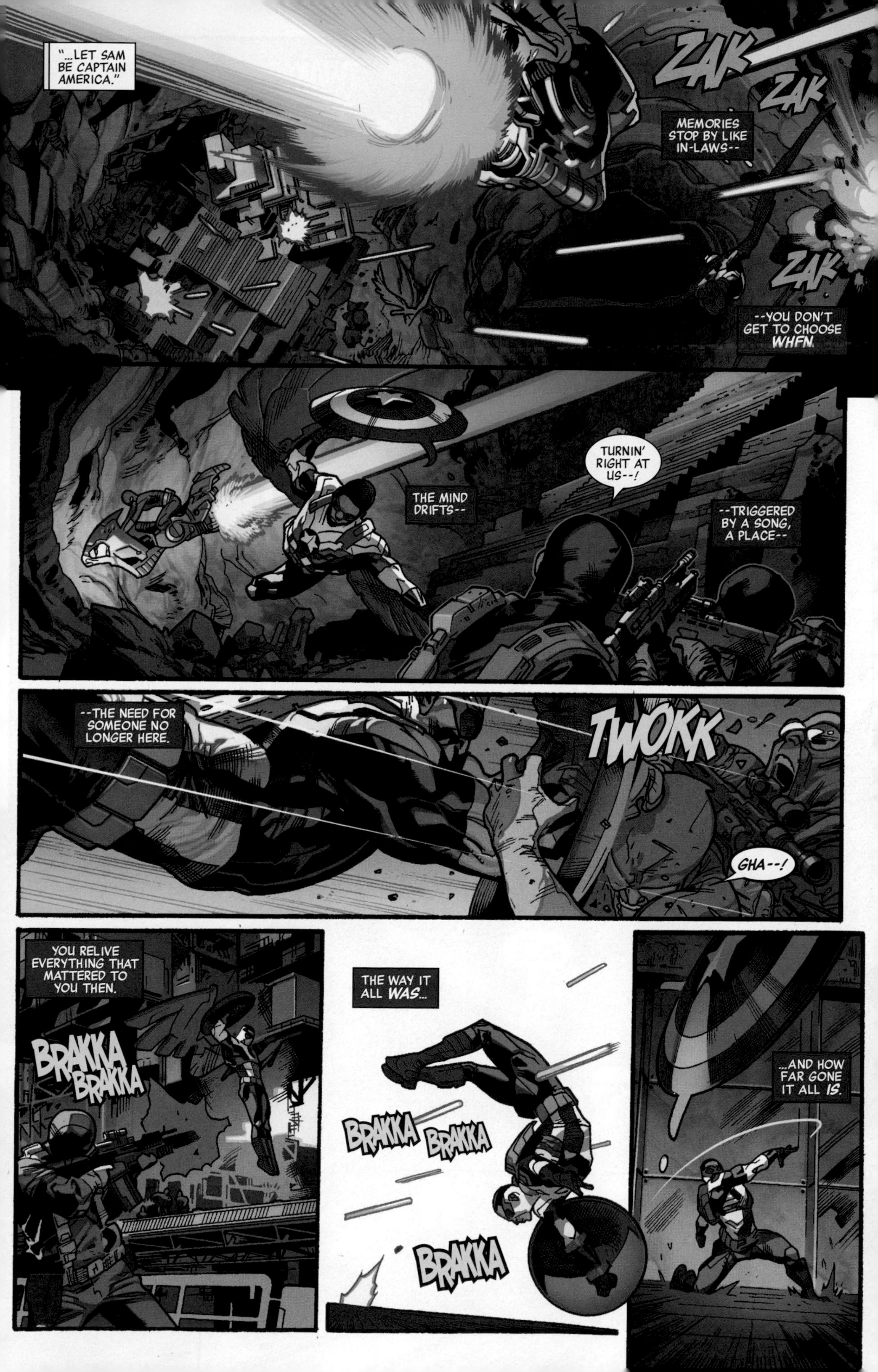
"...LET SAM BE CAPTAIN AMERICA."
ZAK
ZAK
MEMORIES STOP BY LIKE IN-LAWS--
ZAK
--YOU DON'T GET TO CHOOSE WHEN.
THE MIND DRIFTS--
TURNIN' RIGHT AT US--!
--TRIGGERED BY A SONG, A PLACE--
--THE NEED FOR SOMEONE NO LONGER HERE.
TWOKK
GHA--!
YOU RELIVE EVERYTHING THAT MATTERED TO YOU THEN.
BRAKKA BRAKKA
THE WAY IT ALL WAS...
BRAKKA BRAKKA
BRAKKA
...AND HOW FAR GONE IT ALL IS.

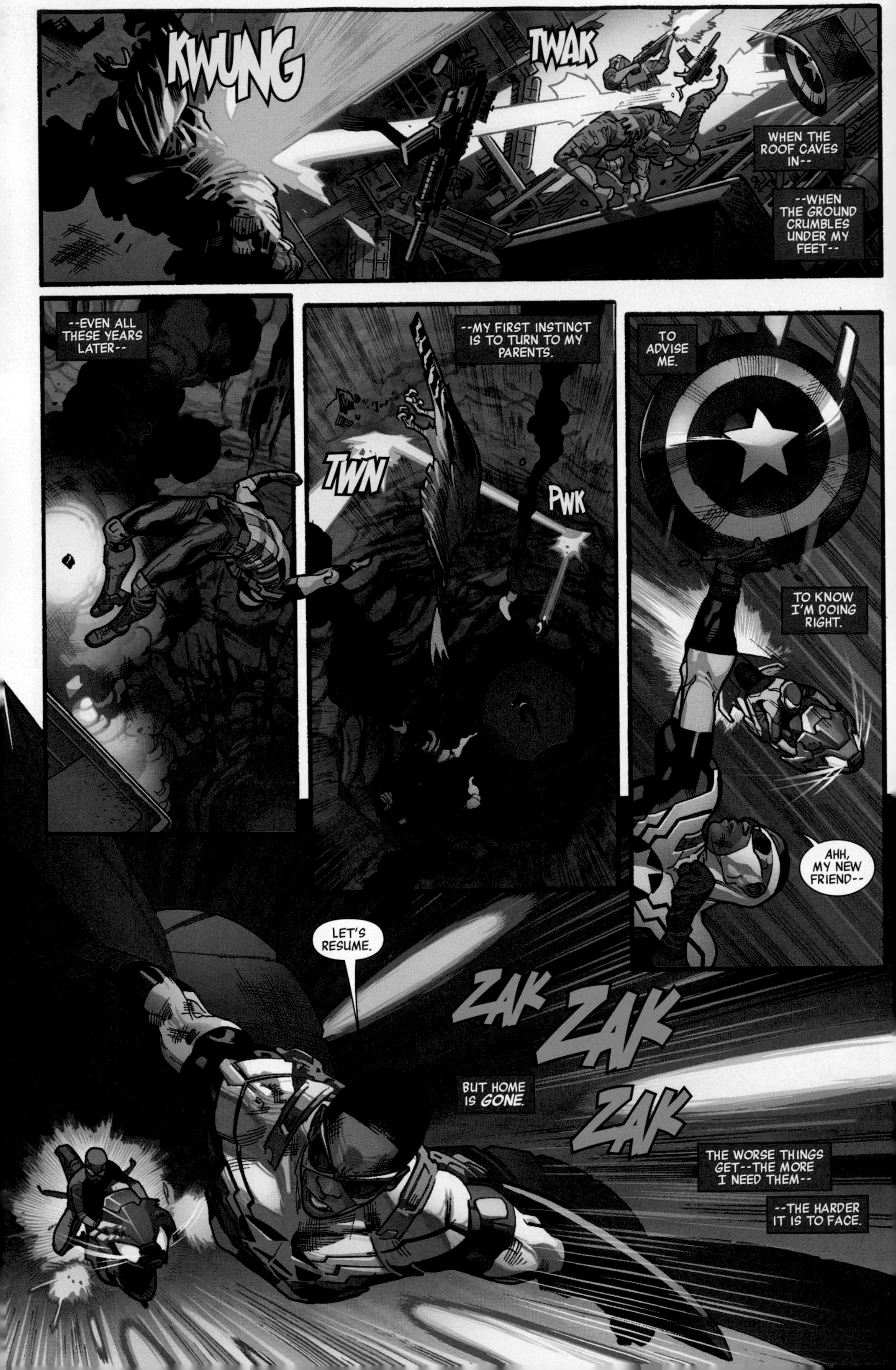
KWUNG
TWAK
WHEN THE ROOF CAVES IN--
--WHEN THE GROUND CRUMBLES UNDER MY FEET--
--EVEN ALL THESE YEARS LATER--
--MY FIRST INSTINCT IS TO TURN TO MY PARENTS.
TWN
PWK
TO ADVISE ME.
TO KNOW I'M DOING RIGHT.
AHH, MY NEW FRIEND--
LET'S RESUME.
ZAK ZAK
BUT HOME IS GONE.
ZAK
THE WORSE THINGS GET--THE MORE I NEED THEM--
--THE HARDER IT IS TO FACE.

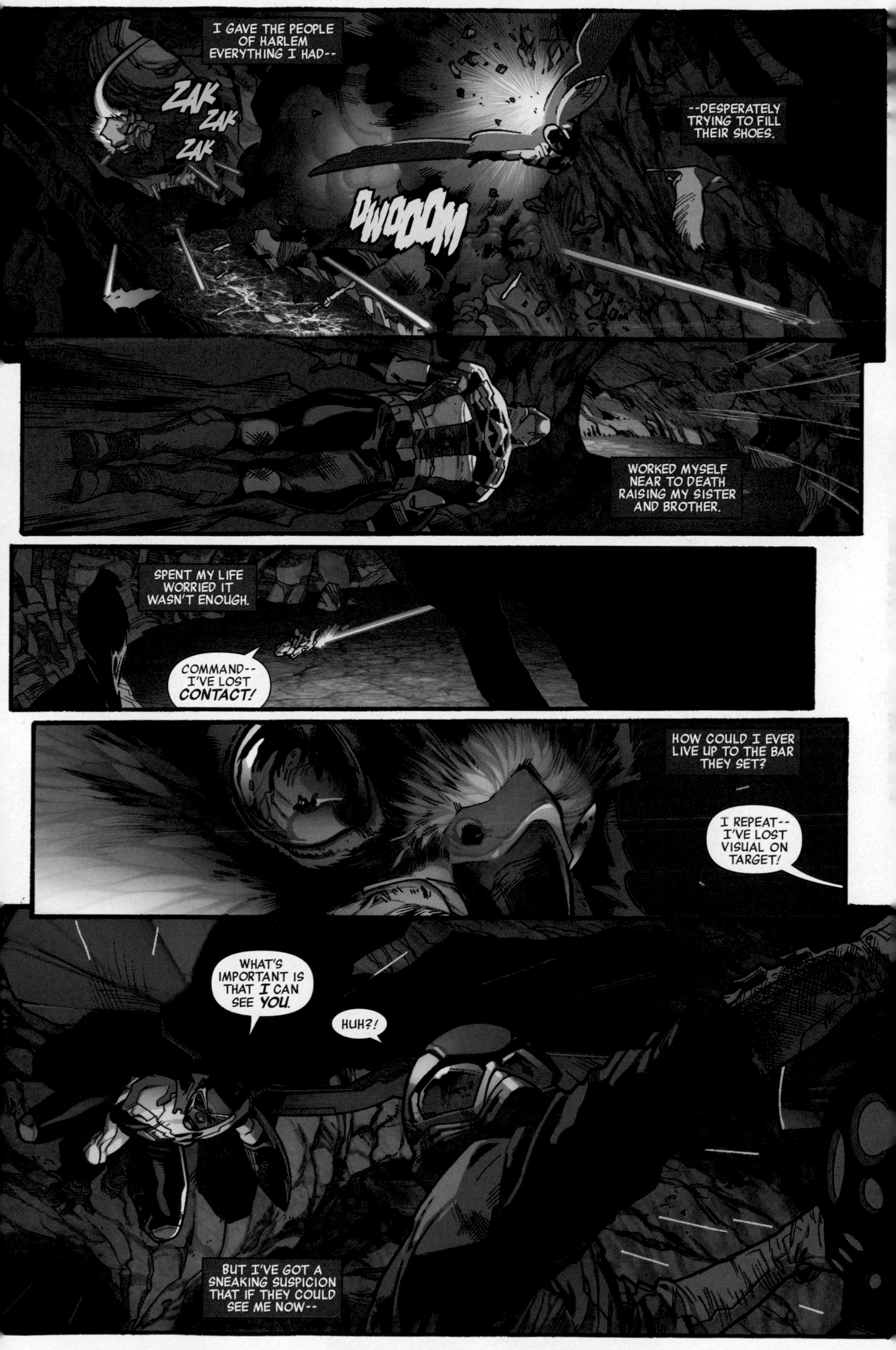
I GAVE THE PEOPLE OF HARLEM EVERYTHING I HAD--
ZAK
ZAK
ZAK
DWOOOM
--DESPERATELY TRYING TO FILL THEIR SHOES.
WORKED MYSELF NEAR TO DEATH RAISING MY SISTER AND BROTHER.
SPENT MY LIFE WORRIED IT WASN'T ENOUGH.
COMMAND-- I'VE LOST CONTACT!
HOW COULD I EVER LIVE UP TO THE BAR THEY SET?
I REPEAT-- I'VE LOST VISUAL ON TARGET!
WHAT'S IMPORTANT IS THAT I CAN SEE YOU.
HUH?!
BUT I'VE GOT A SNEAKING SUSPICION THAT IF THEY COULD SEE ME NOW--

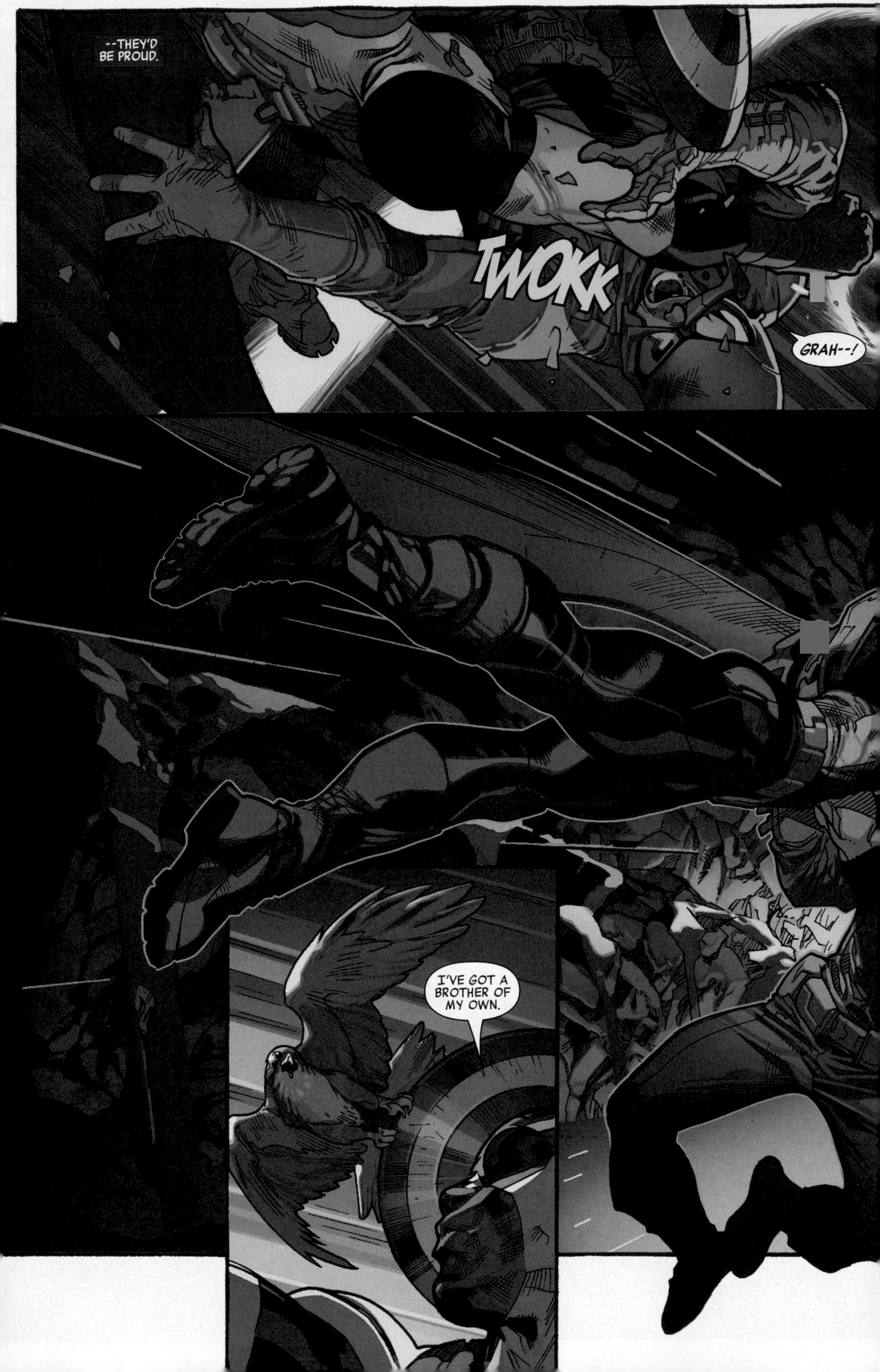
--THEY'D BE PROUD.
TWOKK
GRAH--!
I'VE GOT A BROTHER OF MY OWN.

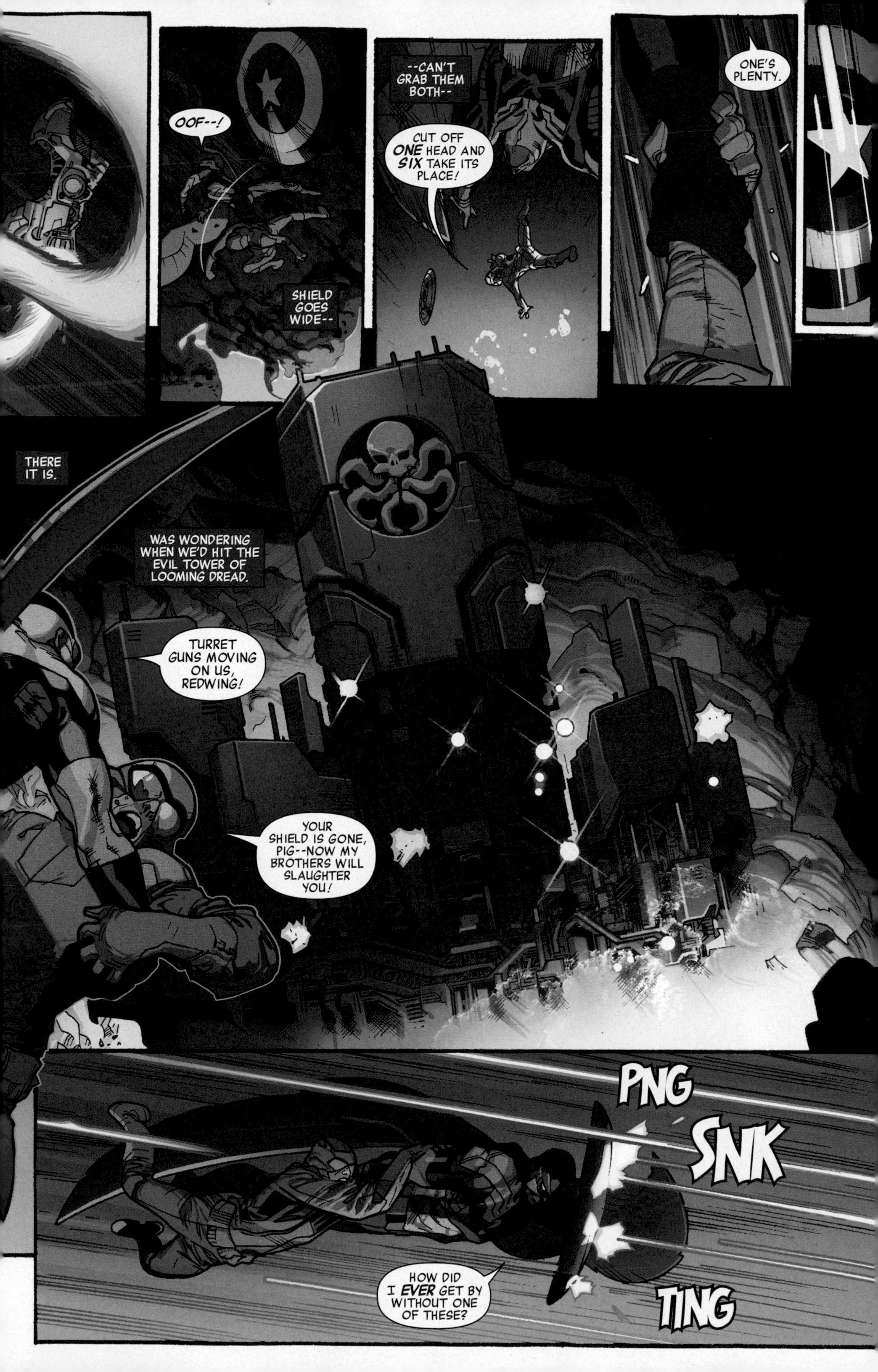
OOF--!
SHIELD GOES WIDE--
--CAN'T GRAB THEM BOTH--
CUT OFF ONE HEAD AND SIX TAKE ITS PLACE!
ONE'S PLENTY.
THERE IT IS.
WAS WONDERING WHEN WE'D HIT THE EVIL TOWER OF LOOMING DREAD.
TURRET GUNS MOVING ON US, REDWING!
YOUR SHIELD IS GONE, PIG--NOW MY BROTHERS WILL SLAUGHTER YOU!
PNG
SNK
HOW DID I EVER GET BY WITHOUT ONE OF THESE?
TING

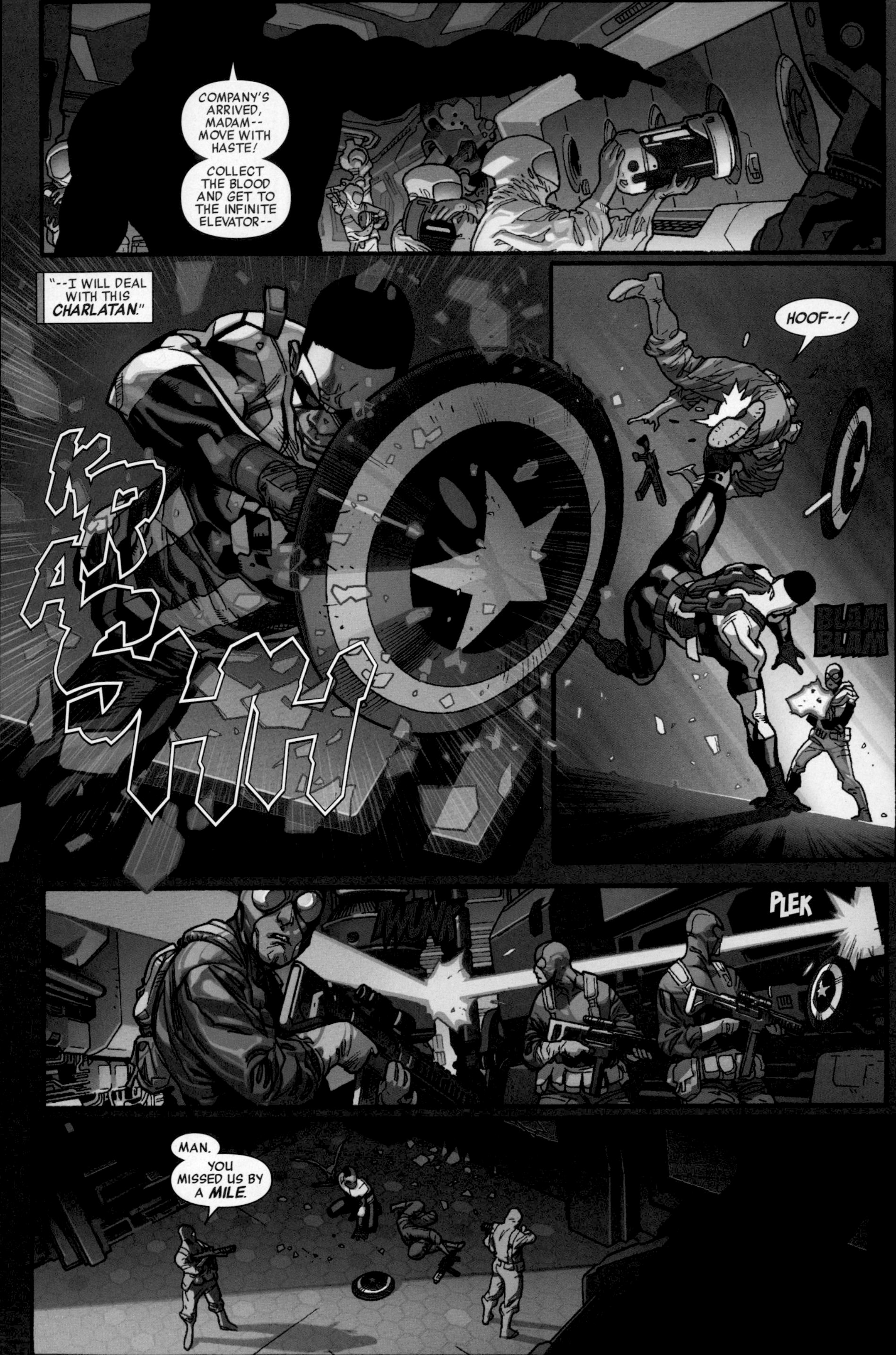
COMPANY'S ARRIVED, MADAM-- MOVE WITH HASTE!
COLLECT THE BLOOD AND GET TO THE INFINITE ELEVATOR--
"--I WILL DEAL WITH THIS CHARLATAN."
HOOF--!
BLAM BLAM
THUNK
PLEK
MAN. YOU MISSED US BY A MILE.

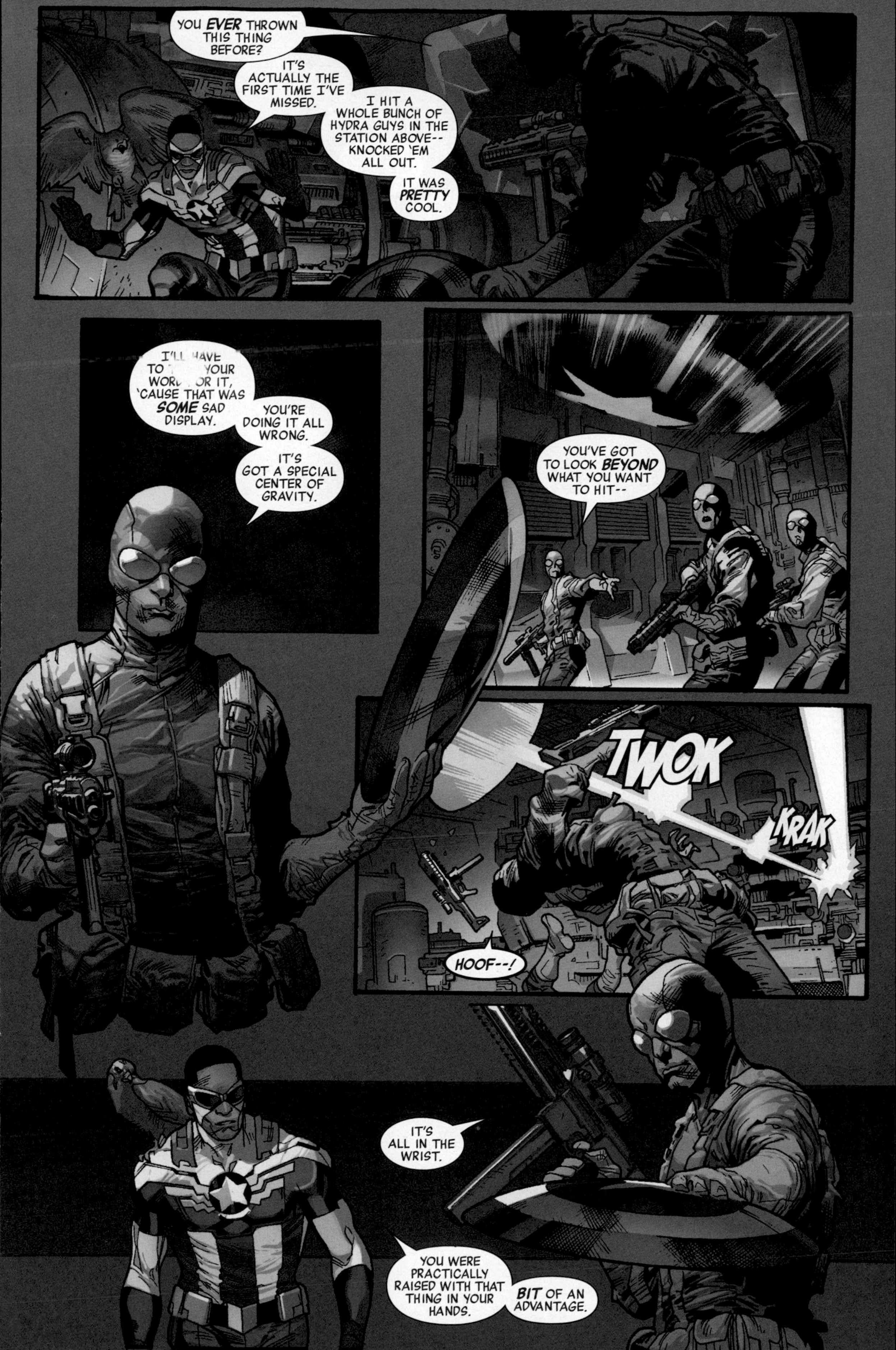
YOU EVER THROWN THIS THING BEFORE?
IT'S ACTUALLY THE FIRST TIME I'VE MISSED.
I HIT A WHOLE BUNCH OF HYDRA GUYS IN THE STATION ABOVE-- KNOCKED 'EM ALL OUT.
IT WAS PRETTY COOL.
I'LL HAVE TO YOUR WOR OR IT, 'CAUSE THAT WAS SOME SAD DISPLAY.
YOU'RE DOING IT ALL WRONG.
IT'S GOT A SPECIAL CENTER OF GRAVITY.
YOU'VE GOT TO LOOK BEYOND WHAT YOU WANT TO HIT--
TWOK
KRAK
HOOF--!
IT'S ALL IN THE WRIST.
YOU WERE PRACTICALLY RAISED WITH THAT THING IN YOUR HANDS.
BIT OF AN ADVANTAGE.

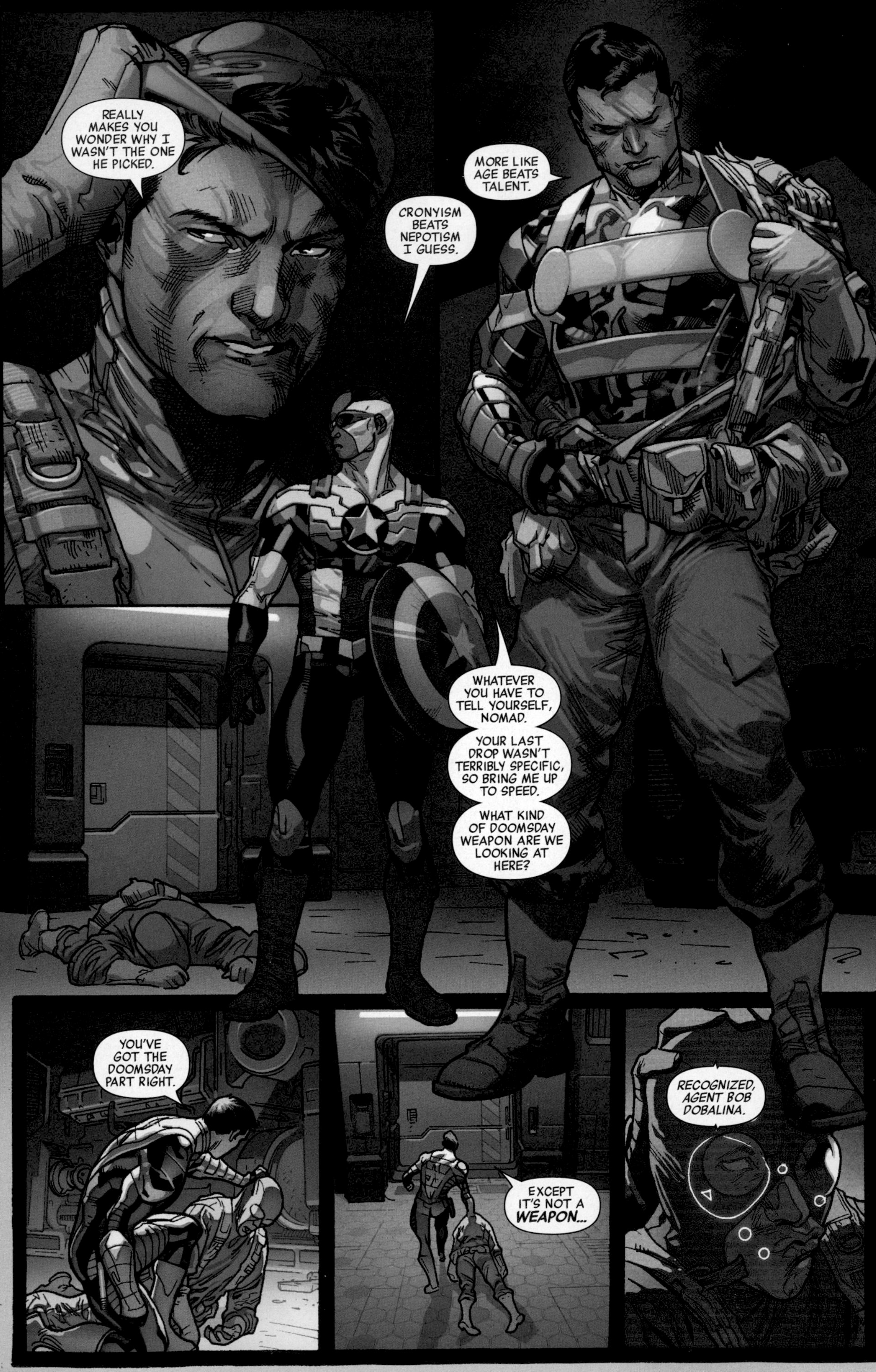
REALLY MAKES YOU WONDER WHY I WASN'T THE ONE HE PICKED.
CRONYISM BEATS NEPOTISM I GUESS.
MORE LIKE AGE BEATS TALENT.
WHATEVER YOU HAVE TO TELL YOURSELF, NOMAD.
YOUR LAST DROP WASN'T TERRIBLY SPECIFIC, SO BRING ME UP TO SPEED.
WHAT KIND OF DOOMSDAY WEAPON ARE WE LOOKING AT HERE?
YOU'VE GOT THE DOOMSDAY PART RIGHT.
EXCEPT IT'S NOT A *WEAPON*...
RECOGNIZED, AGENT BOB DOBALINA.

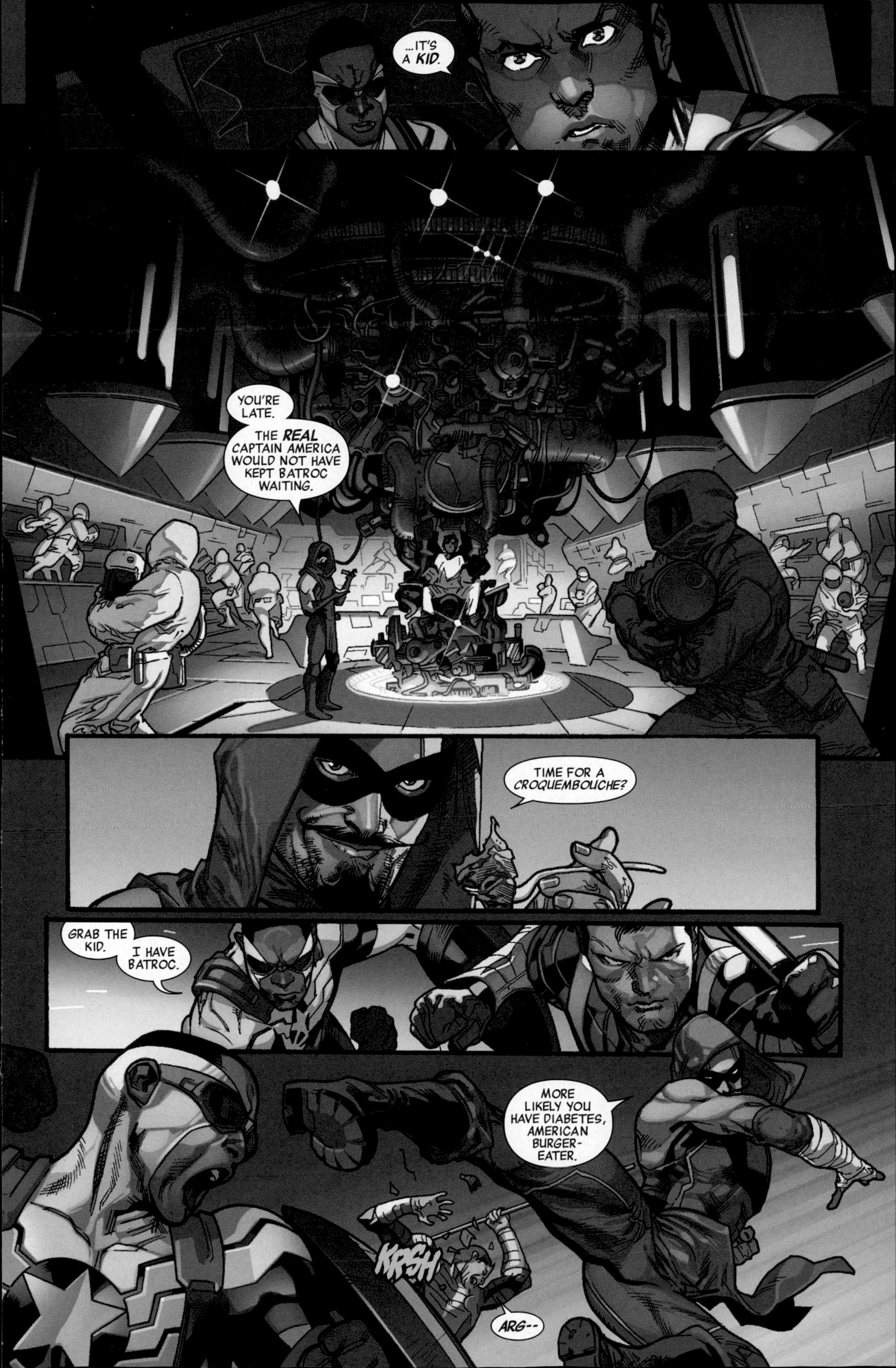

...IT'S A KID.
YOU'RE LATE.
THE REAL CAPTAIN AMERICA WOULD NOT HAVE KEPT BATROC WAITING.
TIME FOR A CROQUEMBOUCHE?
GRAB THE KID.
I HAVE BATROC.
MORE LIKELY YOU HAVE DIABETES, AMERICAN BURGER-EATER.
KRSH
ARG--

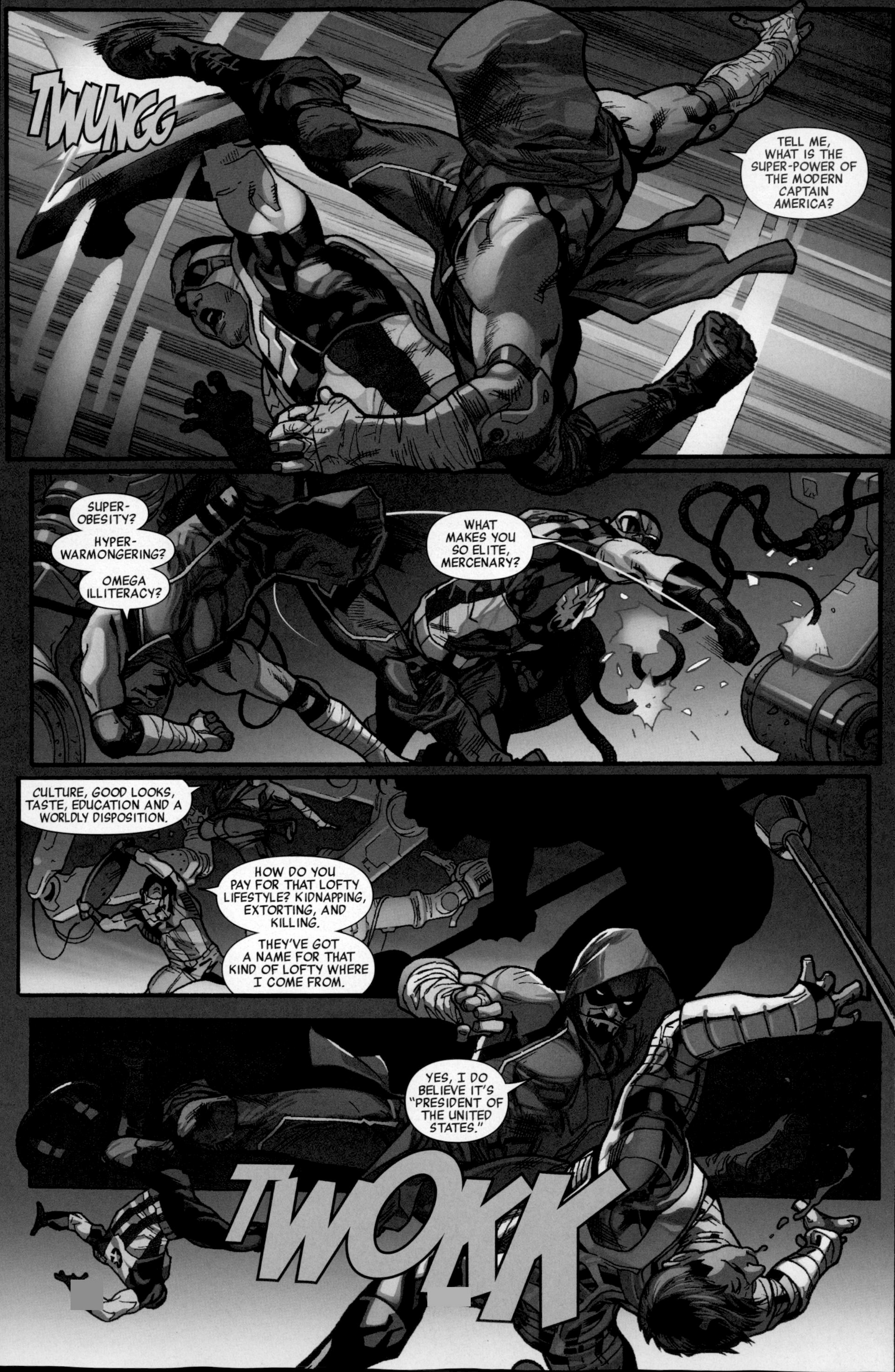
TWUNGG
TELL ME, WHAT IS THE SUPER-POWER OF THE MODERN CAPTAIN AMERICA?
SUPER-OBESITY?
HYPER-WARMONGERING?
OMEGA ILLITERACY?
WHAT MAKES YOU SO ELITE, MERCENARY?
CULTURE, GOOD LOOKS, TASTE, EDUCATION AND A WORLDLY DISPOSITION.
HOW DO YOU PAY FOR THAT LOFTY LIFESTYLE? KIDNAPPING, EXTORTING, AND KILLING.
THEY'VE GOT A NAME FOR THAT KIND OF LOFTY WHERE I COME FROM.
YES, I DO BELIEVE IT'S "PRESIDENT OF THE UNITED STATES."
TWOKK

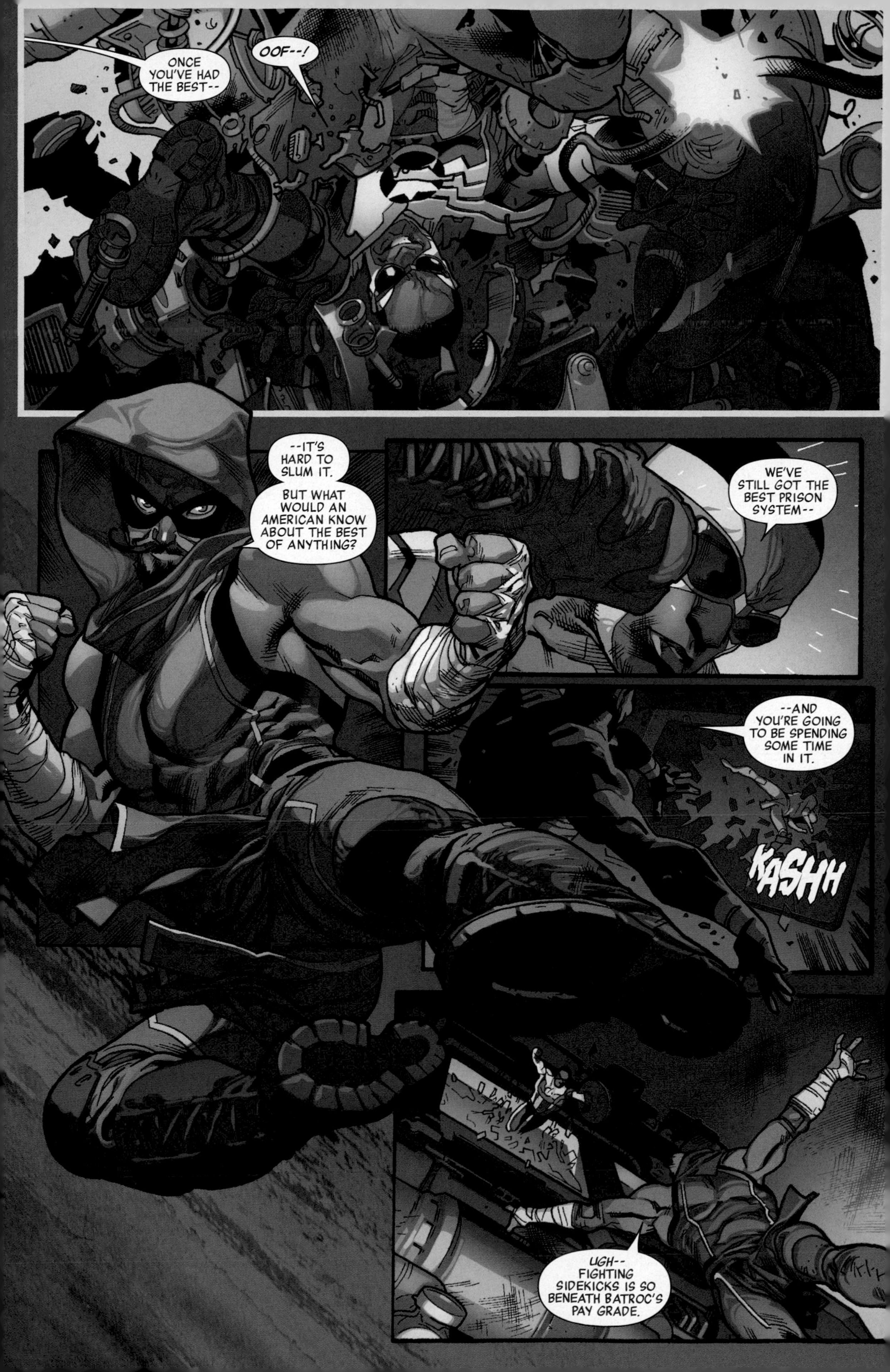
ONCE YOU'VE HAD THE BEST--
OOF--!
--IT'S HARD TO SLUM IT.
BUT WHAT WOULD AN AMERICAN KNOW ABOUT THE BEST OF ANYTHING?
WE'VE STILL GOT THE BEST PRISON SYSTEM--
--AND YOU'RE GOING TO BE SPENDING SOME TIME IN IT.
KASHH
UGH-- FIGHTING SIDEKICKS IS SO BENEATH BATROC'S PAY GRADE.

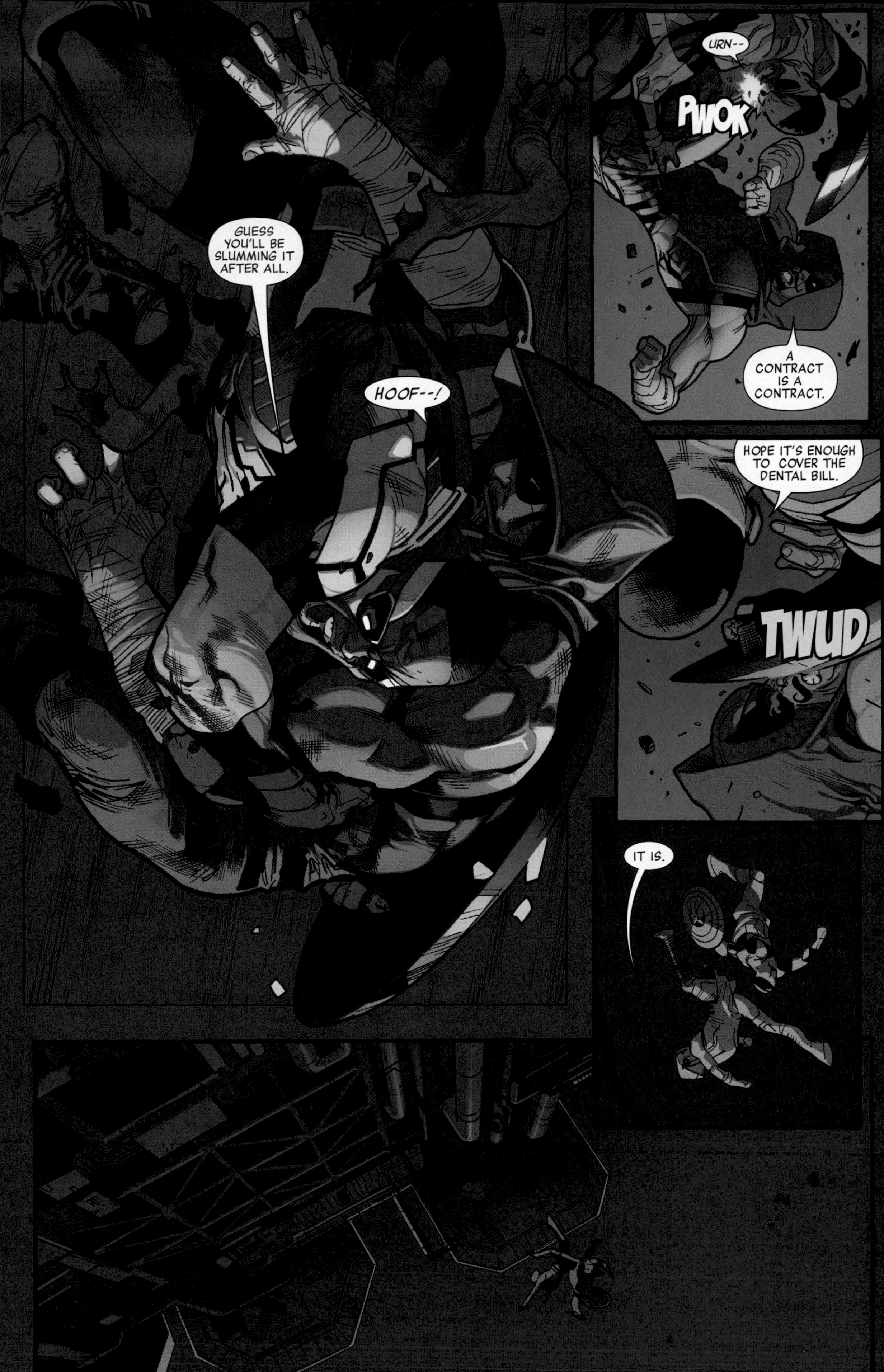
GUESS YOU'LL BE SLUMMING IT AFTER ALL.
HOOF--!
URN--
PWOK
A CONTRACT IS A CONTRACT.
HOPE IT'S ENOUGH TO COVER THE DENTAL BILL.
TWUD
IT IS.

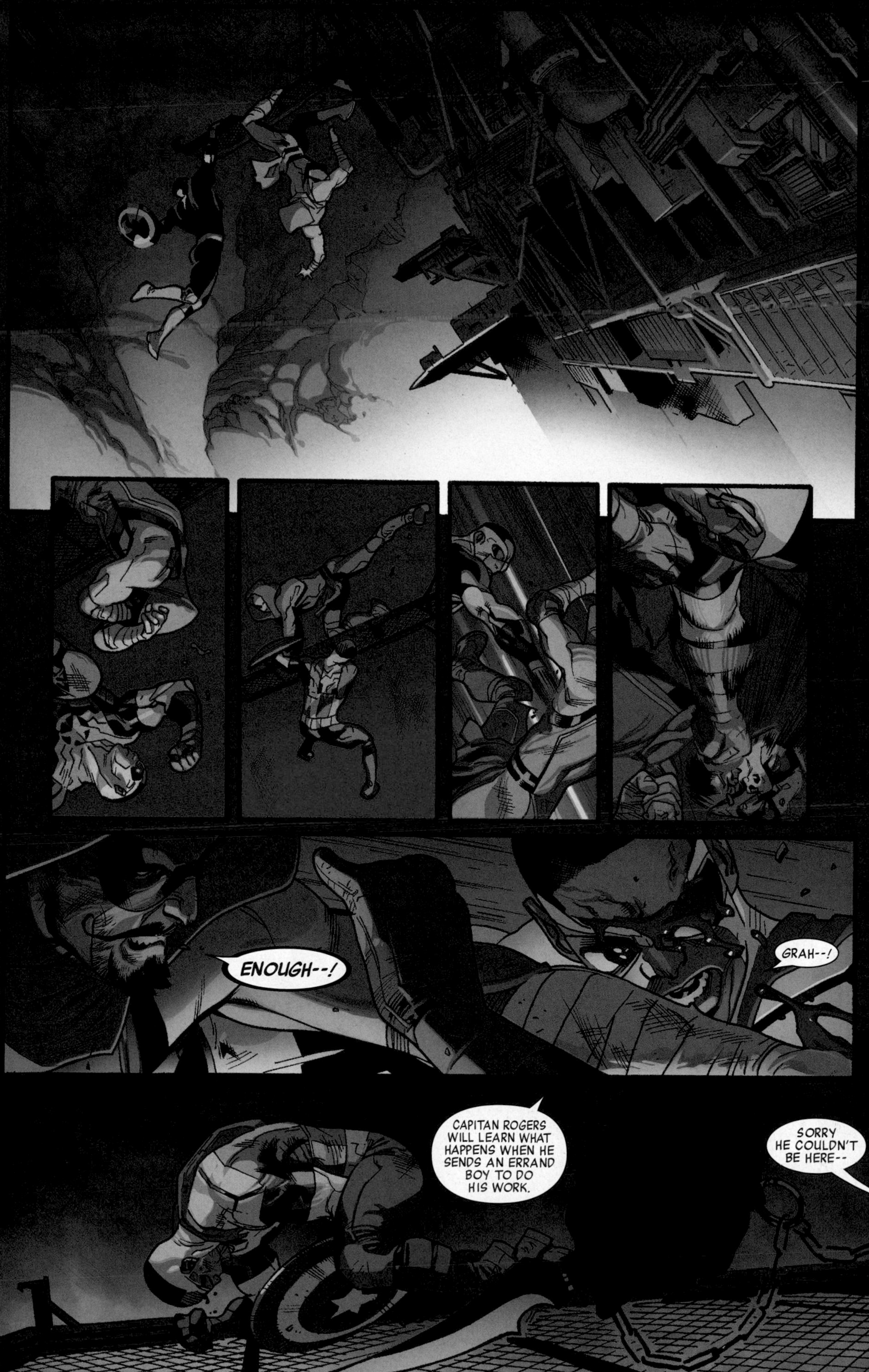
ENOUGH--!
GRAH--!
CAPITAN ROGERS WILL LEARN WHAT HAPPENS WHEN HE SENDS AN ERRAND BOY TO DO HIS WORK.
SORRY HE COULDN'T BE HERE--

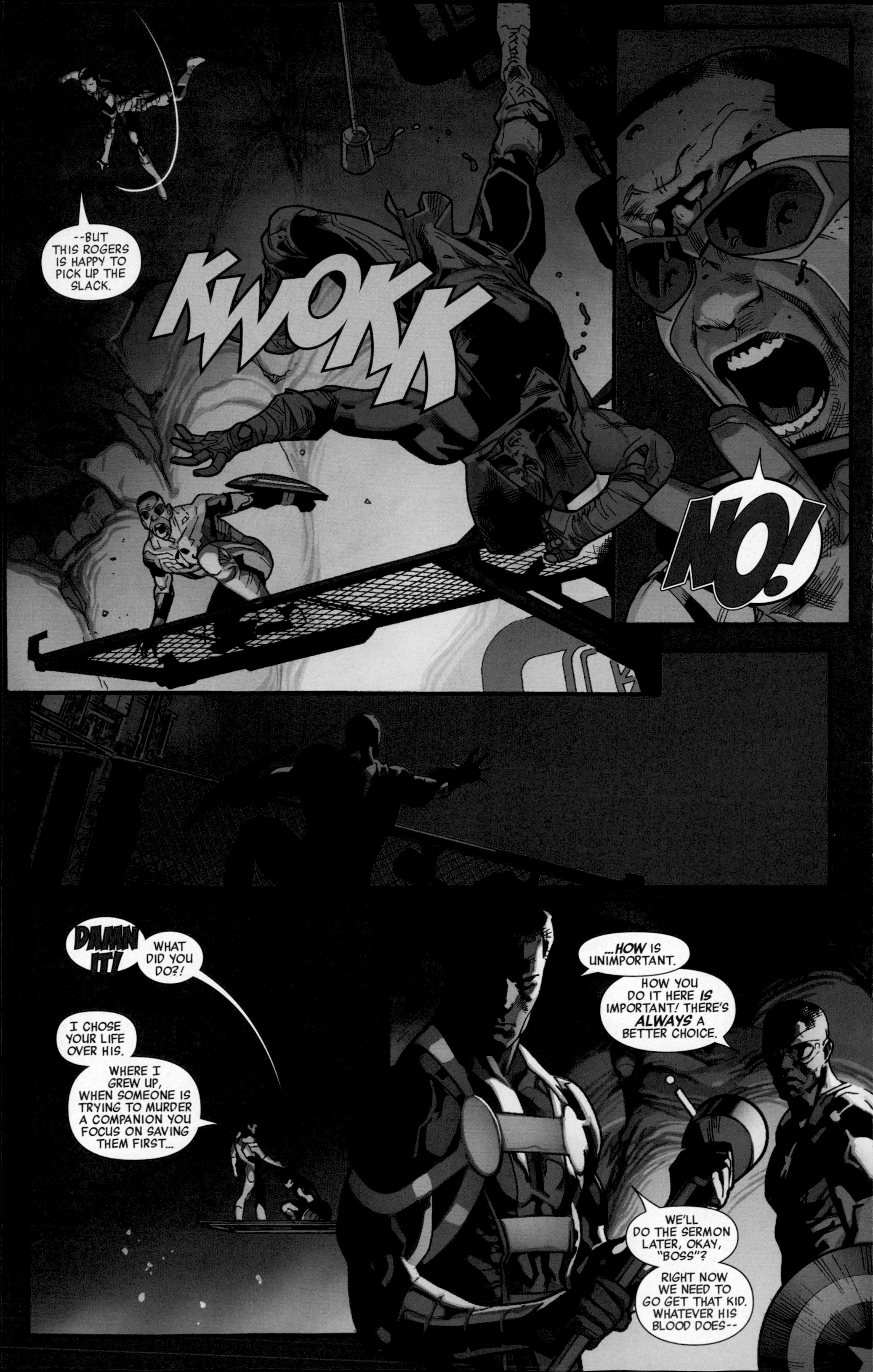
--BUT THIS ROGERS IS HAPPY TO PICK UP THE SLACK.
KWOKK
NO!
DAMN IT!
WHAT DID YOU DO?!
I CHOSE YOUR LIFE OVER HIS.
WHERE I GREW UP, WHEN SOMEONE IS TRYING TO MURDER A COMPANION YOU FOCUS ON SAVING THEM FIRST...
...HOW IS UNIMPORTANT.
HOW YOU DO IT HERE IS IMPORTANT! THERE'S ALWAYS A BETTER CHOICE.
WE'LL DO THE SERMON LATER, OKAY, "BOSS"?
RIGHT NOW WE NEED TO GO GET THAT KID. WHATEVER HIS BLOOD DOES--

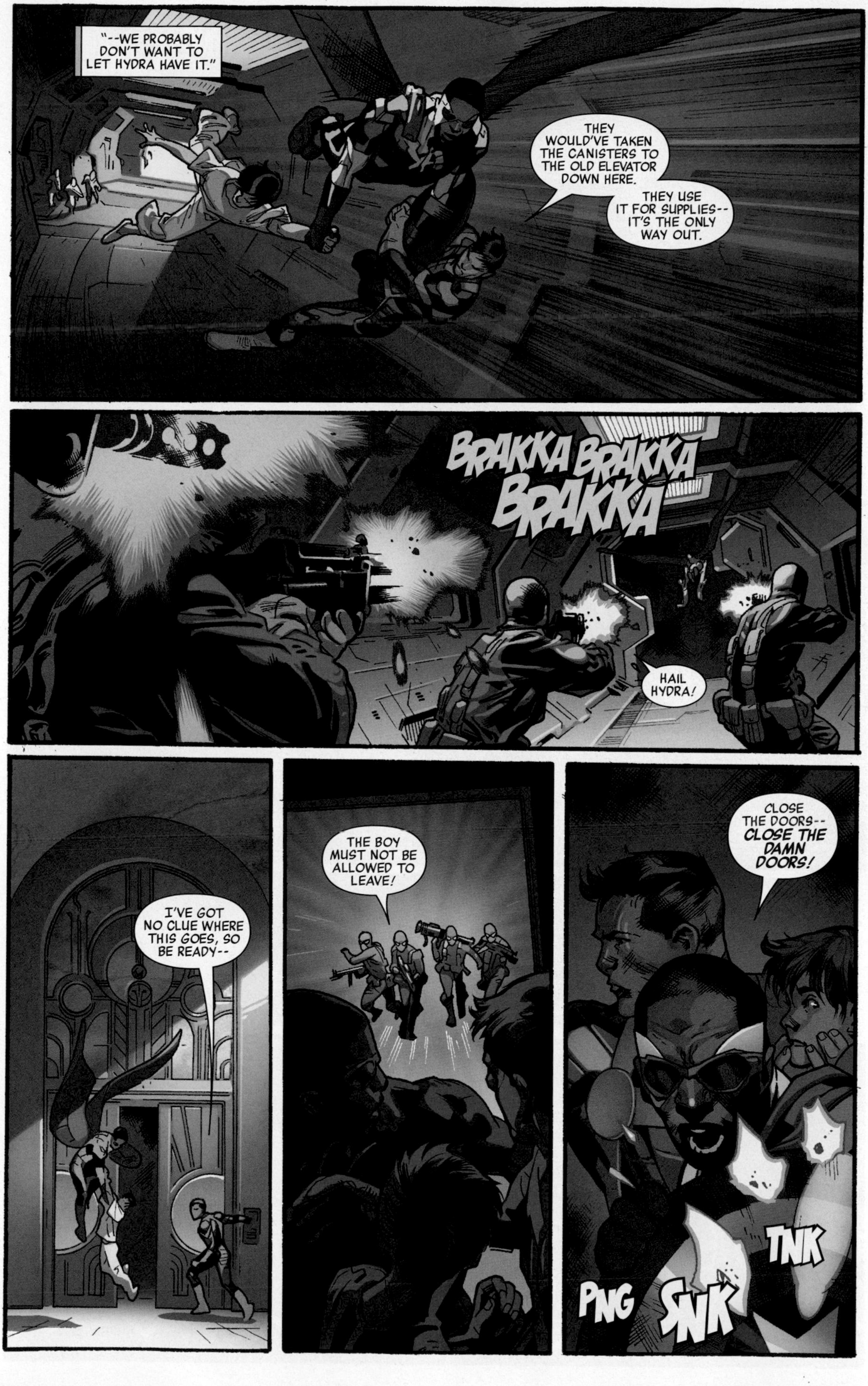
"--WE PROBABLY DON'T WANT TO LET HYDRA HAVE IT."
THEY WOULD'VE TAKEN THE CANISTERS TO THE OLD ELEVATOR DOWN HERE.
THEY USE IT FOR SUPPLIES-- IT'S THE ONLY WAY OUT.
BRAKKA BRAKKA BRAKKA
HAIL HYDRA!
I'VE GOT NO CLUE WHERE THIS GOES, SO BE READY--
THE BOY MUST NOT BE ALLOWED TO LEAVE!
CLOSE THE DOORS-- CLOSE THE DAMN DOORS!
PNG
SNK
TNK

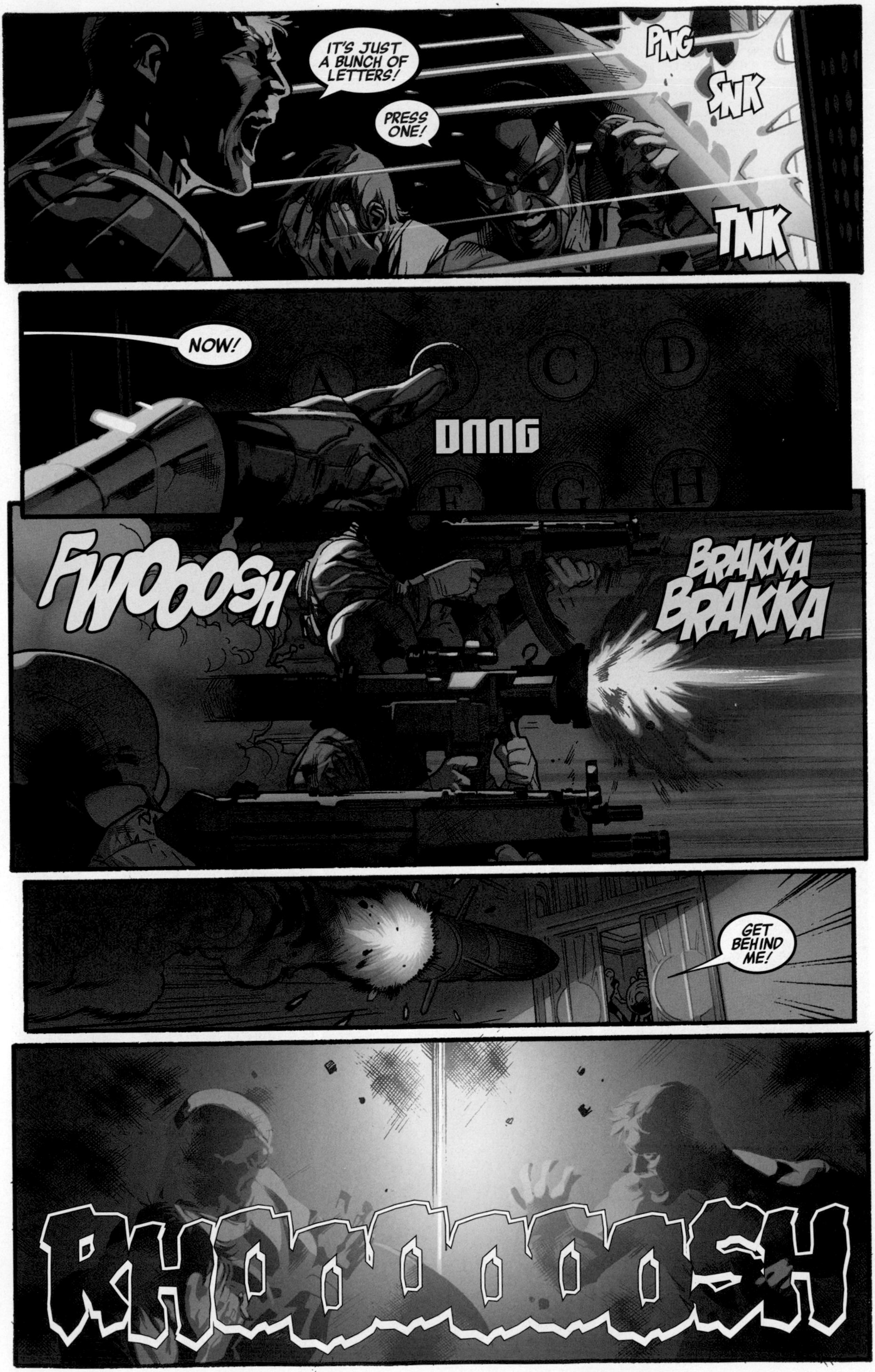
IT'S JUST A BUNCH OF LETTERS!
PRESS ONE!
PNG
SNK
TNK
NOW!
C
D
DNNG
G
H
FWOOOSH
BRAKKA BRAKKA
GET BEHIND ME!
RHOOOOOOSH

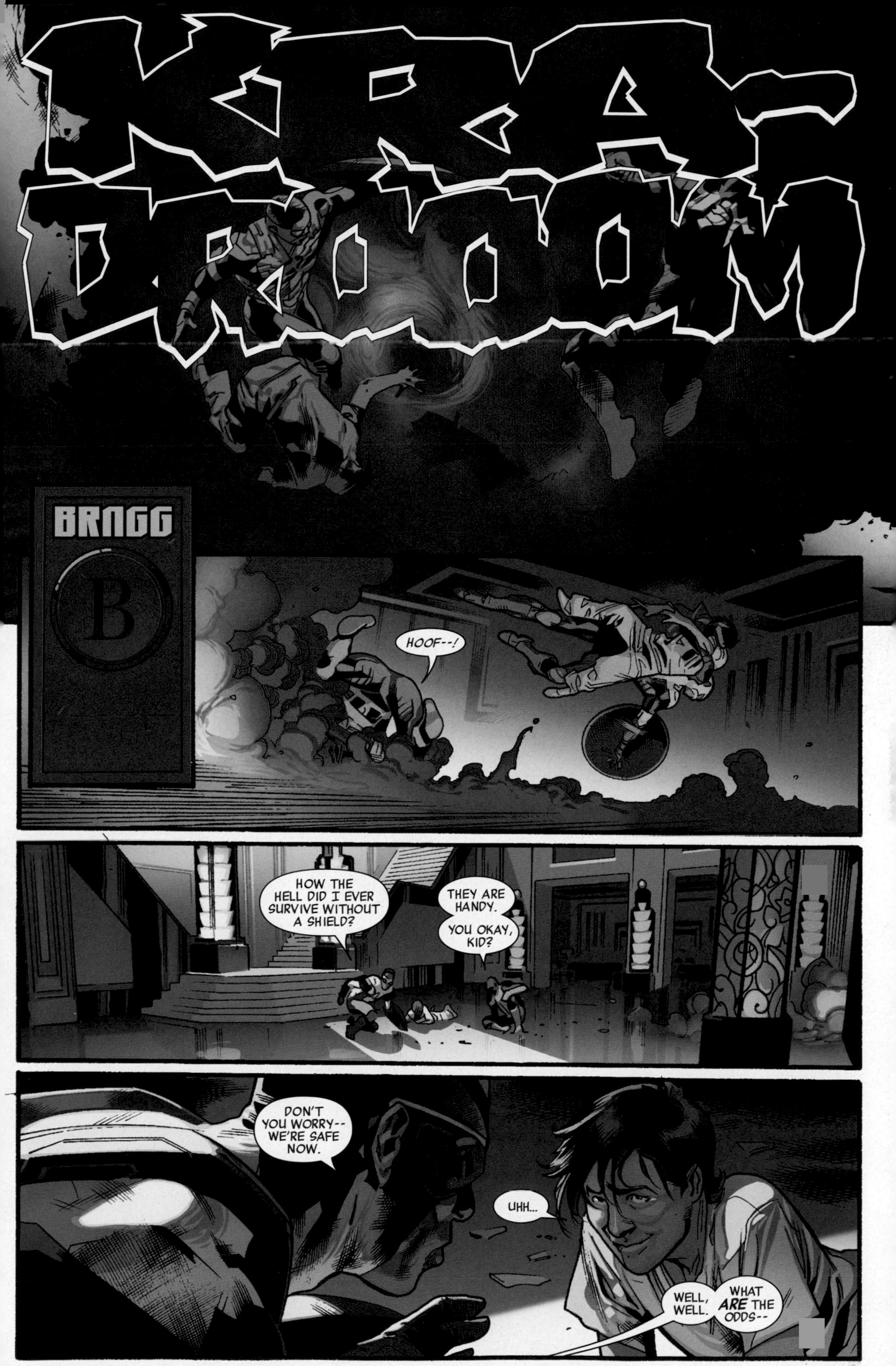
KRA-DROOOM
BRNGG
HOOF--!
HOW THE HELL DID I EVER SURVIVE WITHOUT A SHIELD?
THEY ARE HANDY.
YOU OKAY, KID?
DON'T YOU WORRY-- WE'RE SAFE NOW.
UHH...
WELL, WELL.
WHAT ARE THE ODDS--

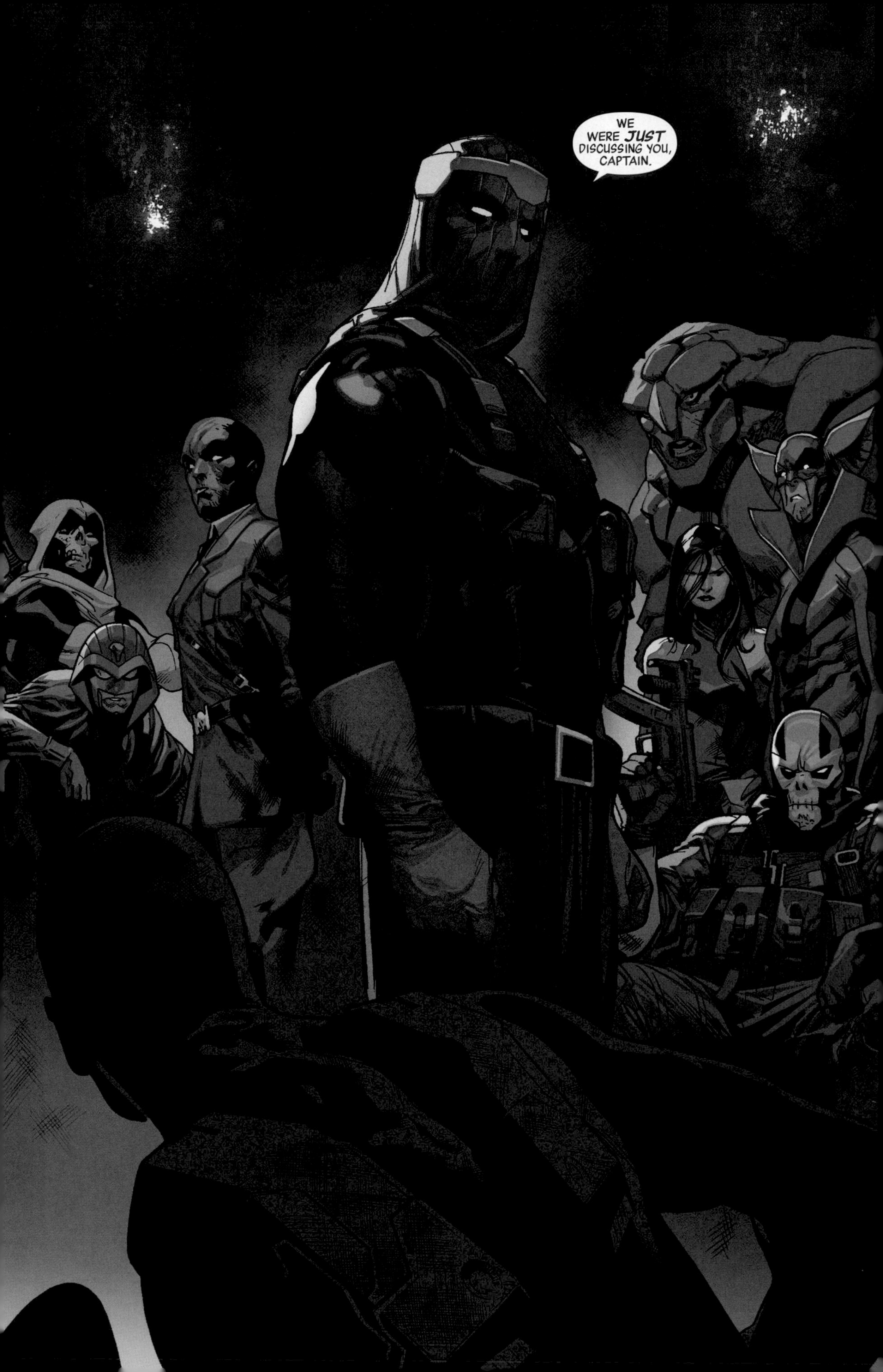
WE WERE JUST DISCUSSING YOU, CAPTAIN.

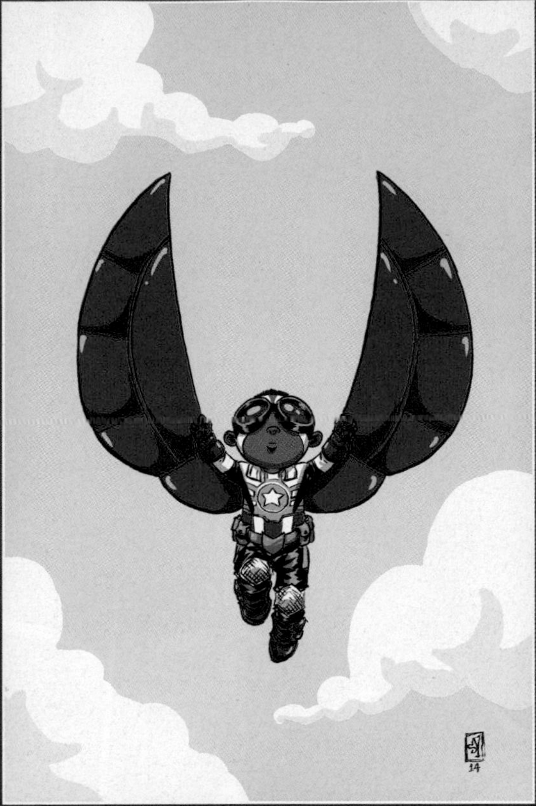

#1 VARIANT BY SKOTTIE YOUNG

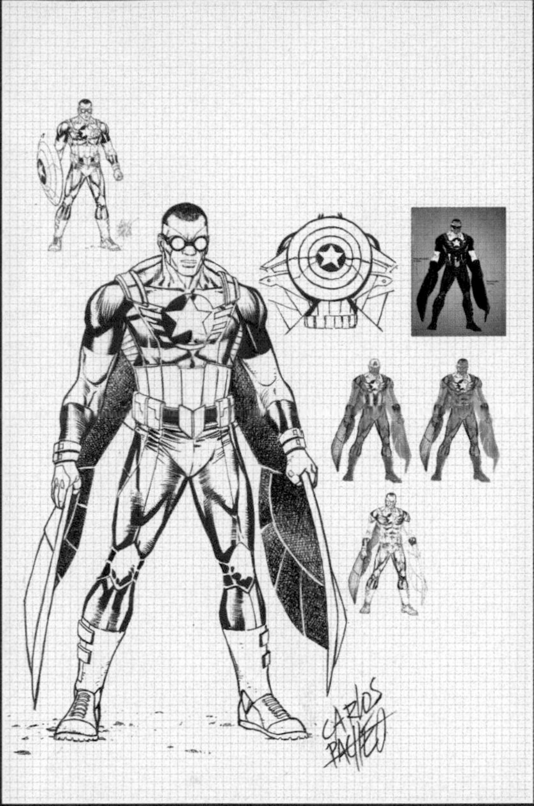

#1 DESIGN VARIANT
BY CARLOS PACHECO

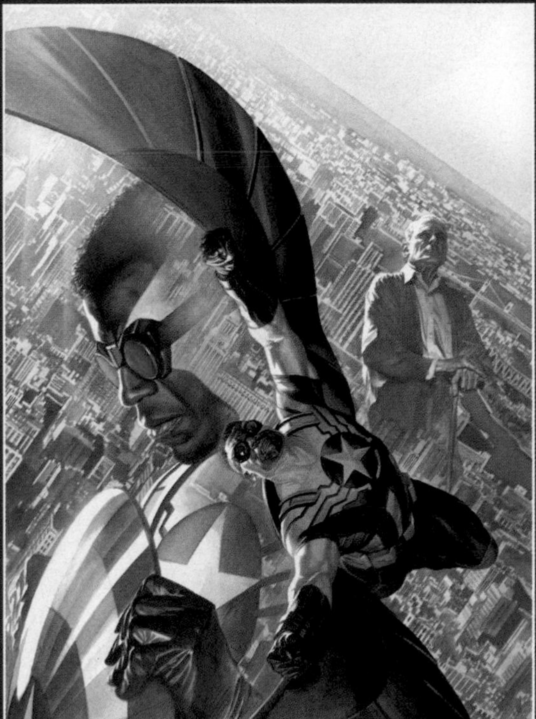

#1 VARIANT BY ALEX ROSS

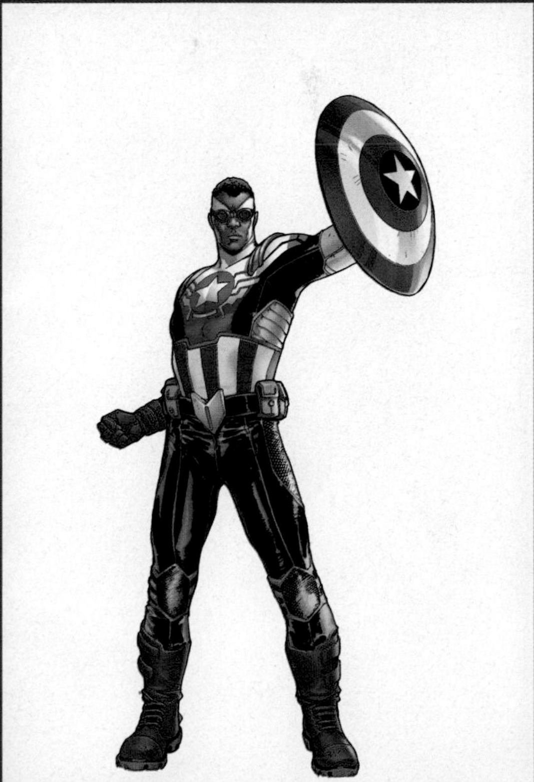

#1 VARIANT
BY SARA PICHELLI & LAURA MARTIN

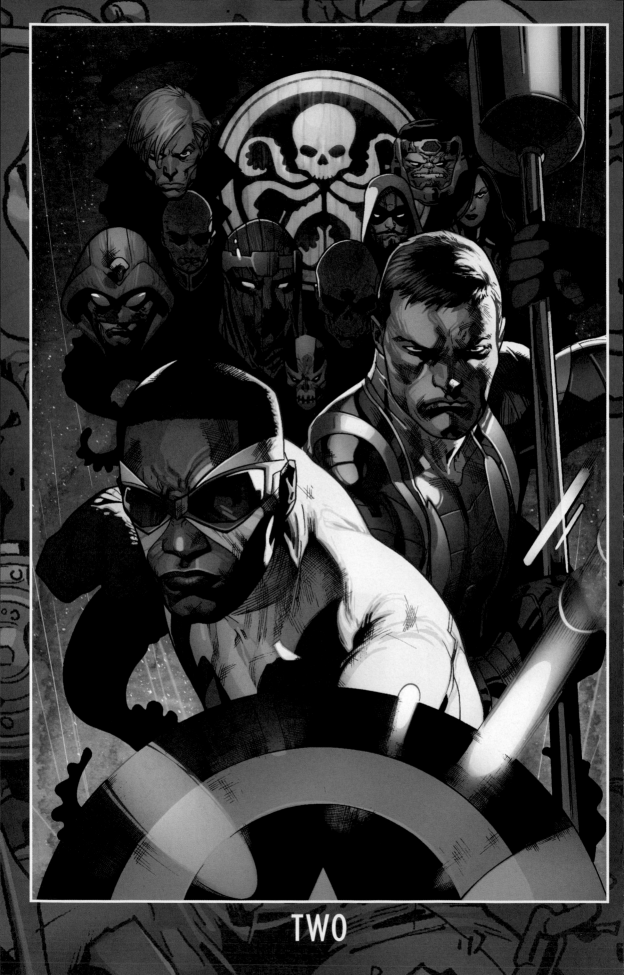

TWO

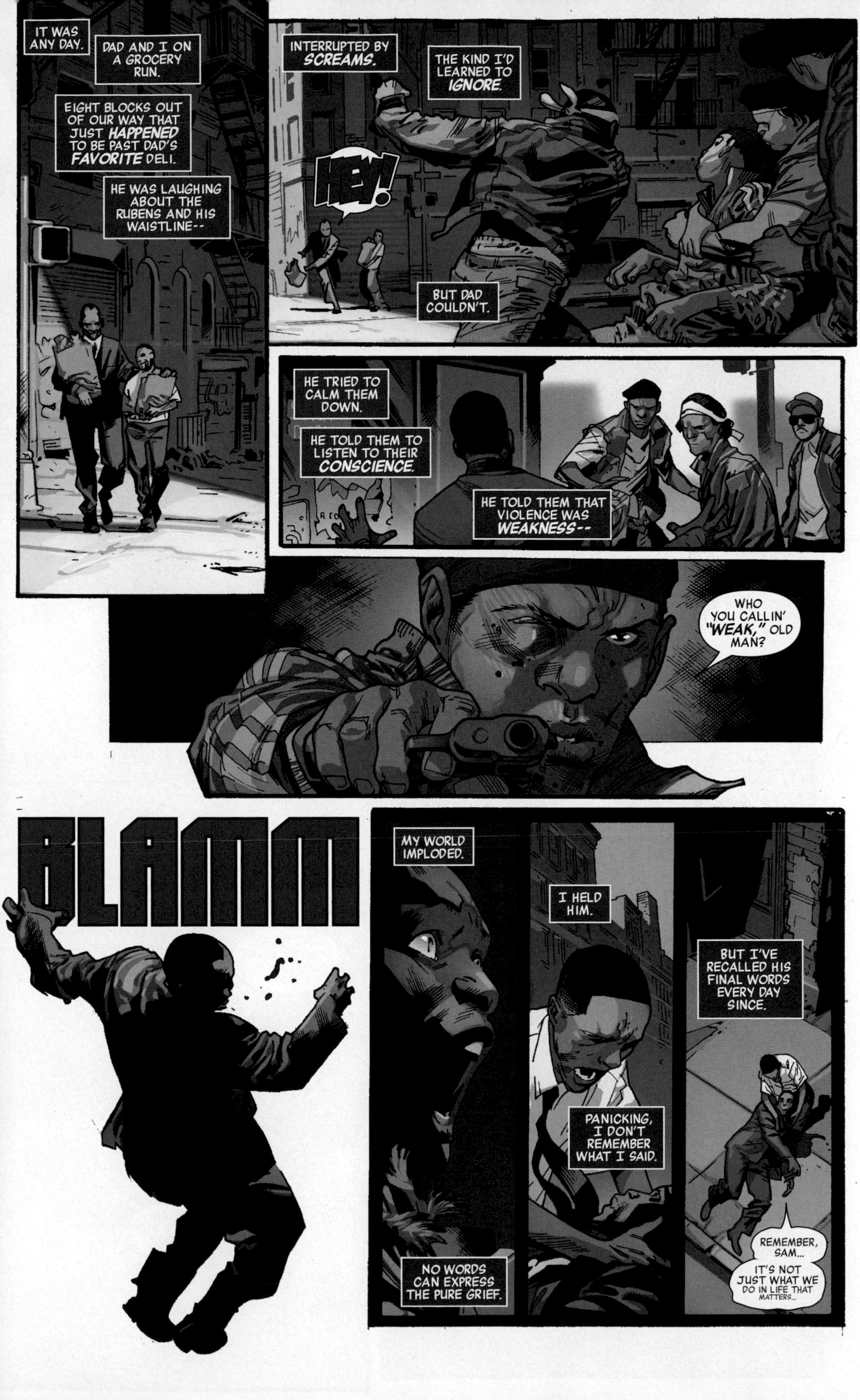

IT WAS ANY DAY.
DAD AND I ON A GROCERY RUN.
EIGHT BLOCKS OUT OF OUR WAY THAT JUST HAPPENED TO BE PAST DAD'S FAVORITE DELI.
HE WAS LAUGHING ABOUT THE RUBENS AND HIS WAISTLINE--
INTERRUPTED BY SCREAMS.
HEY!
THE KIND I'D LEARNED TO IGNORE.
BUT DAD COULDN'T.
HE TRIED TO CALM THEM DOWN.
HE TOLD THEM TO LISTEN TO THEIR CONSCIENCE.
HE TOLD THEM THAT VIOLENCE WAS WEAKNESS--
WHO YOU CALLIN' "WEAK," OLD MAN?
BLAMM
MY WORLD IMPLODED.
NO WORDS CAN EXPRESS THE PURE GRIEF.
I HELD HIM.
PANICKING, I DON'T REMEMBER WHAT I SAID.
BUT I'VE RECALLED HIS FINAL WORDS EVERY DAY SINCE.
REMEMBER, SAM... IT'S NOT JUST WHAT WE DO IN LIFE THAT MATTERS...

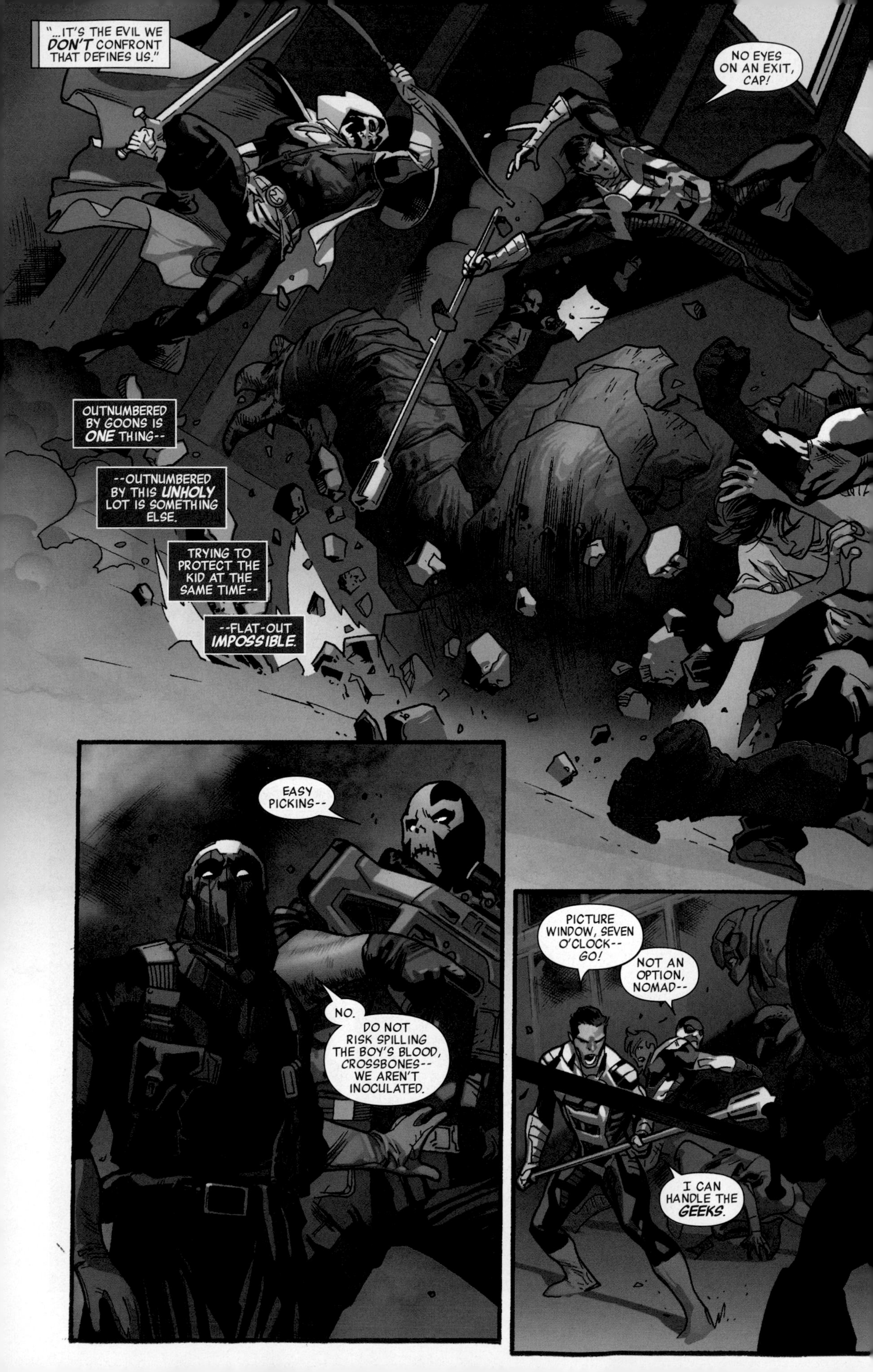
"...IT'S THE EVIL WE DON'T CONFRONT THAT DEFINES US."
NO EYES ON AN EXIT, CAP!
OUTNUMBERED BY GOONS IS ONE THING--
--OUTNUMBERED BY THIS UNHOLY LOT IS SOMETHING ELSE.
TRYING TO PROTECT THE KID AT THE SAME TIME--
--FLAT-OUT IMPOSSIBLE.
EASY PICKINS--
NO.
DO NOT RISK SPILLING THE BOY'S BLOOD, CROSSBONES-- WE AREN'T INOCULATED.
PICTURE WINDOW, SEVEN O'CLOCK-- GO!
NOT AN OPTION, NOMAD--
I CAN HANDLE THE GEEKS.

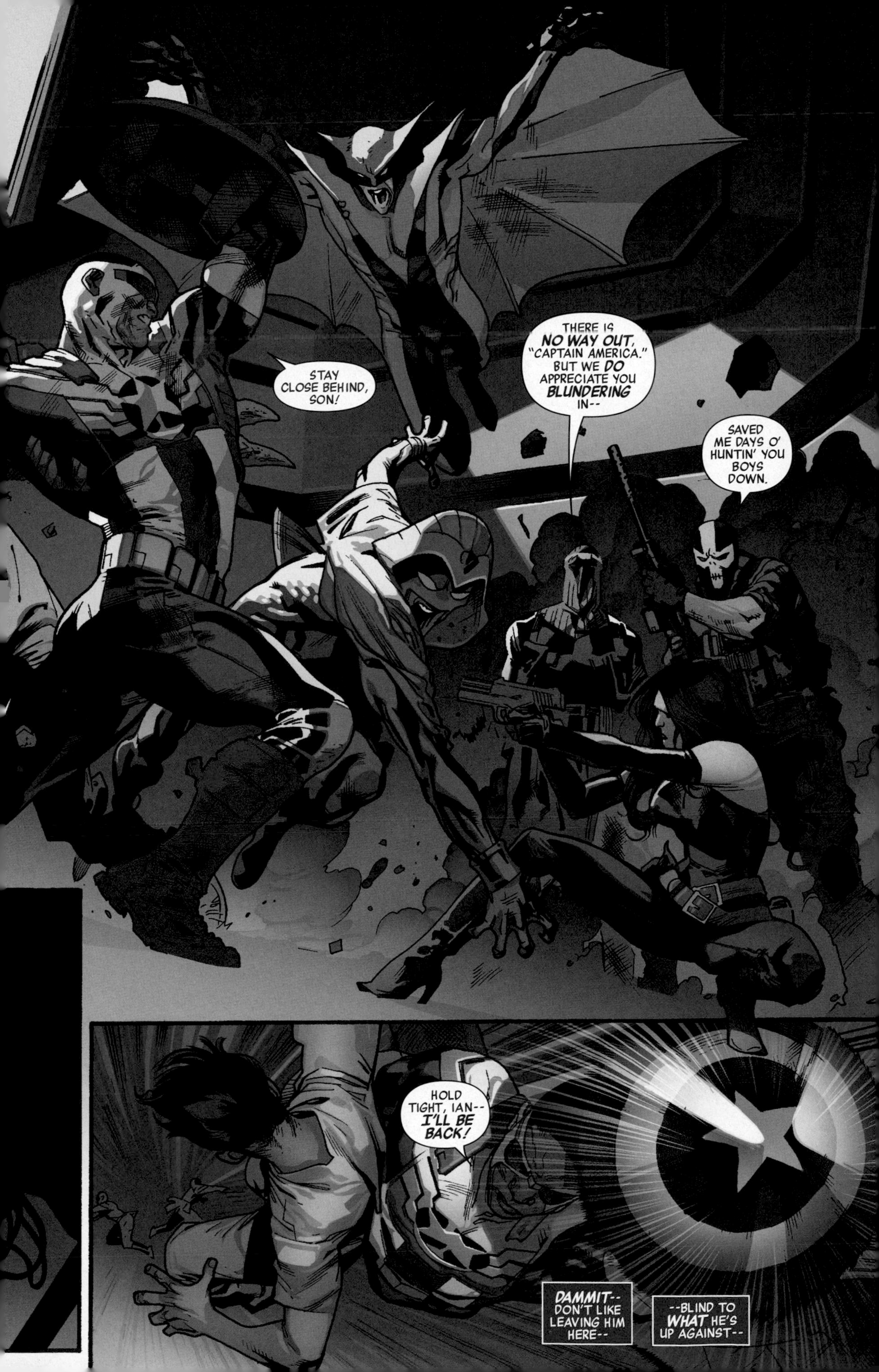
STAY CLOSE BEHIND, SON!
THERE IS NO WAY OUT, "CAPTAIN AMERICA." BUT WE DO APPRECIATE YOU BLUNDERING IN--
SAVED ME DAYS O' HUNTIN' YOU BOYS DOWN.
HOLD TIGHT, IAN-- I'LL BE BACK!
DAMMIT-- DON'T LIKE LEAVING HIM HERE--
--BLIND TO WHAT HE'S UP AGAINST--

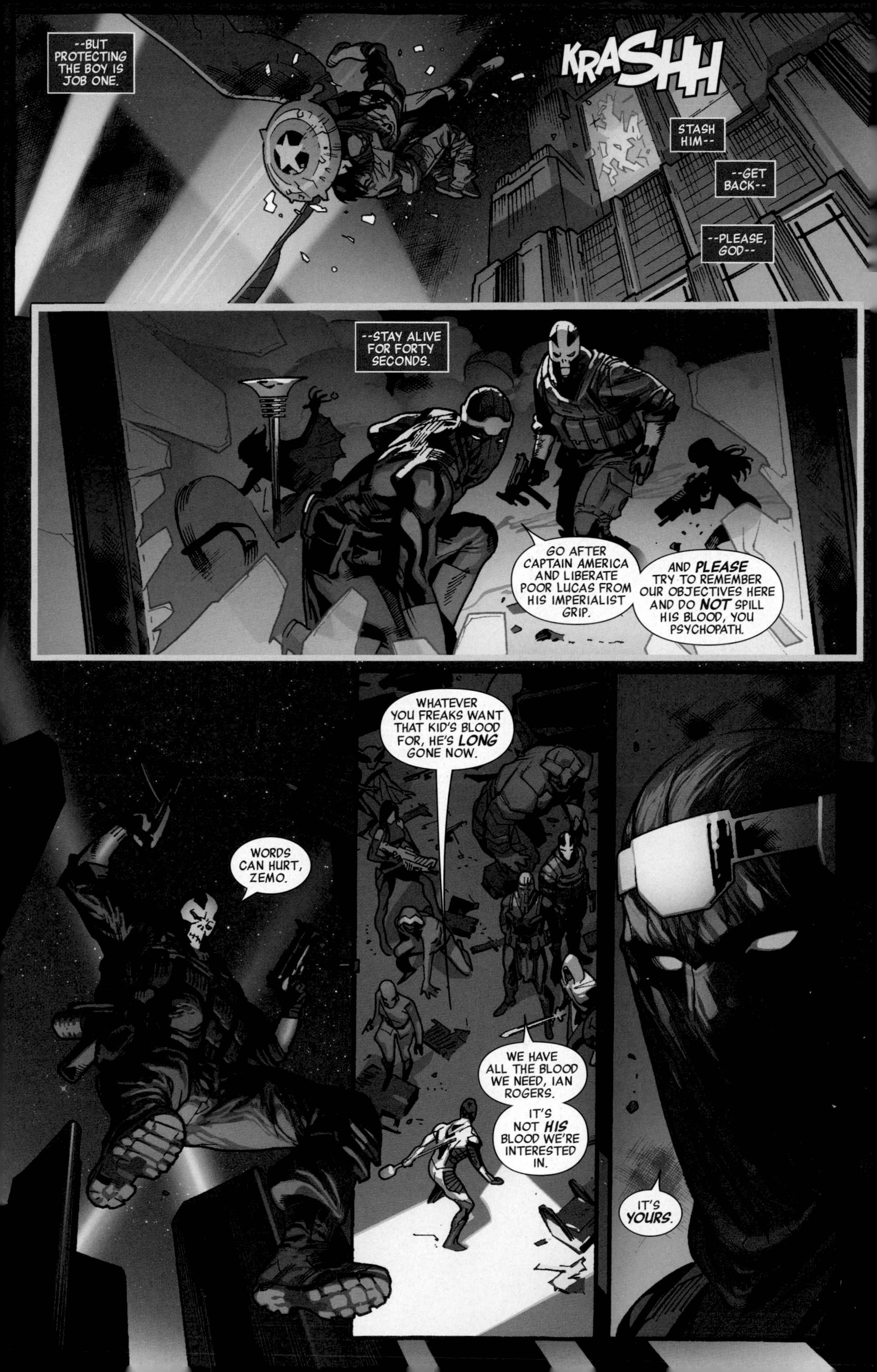
--BUT PROTECTING THE BOY IS JOB ONE.
KRASHH
STASH HIM--
--GET BACK--
--PLEASE, GOD--
--STAY ALIVE FOR FORTY SECONDS.
GO AFTER CAPTAIN AMERICA AND LIBERATE POOR LUCAS FROM HIS IMPERIALIST GRIP.
AND PLEASE TRY TO REMEMBER OUR OBJECTIVES HERE AND DO NOT SPILL HIS BLOOD, YOU PSYCHOPATH.
WORDS CAN HURT, ZEMO.
WHATEVER YOU FREAKS WANT THAT KID'S BLOOD FOR, HE'S LONG GONE NOW.
WE HAVE ALL THE BLOOD WE NEED, IAN ROGERS.
IT'S NOT HIS BLOOD WE'RE INTERESTED IN.
IT'S YOURS.

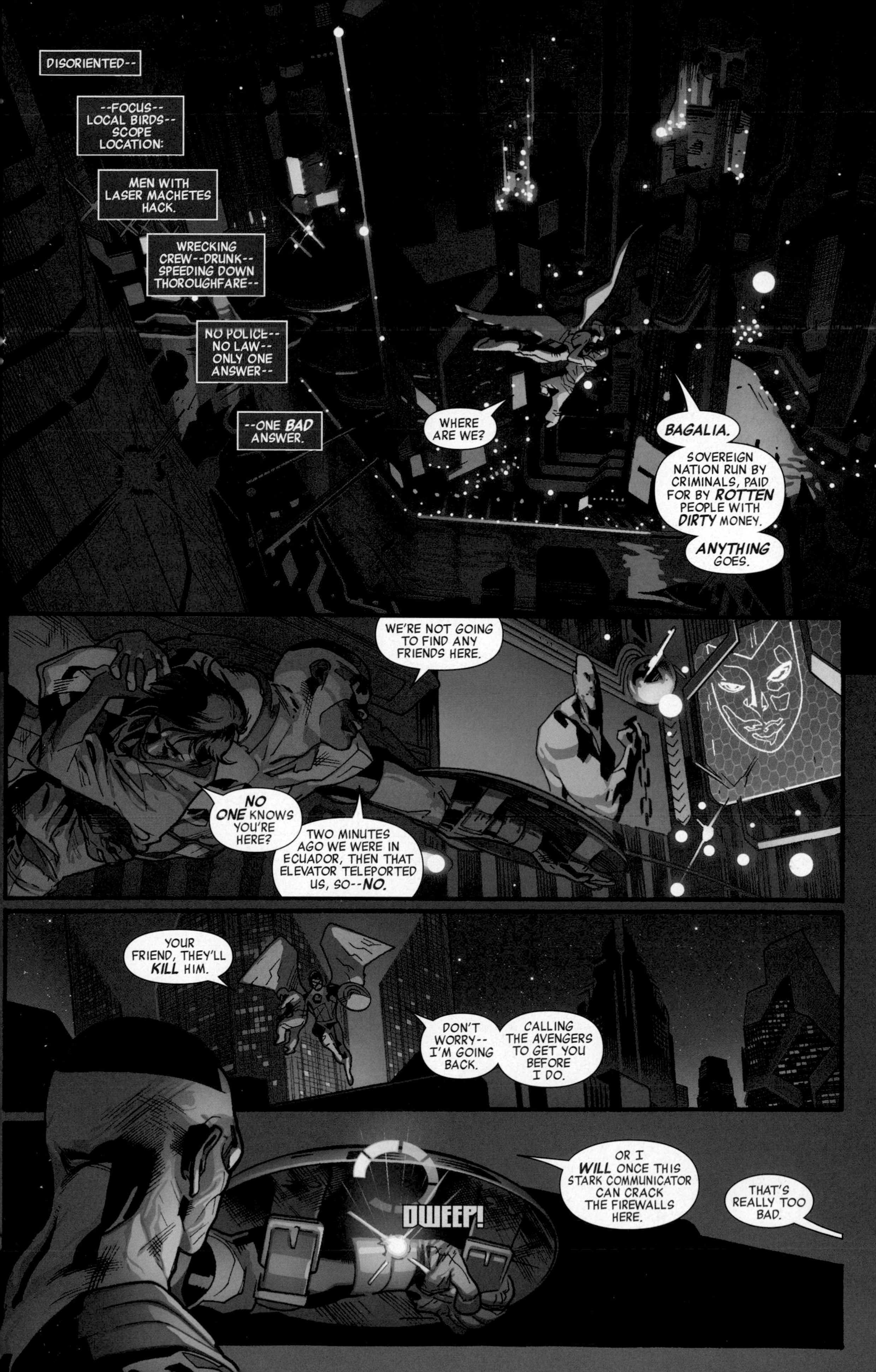
DISORIENTED--
--FOCUS-- LOCAL BIRDS-- SCOPE LOCATION:
MEN WITH LASER MACHETES HACK.
WRECKING CREW--DRUNK-- SPEEDING DOWN THOROUGHFARE--
NO POLICE-- NO LAW-- ONLY ONE ANSWER--
--ONE BAD ANSWER.
WHERE ARE WE?
BAGALIA.
SOVEREIGN NATION RUN BY CRIMINALS, PAID FOR BY ROTTEN PEOPLE WITH DIRTY MONEY.
ANYTHING GOES.
WE'RE NOT GOING TO FIND ANY FRIENDS HERE.
NO ONE KNOWS YOU'RE HERE?
TWO MINUTES AGO WE WERE IN ECUADOR, THEN THAT ELEVATOR TELEPORTED US, SO--NO.
YOUR FRIEND, THEY'LL KILL HIM.
DON'T WORRY-- I'M GOING BACK.
CALLING THE AVENGERS TO GET YOU BEFORE I DO.
OR I WILL ONCE THIS STARK COMMUNICATOR CAN CRACK THE FIREWALLS HERE.
DWEEP!
THAT'S REALLY TOO BAD.

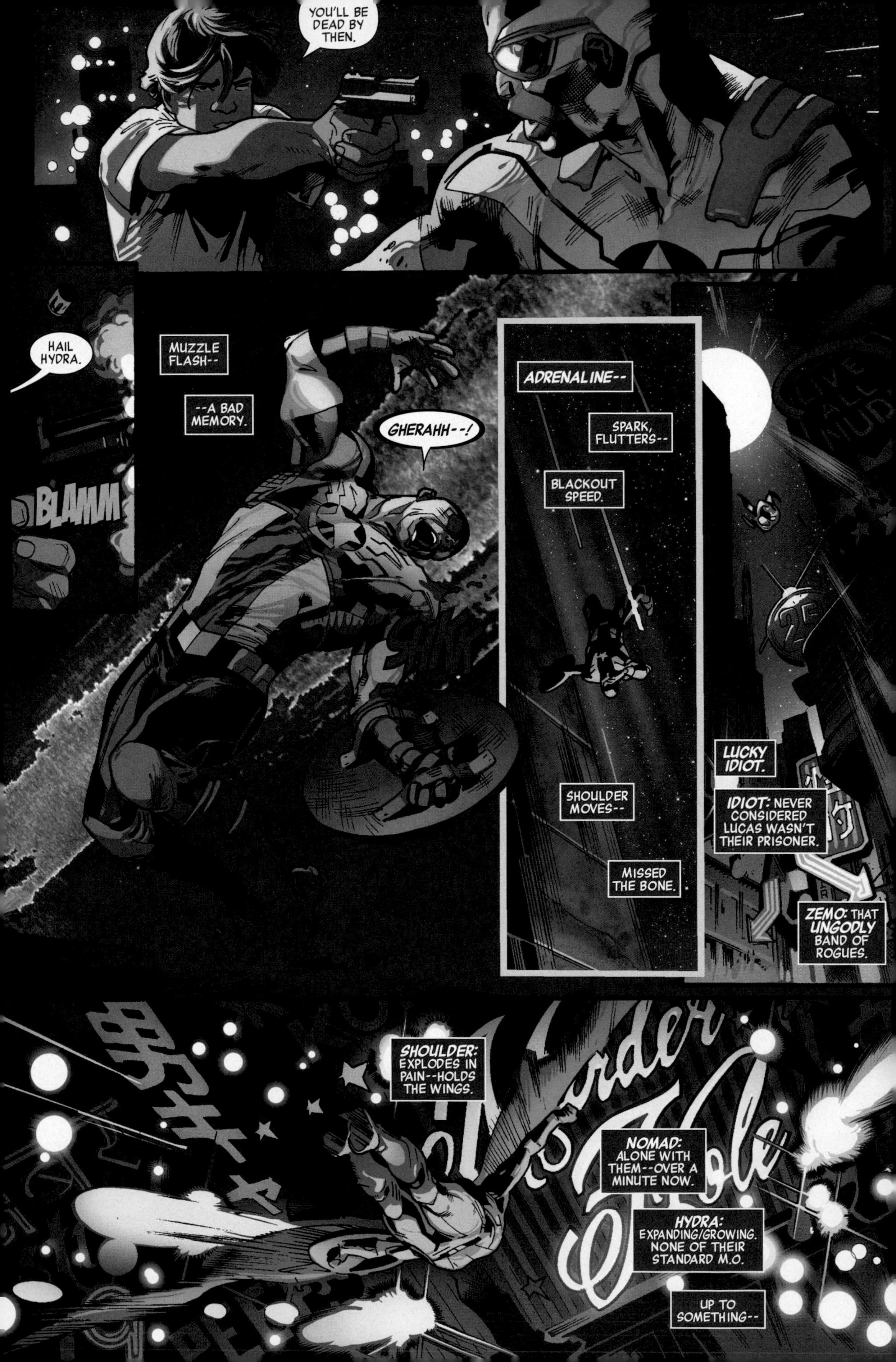
YOU'LL BE DEAD BY THEN.
HAIL HYDRA.
BLAMM
MUZZLE FLASH--
--A BAD MEMORY.
GHERAHH--!
ADRENALINE--
SPARK, FLUTTERS--
BLACKOUT SPEED.
SHOULDER MOVES--
MISSED THE BONE.
LUCKY IDIOT.
IDIOT: NEVER CONSIDERED LUCAS WASN'T THEIR PRISONER.
ZEMO: THAT UNGODLY BAND OF ROGUES.
SHOULDER: EXPLODES IN PAIN--HOLDS THE WINGS.
NOMAD: ALONE WITH THEM--OVER A MINUTE NOW.
HYDRA: EXPANDING/GROWING. NONE OF THEIR STANDARD M.O.
UP TO SOMETHING--

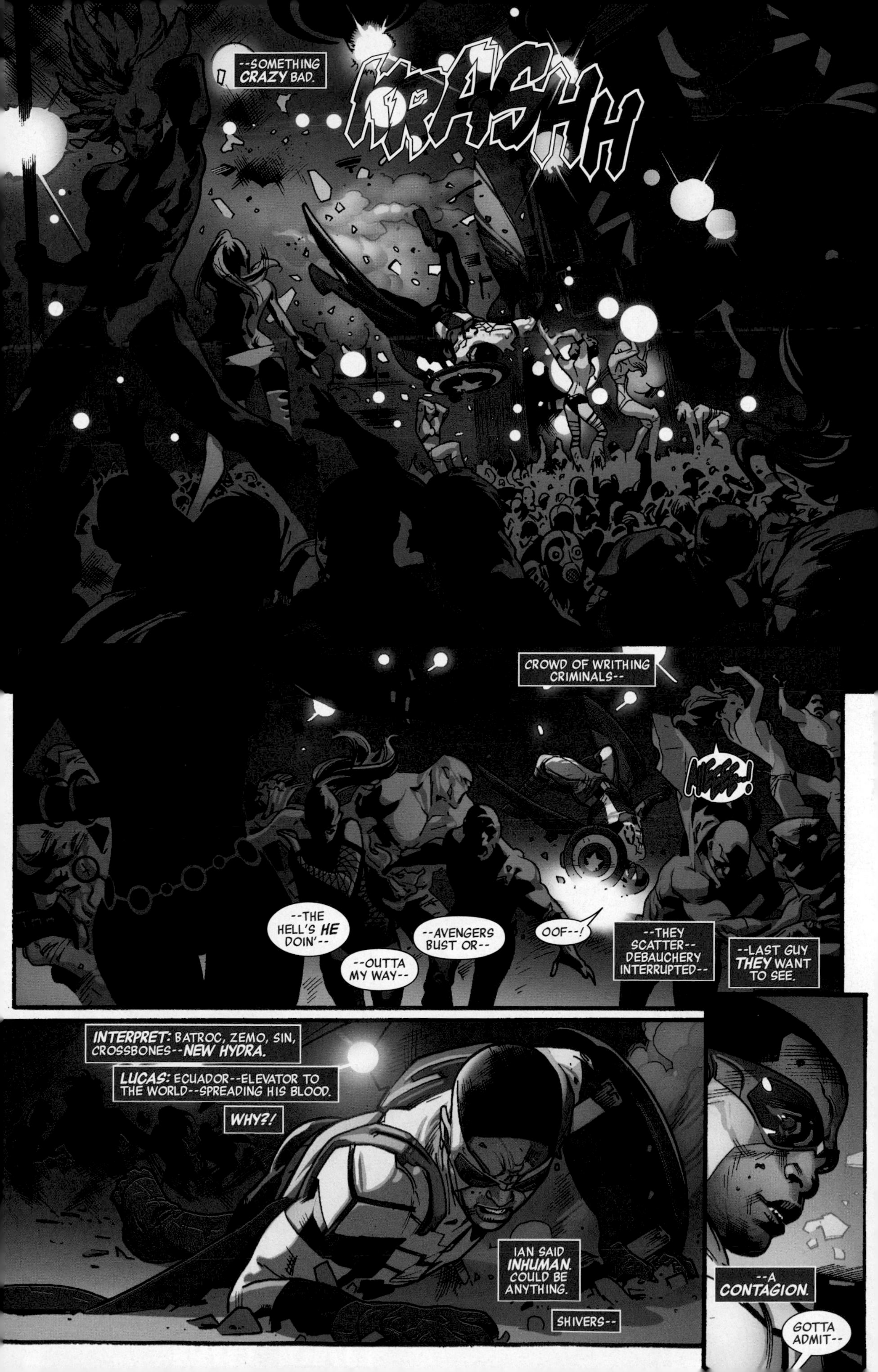
--SOMETHING CRAZY BAD.
KRASHH
CROWD OF WRITHING CRIMINALS--
AIEEE--!
--THE HELL'S HE DOIN'--
--OUTTA MY WAY--
--AVENGERS BUST OR--
OOF--!
--THEY SCATTER--DEBAUCHERY INTERRUPTED--
--LAST GUY THEY WANT TO SEE.
INTERPRET: BATROC, ZEMO, SIN, CROSSBONES--NEW HYDRA.
LUCAS: ECUADOR--ELEVATOR TO THE WORLD--SPREADING HIS BLOOD.
WHY?!
IAN SAID INHUMAN. COULD BE ANYTHING.
SHIVERS--
--A CONTAGION.
GOTTA ADMIT--

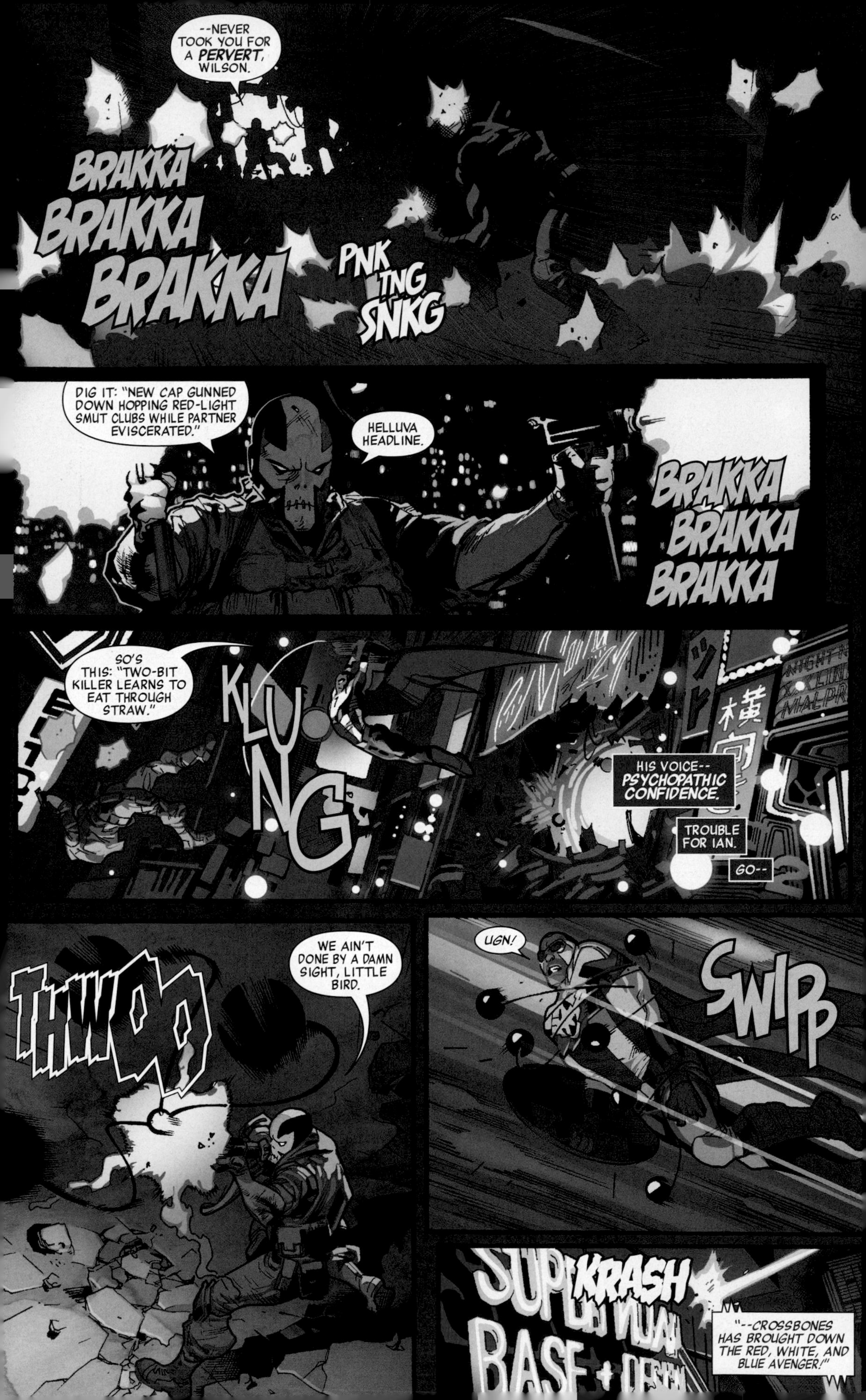
--NEVER TOOK YOU FOR A *PERVERT*, WILSON.
BRAKKA BRAKKA BRAKKA
PNK TNG SNKG
DIG IT: "NEW CAP GUNNED DOWN HOPPING RED-LIGHT SMUT CLUBS WHILE PARTNER EVISCERATED."
HELLUVA HEADLINE.
BRAKKA BRAKKA BRAKKA
SO'S THIS: "TWO-BIT KILLER LEARNS TO EAT THROUGH STRAW."
KLUNG
HIS VOICE-- *PSYCHOPATHIC CONFIDENCE.*
TROUBLE FOR IAN.
GO--
THWOOP
WE AIN'T DONE BY A DAMN SIGHT, LITTLE BIRD.
UGN!
SWIPP
KRASH
"--CROSSBONES HAS BROUGHT DOWN THE RED, WHITE, AND BLUE AVENGER!"

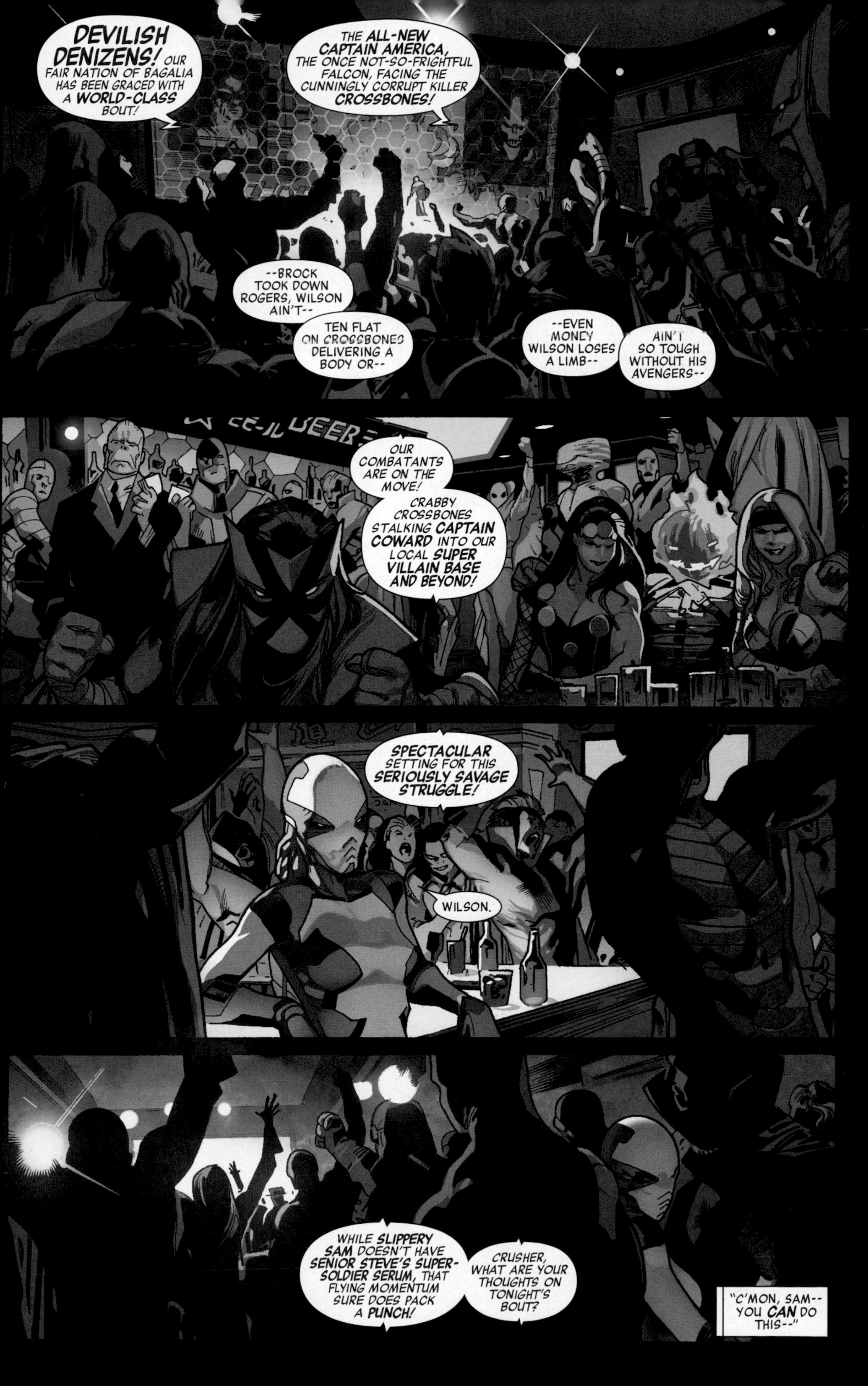
DEVILISH DENIZENS! OUR FAIR NATION OF BAGALIA HAS BEEN GRACED WITH A WORLD-CLASS BOUT!
THE ALL-NEW CAPTAIN AMERICA, THE ONCE NOT-SO-FRIGHTFUL FALCON, FACING THE CUNNINGLY CORRUPT KILLER CROSSBONES!
--BROCK TOOK DOWN ROGERS, WILSON AIN'T--
TEN FLAT ON CROSSBONES DELIVERING A BODY OR--
--EVEN MONEY WILSON LOSES A LIMB--
AIN'T SO TOUGH WITHOUT HIS AVENGERS--
BEER
OUR COMBATANTS ARE ON THE MOVE!
CRABBY CROSSBONES STALKING CAPTAIN COWARD INTO OUR LOCAL SUPER VILLAIN BASE AND BEYOND!
SPECTACULAR SETTING FOR THIS SERIOUSLY SAVAGE STRUGGLE!
WILSON.
WHILE SLIPPERY SAM DOESN'T HAVE SENIOR STEVE'S SUPER-SOLDIER SERUM, THAT FLYING MOMENTUM SURE DOES PACK A PUNCH!
CRUSHER, WHAT ARE YOUR THOUGHTS ON TONIGHT'S BOUT?
"C'MON, SAM-- YOU CAN DO THIS--"

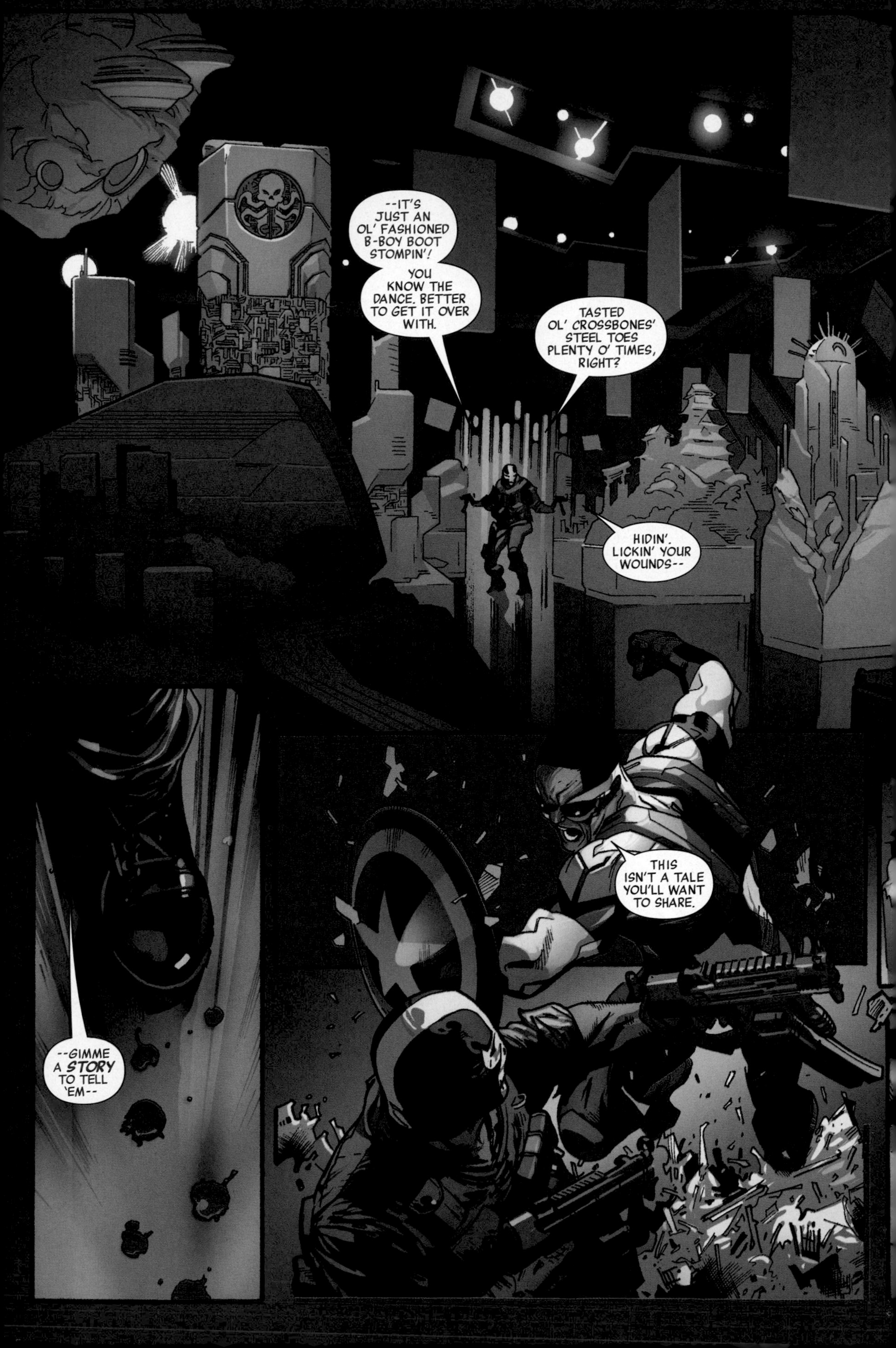
--IT'S JUST AN OL' FASHIONED B-BOY BOOT STOMPIN'!
YOU KNOW THE DANCE. BETTER TO GET IT OVER WITH.
TASTED OL' CROSSBONES' STEEL TOES PLENTY O' TIMES, RIGHT?
HIDIN'. LICKIN' YOUR WOUNDS--
--GIMME A STORY TO TELL 'EM--
THIS ISN'T A TALE YOU'LL WANT TO SHARE.

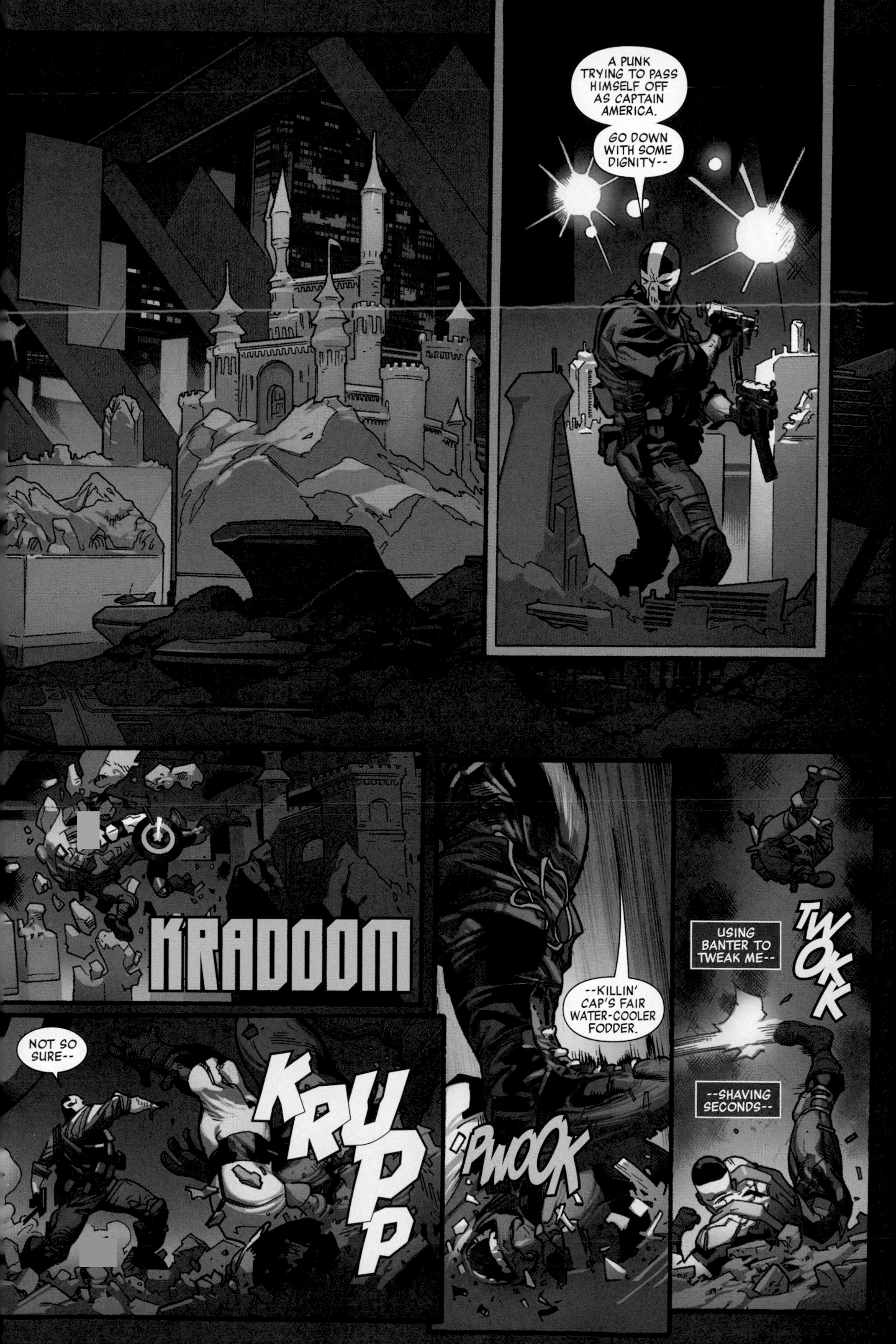

A PUNK TRYING TO PASS HIMSELF OFF AS CAPTAIN AMERICA.
GO DOWN WITH SOME DIGNITY--
KRADOOM
NOT SO SURE--
KRUPP
--KILLIN' CAP'S FAIR WATER-COOLER FODDER.
PWOOK
USING BANTER TO TWEAK ME--
TWOKK
--SHAVING SECONDS--

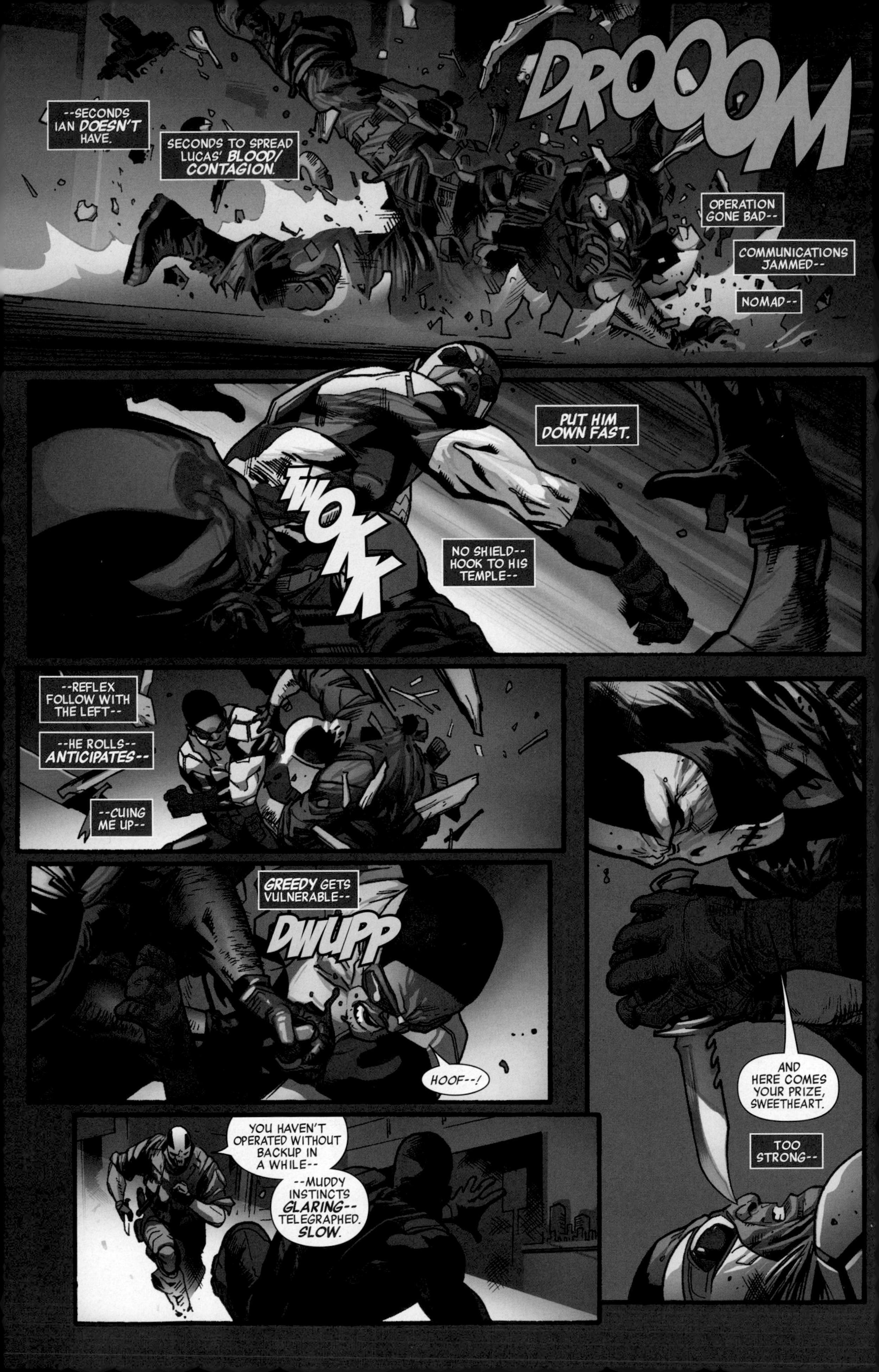
DROOOM
--SECONDS IAN DOESN'T HAVE.
SECONDS TO SPREAD LUCAS' BLOOD/ CONTAGION.
OPERATION GONE BAD--
COMMUNICATIONS JAMMED--
NOMAD--
PUT HIM DOWN FAST.
TWOKK
NO SHIELD-- HOOK TO HIS TEMPLE--
--REFLEX FOLLOW WITH THE LEFT--
--HE ROLLS-- ANTICIPATES--
--CUING ME UP--
GREEDY GETS VULNERABLE--
DWUPP
HOOF--!
YOU HAVEN'T OPERATED WITHOUT BACKUP IN A WHILE--
--MUDDY INSTINCTS GLARING-- TELEGRAPHED. SLOW.
AND HERE COMES YOUR PRIZE, SWEETHEART.
TOO STRONG--

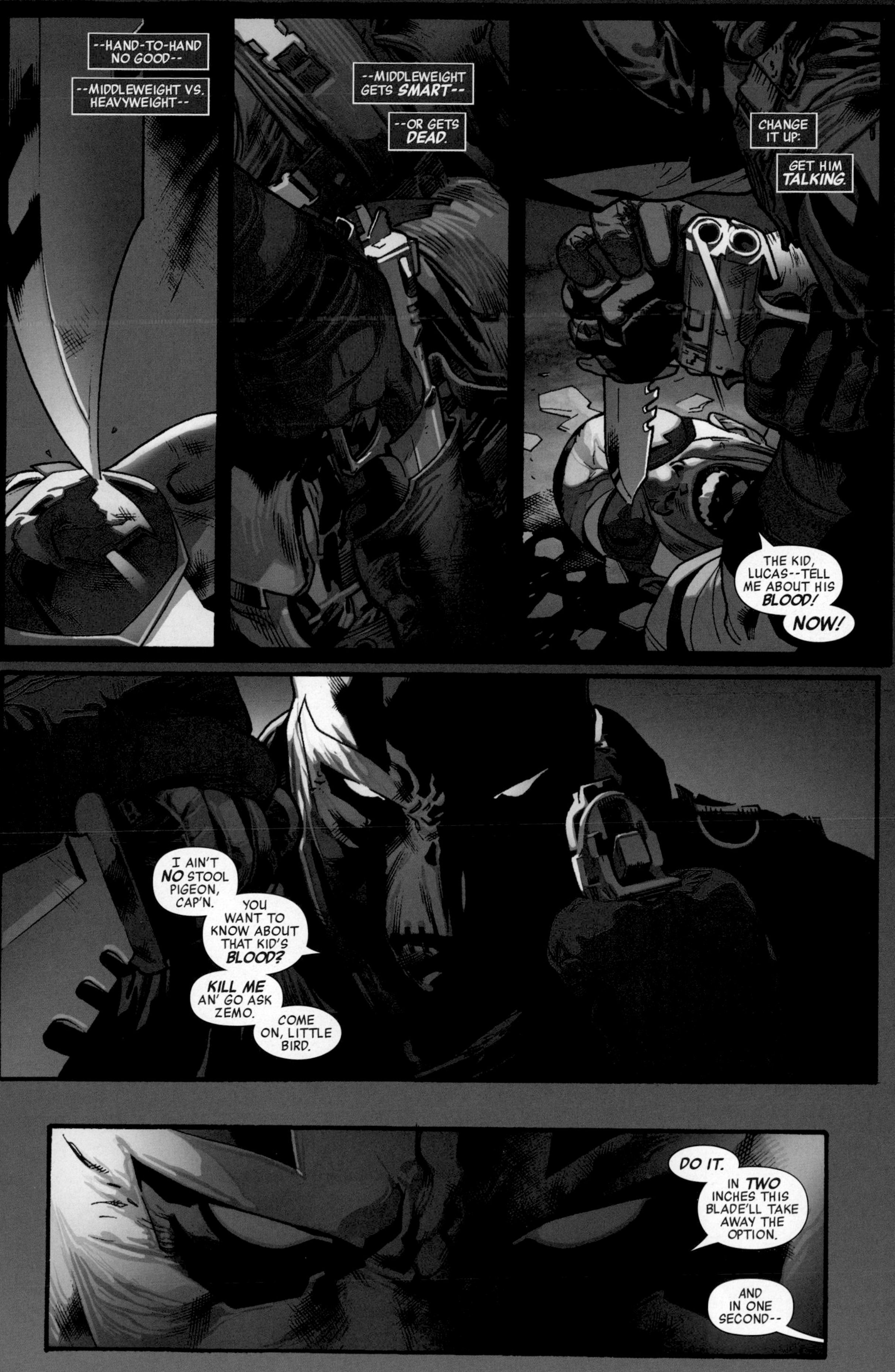

--HAND-TO-HAND NO GOOD--
--MIDDLEWEIGHT VS. HEAVYWEIGHT--
--MIDDLEWEIGHT GETS SMART--
--OR GETS DEAD.
CHANGE IT UP:
GET HIM TALKING.
THE KID, LUCAS--TELL ME ABOUT HIS BLOOD!
NOW!
I AIN'T NO STOOL PIGEON, CAP'N.
YOU WANT TO KNOW ABOUT THAT KID'S BLOOD?
KILL ME AN' GO ASK ZEMO.
COME ON, LITTLE BIRD.
DO IT.
IN TWO INCHES THIS BLADE'LL TAKE AWAY THE OPTION.
AND IN ONE SECOND--

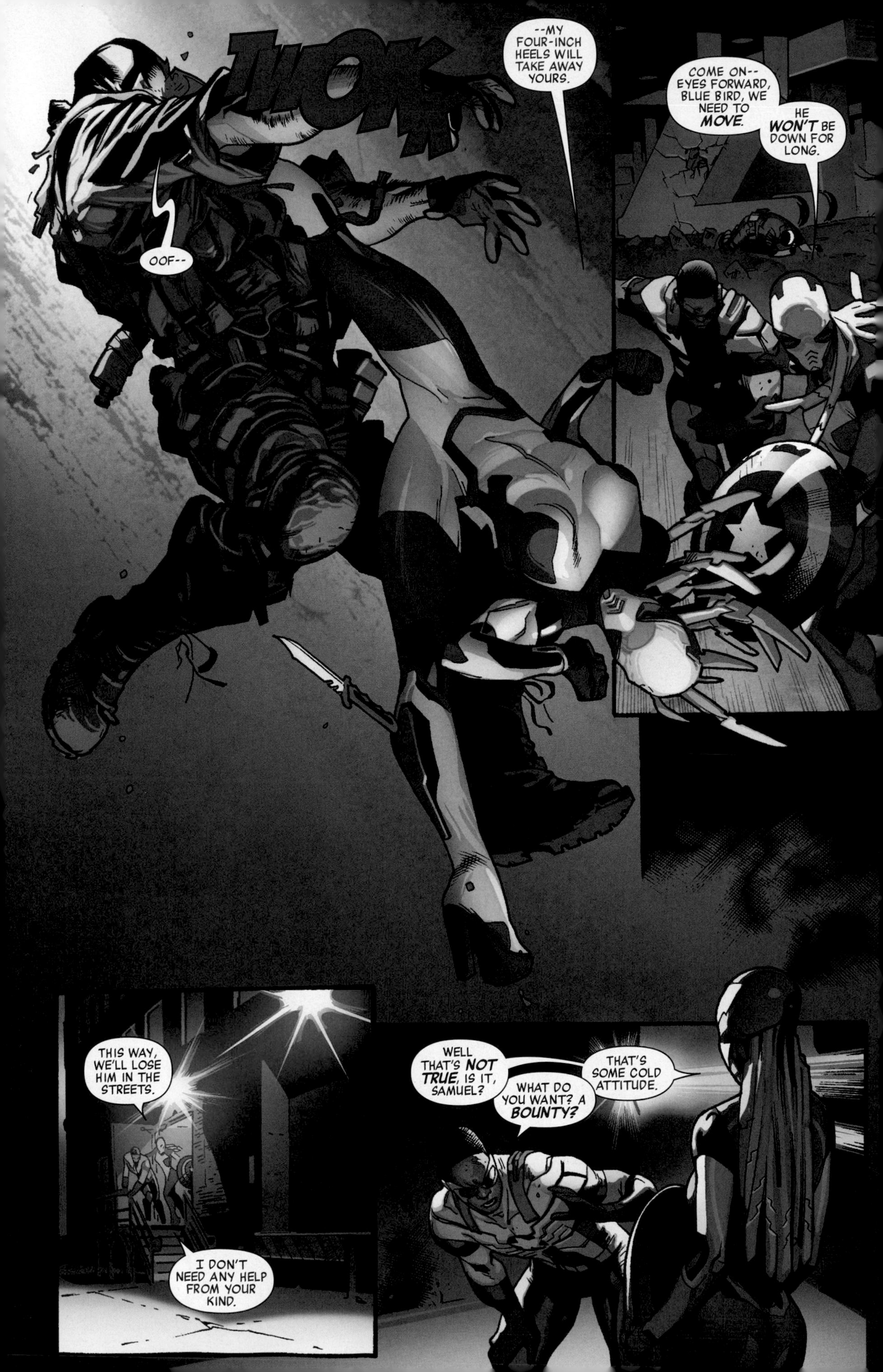
THOK
OOF--
--MY FOUR-INCH HEELS WILL TAKE AWAY YOURS.
COME ON-- EYES FORWARD, BLUE BIRD, WE NEED TO MOVE.
HE WON'T BE DOWN FOR LONG.
THIS WAY, WE'LL LOSE HIM IN THE STREETS.
I DON'T NEED ANY HELP FROM YOUR KIND.
WELL THAT'S NOT TRUE, IS IT, SAMUEL?
THAT'S SOME COLD ATTITUDE.
WHAT DO YOU WANT? A BOUNTY?

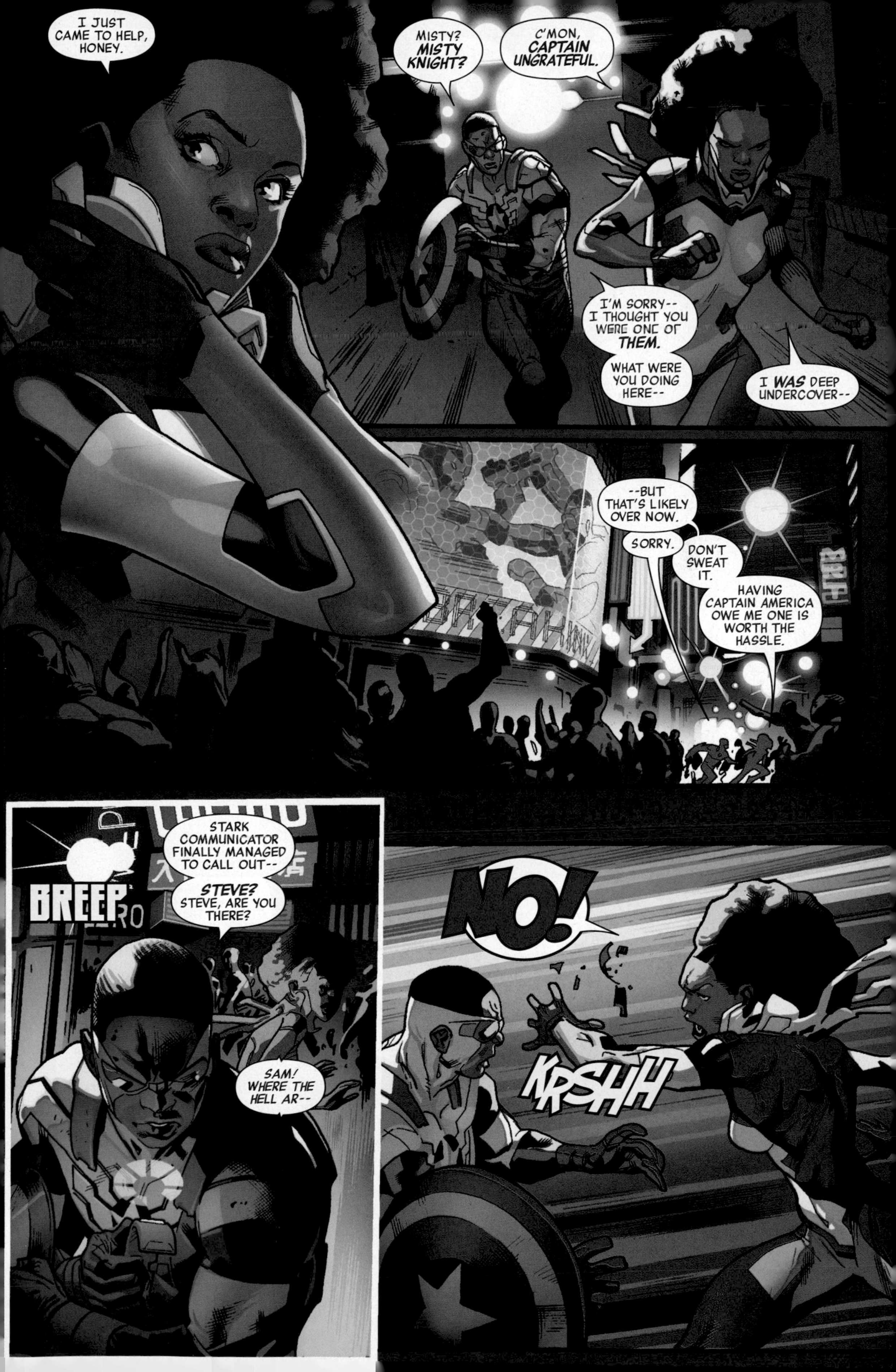
I JUST CAME TO HELP, HONEY.
MISTY? MISTY KNIGHT?
C'MON, CAPTAIN UNGRATEFUL.
I'M SORRY-- I THOUGHT YOU WERE ONE OF THEM.
WHAT WERE YOU DOING HERE--
I WAS DEEP UNDERCOVER--
--BUT THAT'S LIKELY OVER NOW.
SORRY.
DON'T SWEAT IT.
HAVING CAPTAIN AMERICA OWE ME ONE IS WORTH THE HASSLE.
BREEP
STARK COMMUNICATOR FINALLY MANAGED TO CALL OUT--
STEVE? STEVE, ARE YOU THERE?
SAM! WHERE THE HELL AR--
NO!
KRSHH

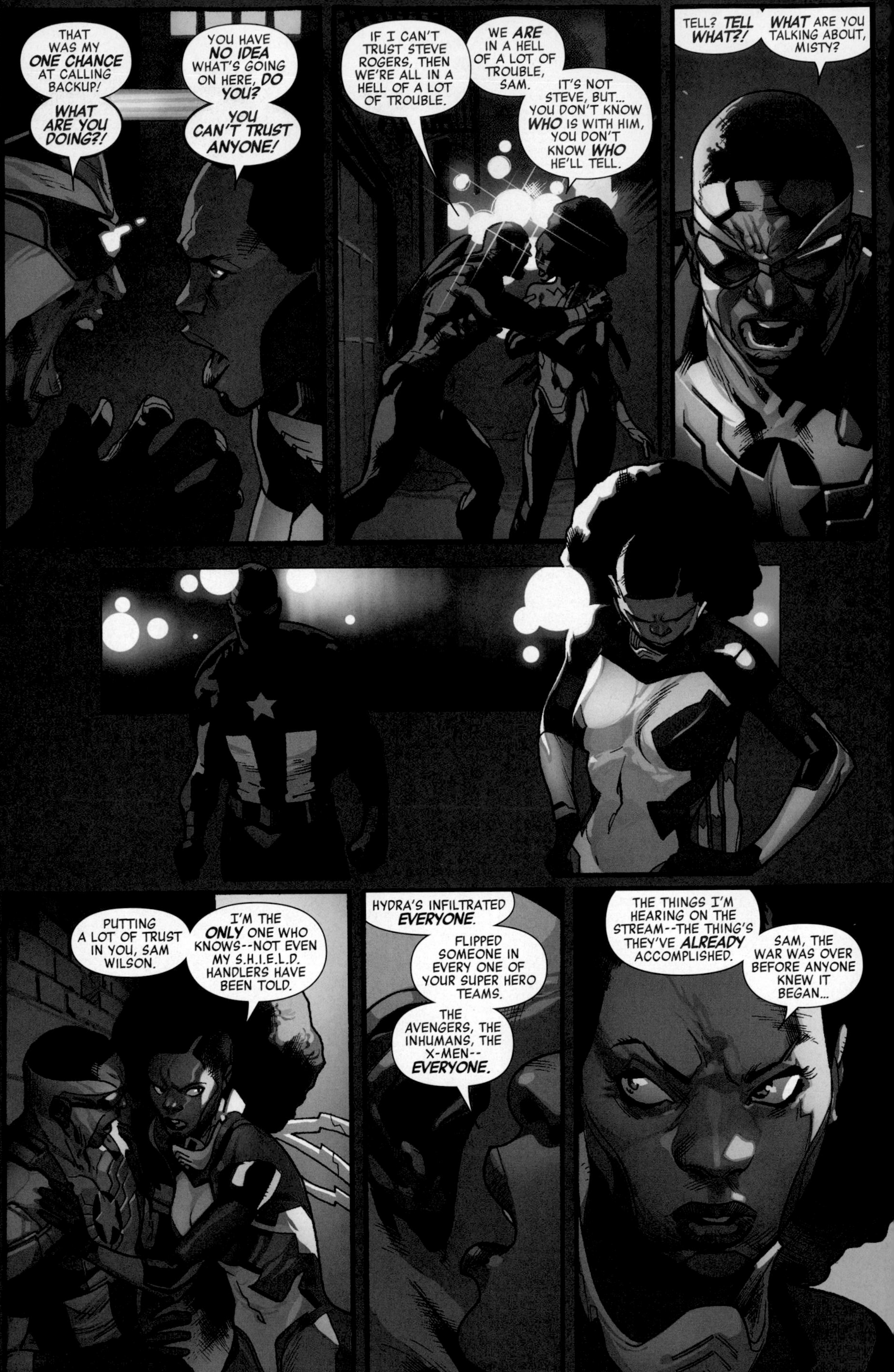
THAT WAS MY ONE CHANCE AT CALLING BACKUP!
WHAT ARE YOU DOING?!
YOU HAVE NO IDEA WHAT'S GOING ON HERE, DO YOU?
YOU CAN'T TRUST ANYONE!
IF I CAN'T TRUST STEVE ROGERS, THEN WE'RE ALL IN A HELL OF A LOT OF TROUBLE.
WE ARE IN A HELL OF A LOT OF TROUBLE, SAM.
IT'S NOT STEVE, BUT... YOU DON'T KNOW WHO IS WITH HIM, YOU DON'T KNOW WHO HE'LL TELL.
TELL? TELL WHAT?!
WHAT ARE YOU TALKING ABOUT, MISTY?
PUTTING A LOT OF TRUST IN YOU, SAM WILSON.
I'M THE ONLY ONE WHO KNOWS--NOT EVEN MY S.H.I.E.L.D. HANDLERS HAVE BEEN TOLD.
HYDRA'S INFILTRATED EVERYONE.
FLIPPED SOMEONE IN EVERY ONE OF YOUR SUPER HERO TEAMS.
THE AVENGERS, THE INHUMANS, THE X-MEN--EVERYONE.
THE THINGS I'M HEARING ON THE STREAM--THE THING'S THEY'VE ALREADY ACCOMPLISHED.
SAM, THE WAR WAS OVER BEFORE ANYONE KNEW IT BEGAN...

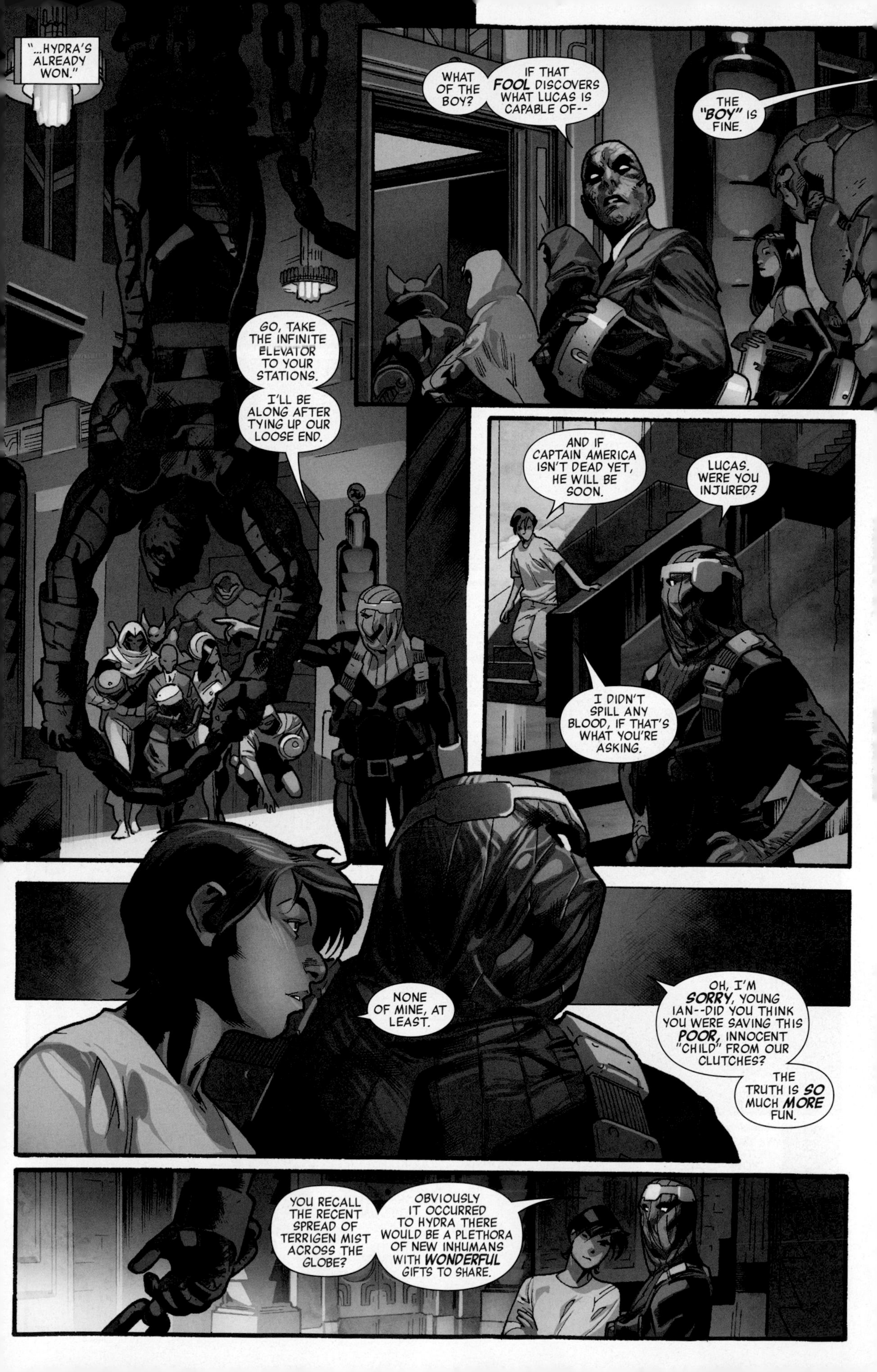
"...HYDRA'S ALREADY WON."
WHAT OF THE BOY?
IF THAT FOOL DISCOVERS WHAT LUCAS IS CAPABLE OF--
THE "BOY" IS FINE.
GO, TAKE THE INFINITE ELEVATOR TO YOUR STATIONS.
I'LL BE ALONG AFTER TYING UP OUR LOOSE END.
AND IF CAPTAIN AMERICA ISN'T DEAD YET, HE WILL BE SOON.
LUCAS. WERE YOU INJURED?
I DIDN'T SPILL ANY BLOOD, IF THAT'S WHAT YOU'RE ASKING.
NONE OF MINE, AT LEAST.
OH, I'M SORRY, YOUNG IAN--DID YOU THINK YOU WERE SAVING THIS POOR, INNOCENT "CHILD" FROM OUR CLUTCHES?
THE TRUTH IS SO MUCH MORE FUN.
YOU RECALL THE RECENT SPREAD OF TERRIGEN MIST ACROSS THE GLOBE?
OBVIOUSLY IT OCCURRED TO HYDRA THERE WOULD BE A PLETHORA OF NEW INHUMANS WITH WONDERFUL GIFTS TO SHARE.

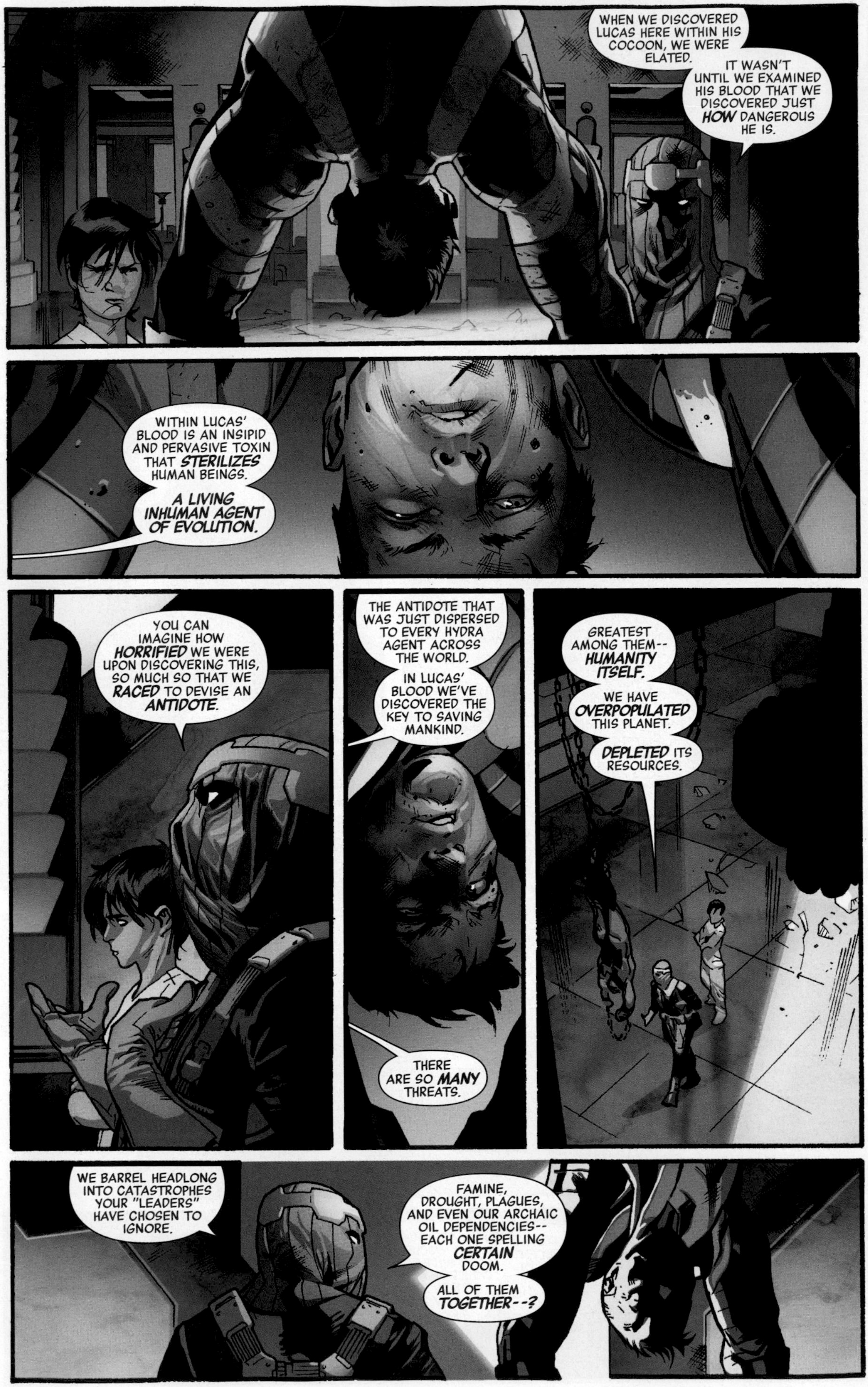
WHEN WE DISCOVERED LUCAS HERE WITHIN HIS COCOON, WE WERE ELATED.
IT WASN'T UNTIL WE EXAMINED HIS BLOOD THAT WE DISCOVERED JUST HOW DANGEROUS HE IS.
WITHIN LUCAS' BLOOD IS AN INSIPID AND PERVASIVE TOXIN THAT STERILIZES HUMAN BEINGS.
A LIVING INHUMAN AGENT OF EVOLUTION.
YOU CAN IMAGINE HOW HORRIFIED WE WERE UPON DISCOVERING THIS, SO MUCH SO THAT WE RACED TO DEVISE AN ANTIDOTE.
THE ANTIDOTE THAT WAS JUST DISPERSED TO EVERY HYDRA AGENT ACROSS THE WORLD.
IN LUCAS' BLOOD WE'VE DISCOVERED THE KEY TO SAVING MANKIND.
THERE ARE SO MANY THREATS.
GREATEST AMONG THEM-- HUMANITY ITSELF.
WE HAVE OVERPOPULATED THIS PLANET.
DEPLETED ITS RESOURCES.
WE BARREL HEADLONG INTO CATASTROPHES YOUR "LEADERS" HAVE CHOSEN TO IGNORE.
FAMINE, DROUGHT, PLAGUES, AND EVEN OUR ARCHAIC OIL DEPENDENCIES-- EACH ONE SPELLING CERTAIN DOOM.
ALL OF THEM TOGETHER--?

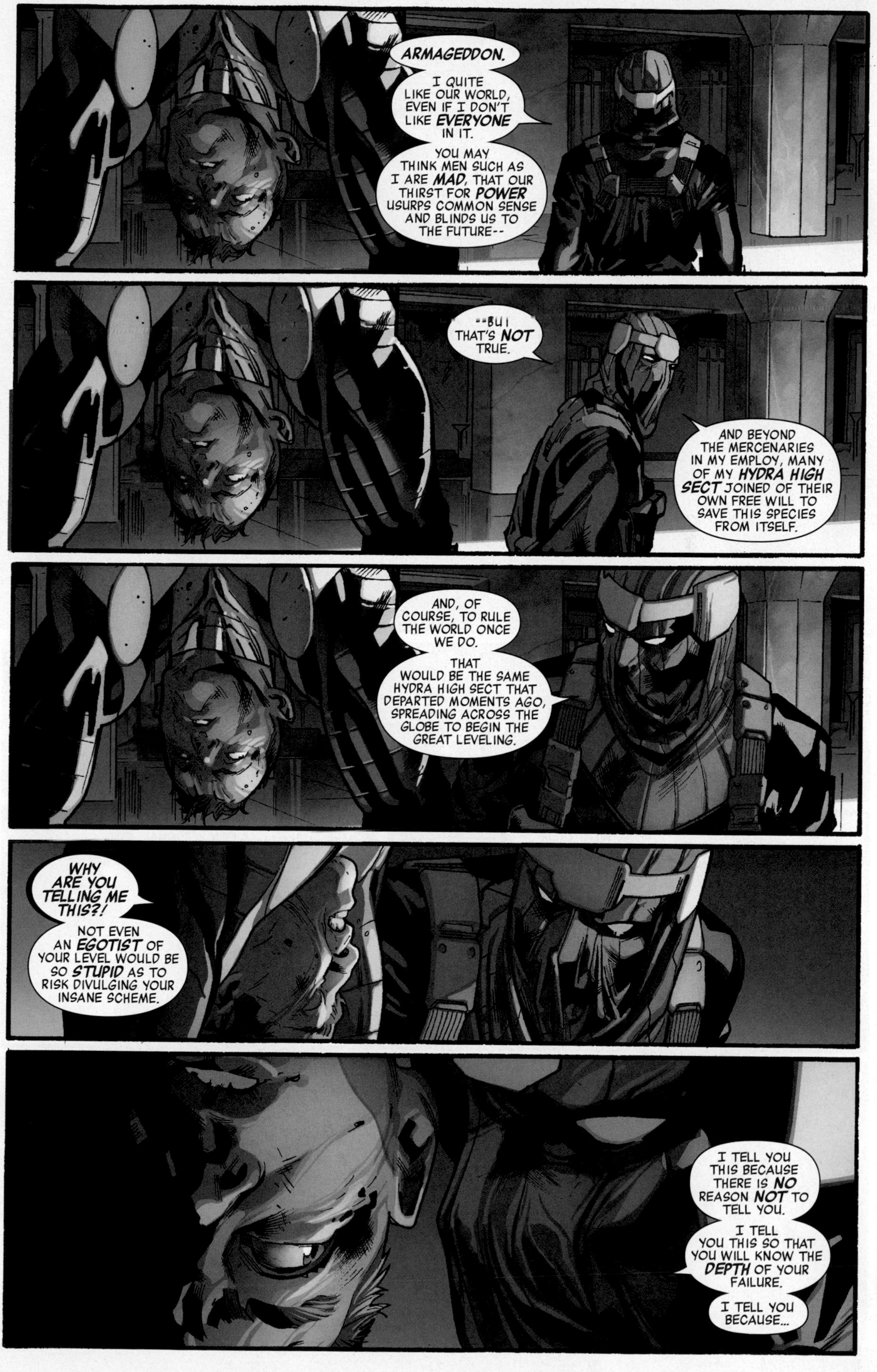
ARMAGEDDON.
I QUITE LIKE OUR WORLD, EVEN IF I DON'T LIKE EVERYONE IN IT.
YOU MAY THINK MEN SUCH AS I ARE MAD, THAT OUR THIRST FOR POWER USURPS COMMON SENSE AND BLINDS US TO THE FUTURE--
--BUT THAT'S NOT TRUE.
AND BEYOND THE MERCENARIES IN MY EMPLOY, MANY OF MY HYDRA HIGH SECT JOINED OF THEIR OWN FREE WILL TO SAVE THIS SPECIES FROM ITSELF.
AND, OF COURSE, TO RULE THE WORLD ONCE WE DO.
THAT WOULD BE THE SAME HYDRA HIGH SECT THAT DEPARTED MOMENTS AGO, SPREADING ACROSS THE GLOBE TO BEGIN THE GREAT LEVELING.
WHY ARE YOU TELLING ME THIS?!
NOT EVEN AN EGOTIST OF YOUR LEVEL WOULD BE SO STUPID AS TO RISK DIVULGING YOUR INSANE SCHEME.
I TELL YOU THIS BECAUSE THERE IS NO REASON NOT TO TELL YOU.
I TELL YOU THIS SO THAT YOU WILL KNOW THE DEPTH OF YOUR FAILURE.
I TELL YOU BECAUSE...

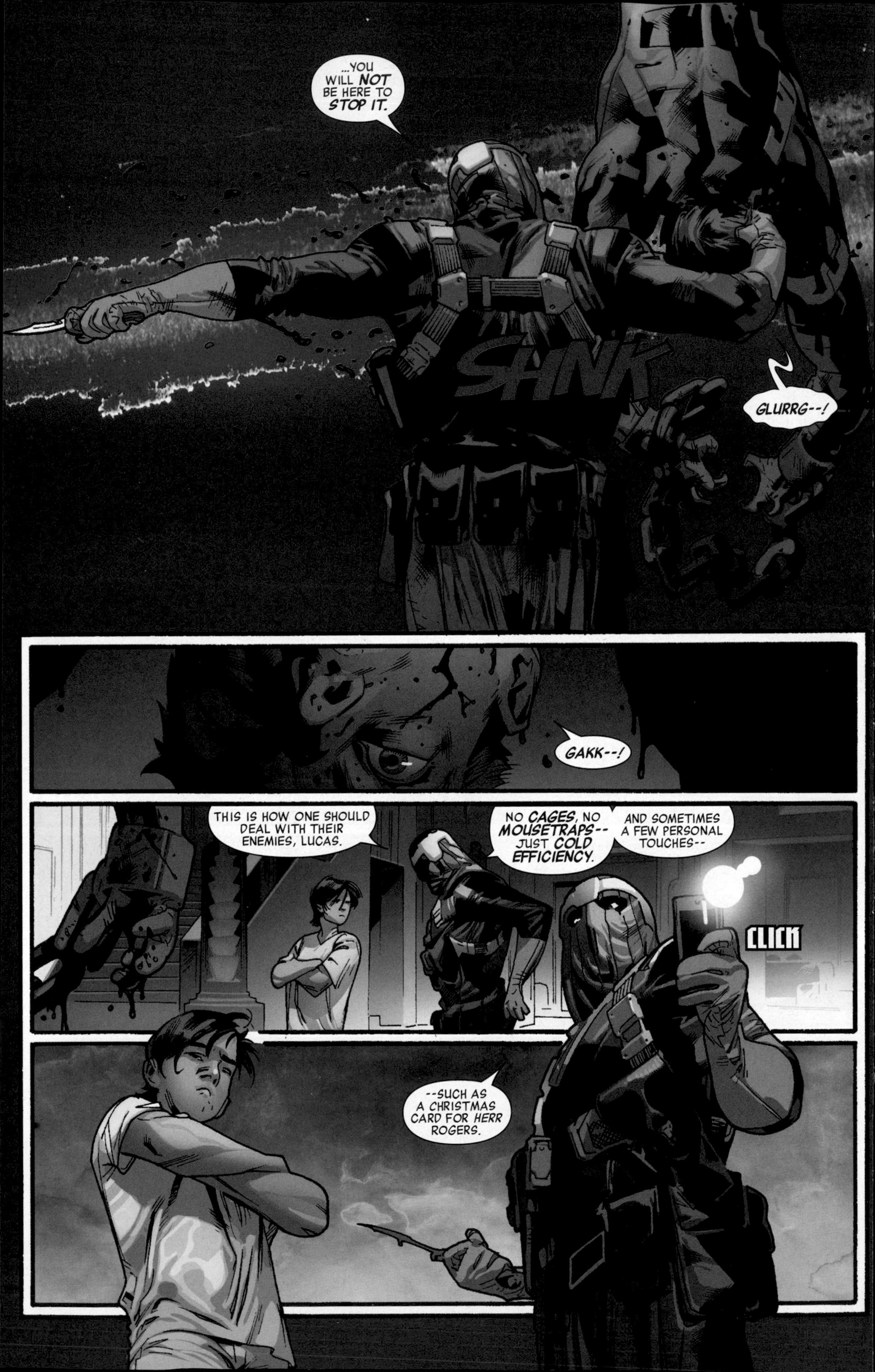

...YOU WILL NOT BE HERE TO STOP IT.
SHINK
GLURRG--!
GAKK--!
THIS IS HOW ONE SHOULD DEAL WITH THEIR ENEMIES, LUCAS.
NO CAGES, NO MOUSETRAPS-- JUST COLD EFFICIENCY.
AND SOMETIMES A FEW PERSONAL TOUCHES--
CLICK
--SUCH AS A CHRISTMAS CARD FOR HERR ROGERS.

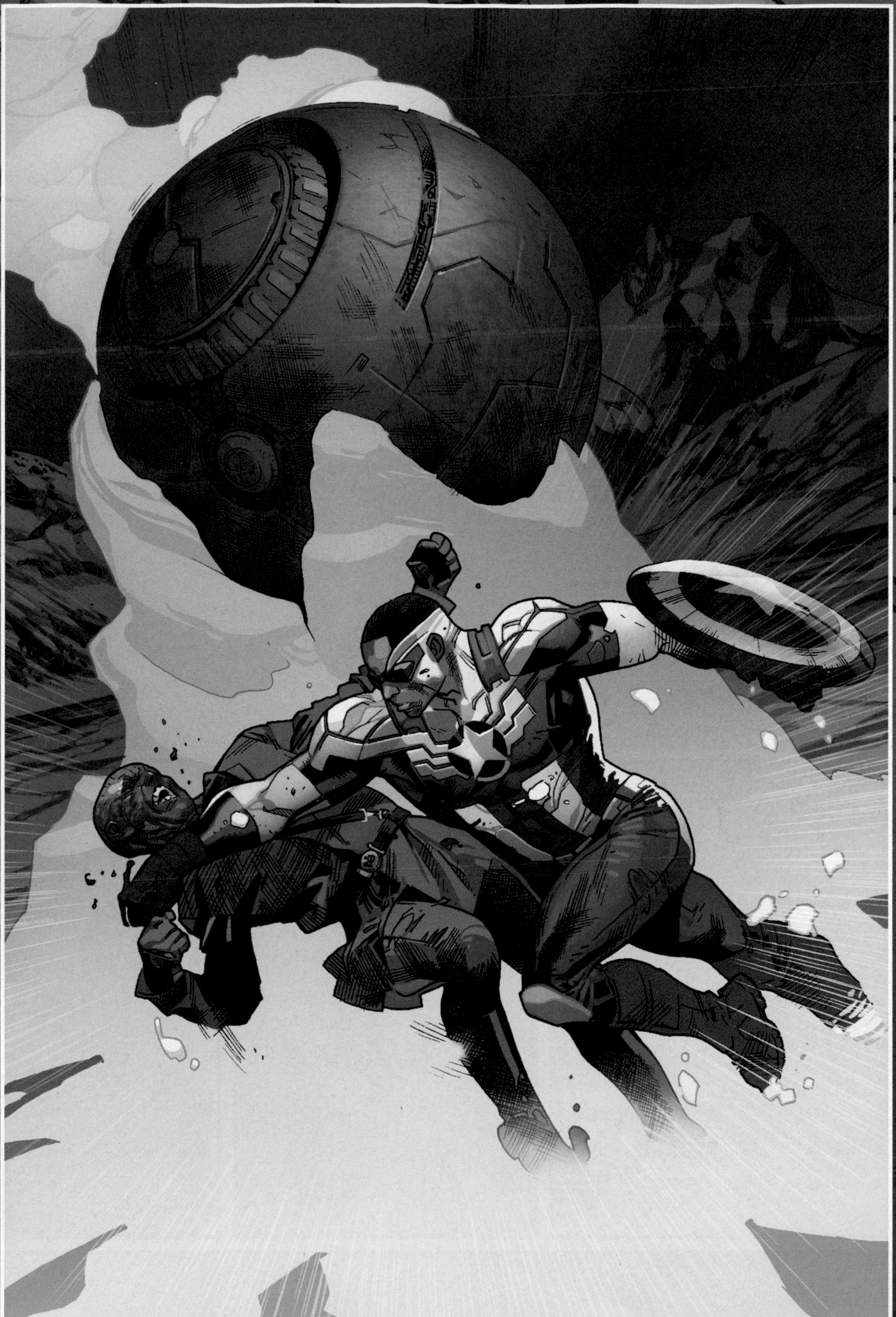

THREE

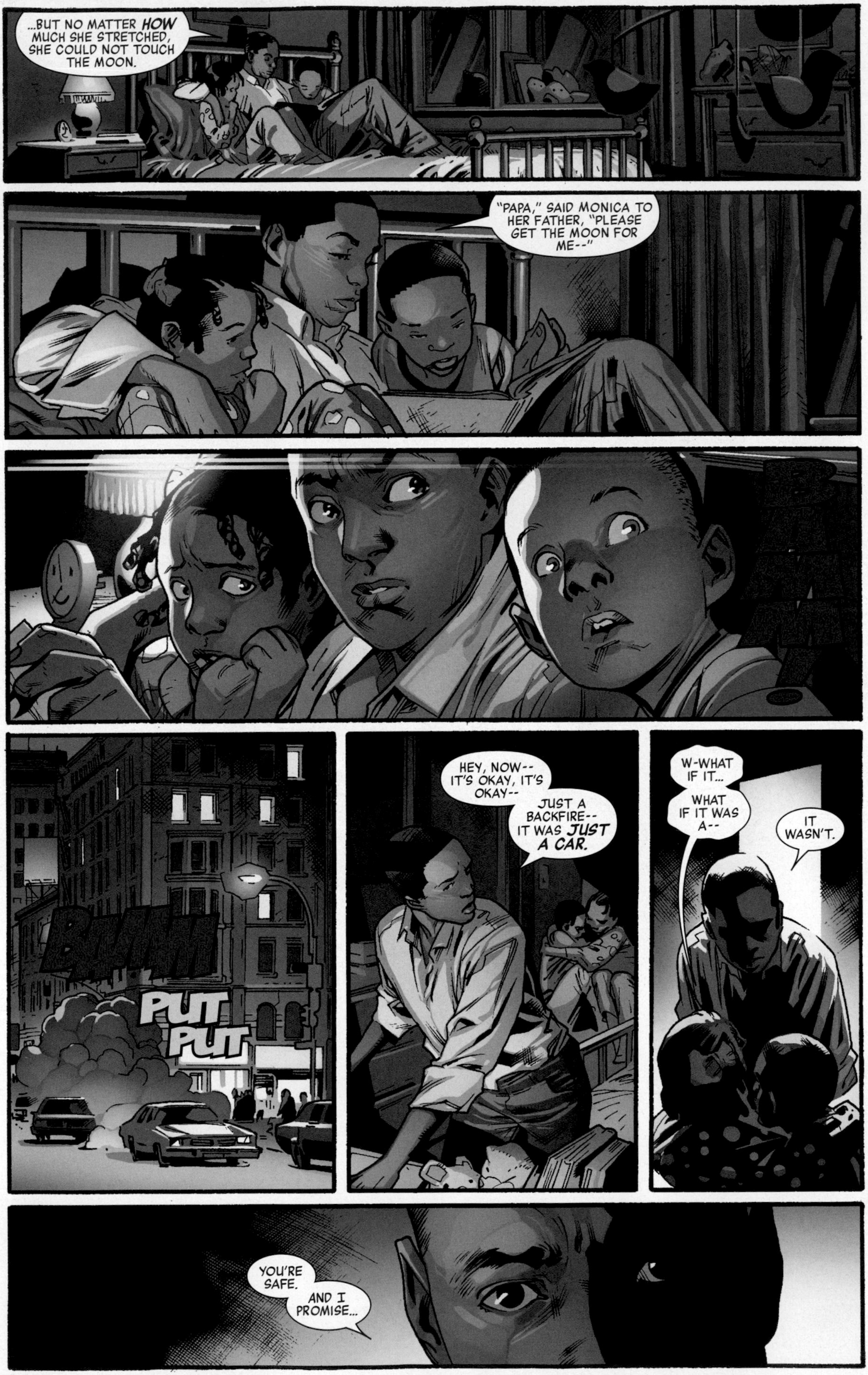
...BUT NO MATTER HOW MUCH SHE STRETCHED, SHE COULD NOT TOUCH THE MOON.
"PAPA," SAID MONICA TO HER FATHER, "PLEASE GET THE MOON FOR ME--"
PUT PUT
HEY, NOW-- IT'S OKAY, IT'S OKAY--
JUST A BACKFIRE-- IT WAS JUST A CAR.
W-WHAT IF IT...
WHAT IF IT WAS A--
IT WASN'T.
YOU'RE SAFE.
AND I PROMISE...

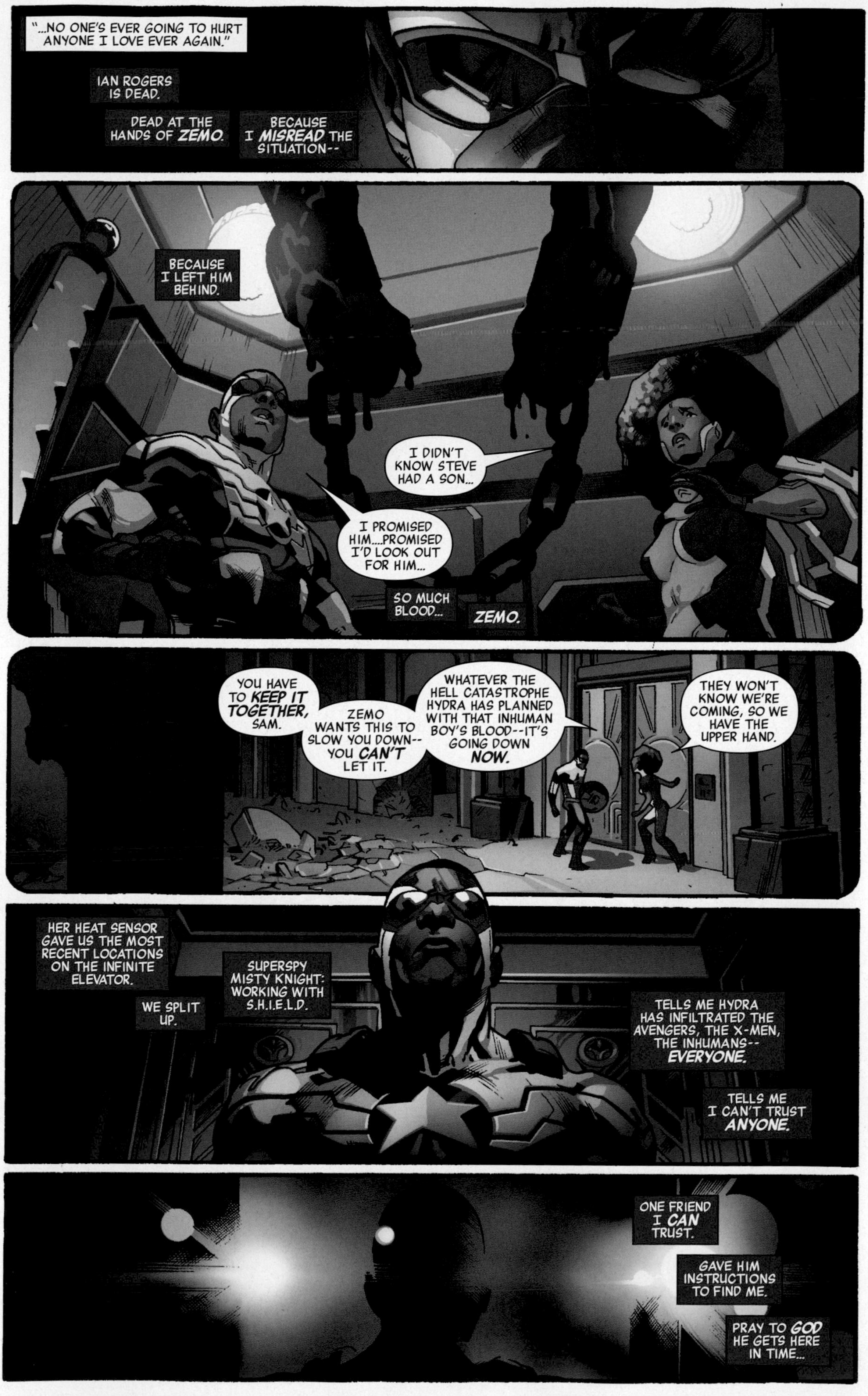

"...NO ONE'S EVER GOING TO HURT ANYONE I LOVE EVER AGAIN."
IAN ROGERS IS DEAD.
DEAD AT THE HANDS OF ZEMO.
BECAUSE I MISREAD THE SITUATION--
BECAUSE I LEFT HIM BEHIND.
I DIDN'T KNOW STEVE HAD A SON...
I PROMISED HIM....PROMISED I'D LOOK OUT FOR HIM...
SO MUCH BLOOD...
ZEMO.
YOU HAVE TO KEEP IT TOGETHER, SAM.
ZEMO WANTS THIS TO SLOW YOU DOWN-- YOU CAN'T LET IT.
WHATEVER THE HELL CATASTROPHE HYDRA HAS PLANNED WITH THAT INHUMAN BOY'S BLOOD--IT'S GOING DOWN NOW.
THEY WON'T KNOW WE'RE COMING, SO WE HAVE THE UPPER HAND.
HER HEAT SENSOR GAVE US THE MOST RECENT LOCATIONS ON THE INFINITE ELEVATOR.
WE SPLIT UP.
SUPERSPY MISTY KNIGHT: WORKING WITH S.H.I.E.L.D.
TELLS ME HYDRA HAS INFILTRATED THE AVENGERS, THE X-MEN, THE INHUMANS-- EVERYONE.
TELLS ME I CAN'T TRUST ANYONE.
ONE FRIEND I CAN TRUST.
GAVE HIM INSTRUCTIONS TO FIND ME.
PRAY TO GOD HE GETS HERE IN TIME...

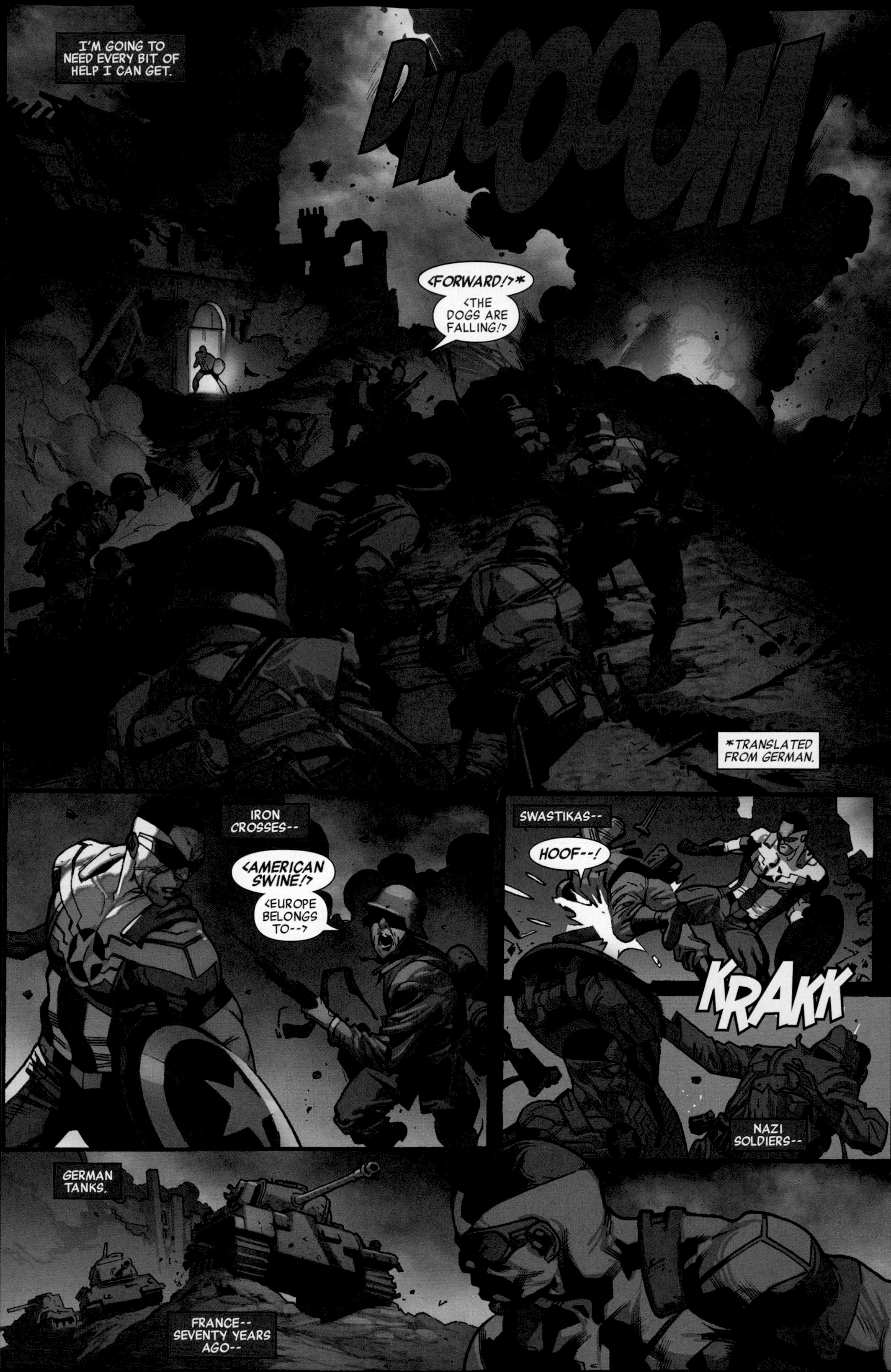
I'M GOING TO NEED EVERY BIT OF HELP I CAN GET.
<FORWARD!>*
<THE DOGS ARE FALLING!>
*TRANSLATED FROM GERMAN.
IRON CROSSES--
<AMERICAN SWINE!>
<EUROPE BELONGS TO-->
SWASTIKAS--
HOOF--!
KRAKK
NAZI SOLDIERS--
GERMAN TANKS.
FRANCE-- SEVENTY YEARS AGO--

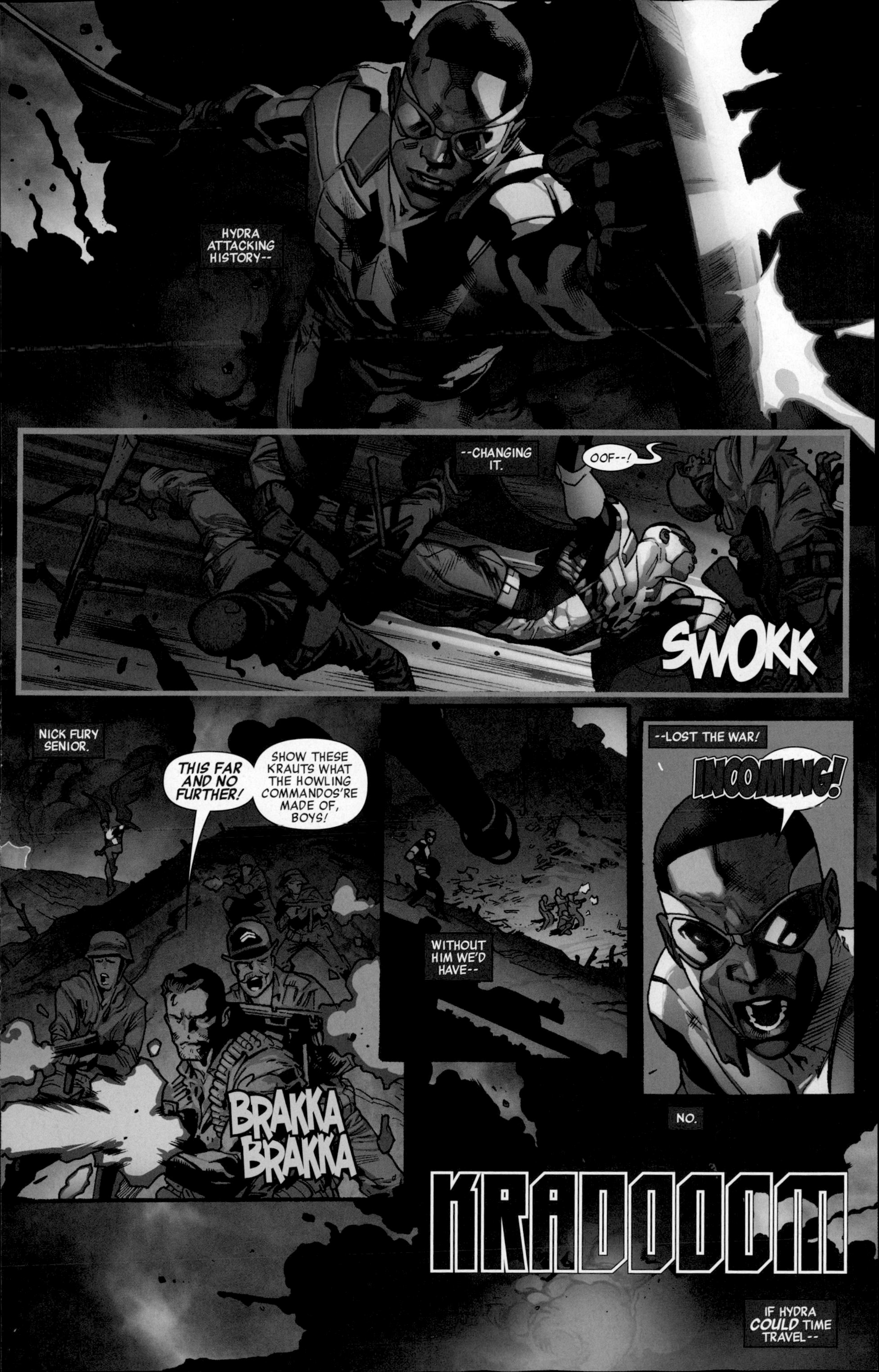
HYDRA ATTACKING HISTORY--
--CHANGING IT.
OOF--!
SWOKK
NICK FURY SENIOR.
THIS FAR AND NO FURTHER!
SHOW THESE KRAUTS WHAT THE HOWLING COMMANDOS'RE MADE OF, BOYS!
BRAKKA BRAKKA
WITHOUT HIM WE'D HAVE--
--LOST THE WAR!
INCOMING!
NO.
KRADOOOM
IF HYDRA COULD TIME TRAVEL--

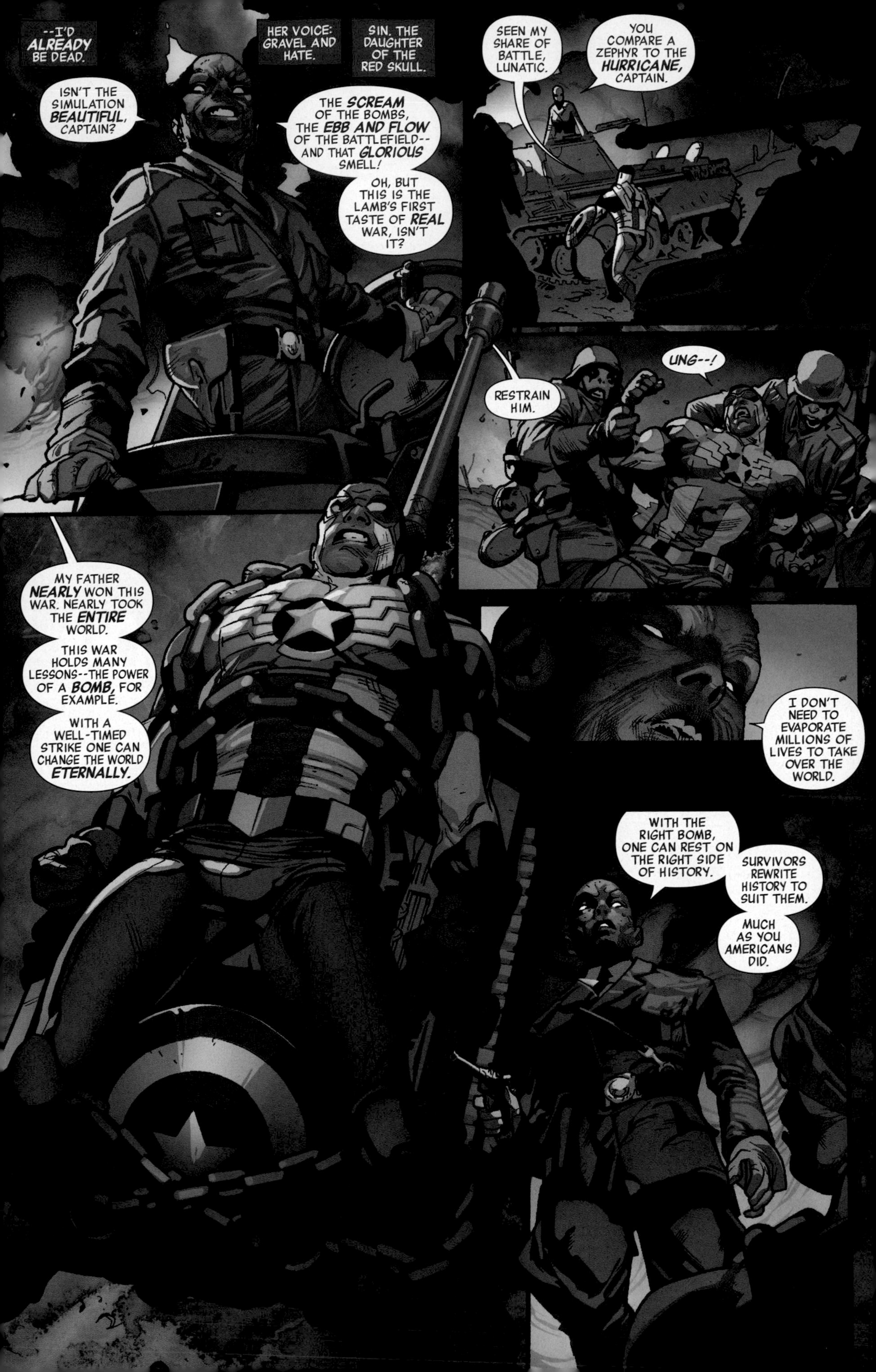
--I'D ALREADY BE DEAD.
HER VOICE: GRAVEL AND HATE.
SIN. THE DAUGHTER OF THE RED SKULL.
ISN'T THE SIMULATION BEAUTIFUL, CAPTAIN?
THE SCREAM OF THE BOMBS, THE EBB AND FLOW OF THE BATTLEFIELD-- AND THAT GLORIOUS SMELL!
OH, BUT THIS IS THE LAMB'S FIRST TASTE OF REAL WAR, ISN'T IT?
SEEN MY SHARE OF BATTLE, LUNATIC.
YOU COMPARE A ZEPHYR TO THE HURRICANE, CAPTAIN.
RESTRAIN HIM.
UNG--!
MY FATHER NEARLY WON THIS WAR. NEARLY TOOK THE ENTIRE WORLD.
THIS WAR HOLDS MANY LESSONS--THE POWER OF A BOMB, FOR EXAMPLE.
WITH A WELL-TIMED STRIKE ONE CAN CHANGE THE WORLD ETERNALLY.
I DON'T NEED TO EVAPORATE MILLIONS OF LIVES TO TAKE OVER THE WORLD.
WITH THE RIGHT BOMB, ONE CAN REST ON THE RIGHT SIDE OF HISTORY.
SURVIVORS REWRITE HISTORY TO SUIT THEM.
MUCH AS YOU AMERICANS DID.

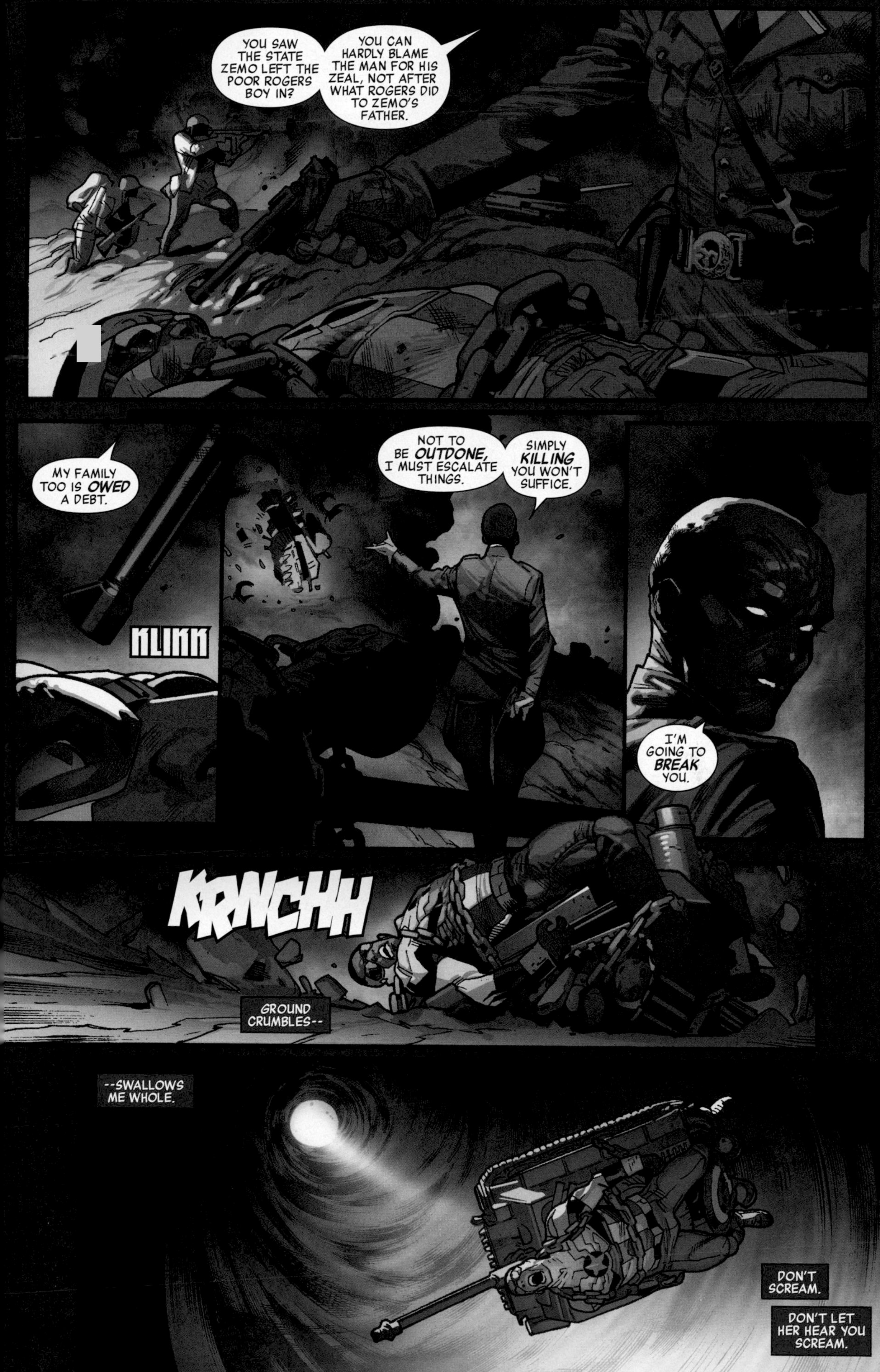
YOU SAW THE STATE ZEMO LEFT THE POOR ROGERS BOY IN?
YOU CAN HARDLY BLAME THE MAN FOR HIS ZEAL, NOT AFTER WHAT ROGERS DID TO ZEMO'S FATHER.
MY FAMILY TOO IS OWED A DEBT.
KLIKK
NOT TO BE OUTDONE, I MUST ESCALATE THINGS.
SIMPLY KILLING YOU WON'T SUFFICE.
I'M GOING TO BREAK YOU.
KRNCHH
GROUND CRUMBLES--
--SWALLOWS ME WHOLE.
DON'T SCREAM.
DON'T LET HER HEAR YOU SCREAM.

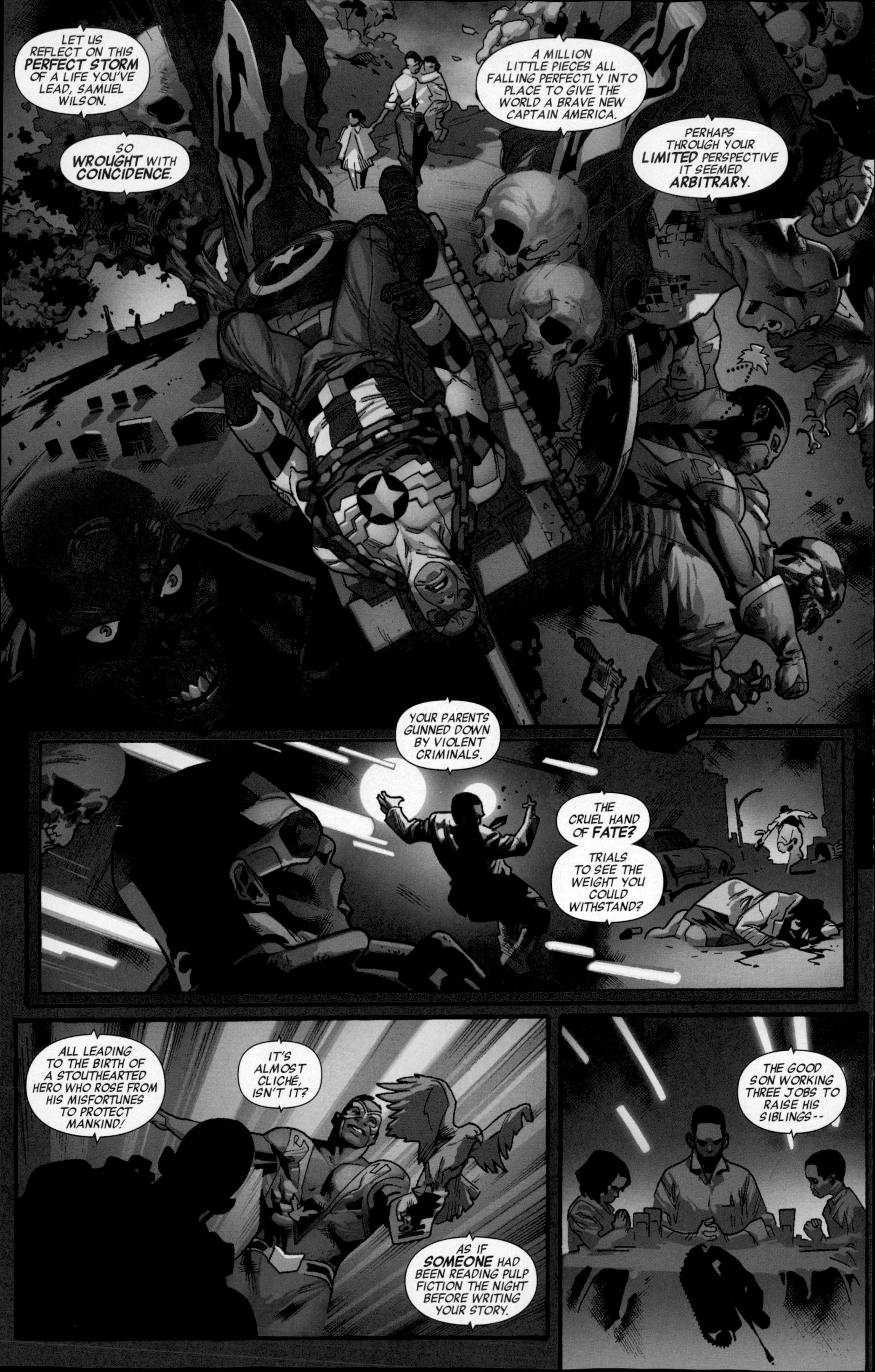
LET US REFLECT ON THIS PERFECT STORM OF A LIFE YOU'VE LEAD, SAMUEL WILSON.
SO WROUGHT WITH COINCIDENCE.
A MILLION LITTLE PIECES ALL FALLING PERFECTLY INTO PLACE TO GIVE THE WORLD A BRAVE NEW CAPTAIN AMERICA.
PERHAPS THROUGH YOUR LIMITED PERSPECTIVE IT SEEMED ARBITRARY.
YOUR PARENTS GUNNED DOWN BY VIOLENT CRIMINALS.
THE CRUEL HAND OF FATE?
TRIALS TO SEE THE WEIGHT YOU COULD WITHSTAND?
ALL LEADING TO THE BIRTH OF A STOUTHEARTED HERO WHO ROSE FROM HIS MISFORTUNES TO PROTECT MANKIND!
IT'S ALMOST CLICHÉ, ISN'T IT?
AS IF SOMEONE HAD BEEN READING PULP FICTION THE NIGHT BEFORE WRITING YOUR STORY.
THE GOOD SON WORKING THREE JOBS TO RAISE HIS SIBLINGS--

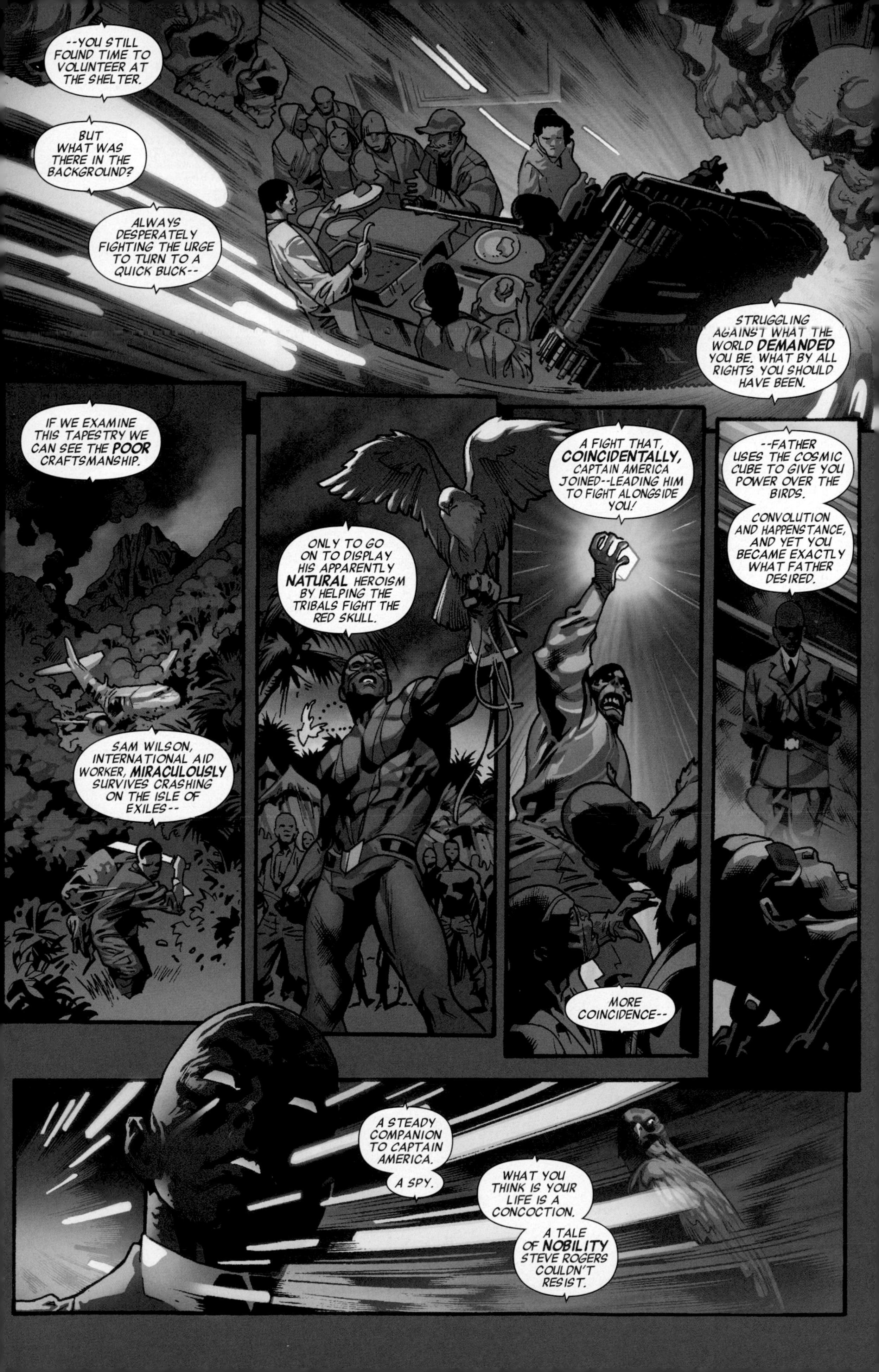
--YOU STILL FOUND TIME TO VOLUNTEER AT THE SHELTER.
BUT WHAT WAS THERE IN THE BACKGROUND?
ALWAYS DESPERATELY FIGHTING THE URGE TO TURN TO A QUICK BUCK--
STRUGGLING AGAINST WHAT THE WORLD DEMANDED YOU BE. WHAT BY ALL RIGHTS YOU SHOULD HAVE BEEN.
IF WE EXAMINE THIS TAPESTRY WE CAN SEE THE POOR CRAFTSMANSHIP.
SAM WILSON, INTERNATIONAL AID WORKER, MIRACULOUSLY SURVIVES CRASHING ON THE ISLE OF EXILES--
ONLY TO GO ON TO DISPLAY HIS APPARENTLY NATURAL HEROISM BY HELPING THE TRIBALS FIGHT THE RED SKULL.
A FIGHT THAT, COINCIDENTALLY, CAPTAIN AMERICA JOINED--LEADING HIM TO FIGHT ALONGSIDE YOU!
MORE COINCIDENCE--
--FATHER USES THE COSMIC CUBE TO GIVE YOU POWER OVER THE BIRDS.
CONVOLUTION AND HAPPENSTANCE, AND YET YOU BECAME EXACTLY WHAT FATHER DESIRED.
A STEADY COMPANION TO CAPTAIN AMERICA.
A SPY.
WHAT YOU THINK IS YOUR LIFE IS A CONCOCTION.
A TALE OF NOBILITY STEVE ROGERS COULDN'T RESIST.

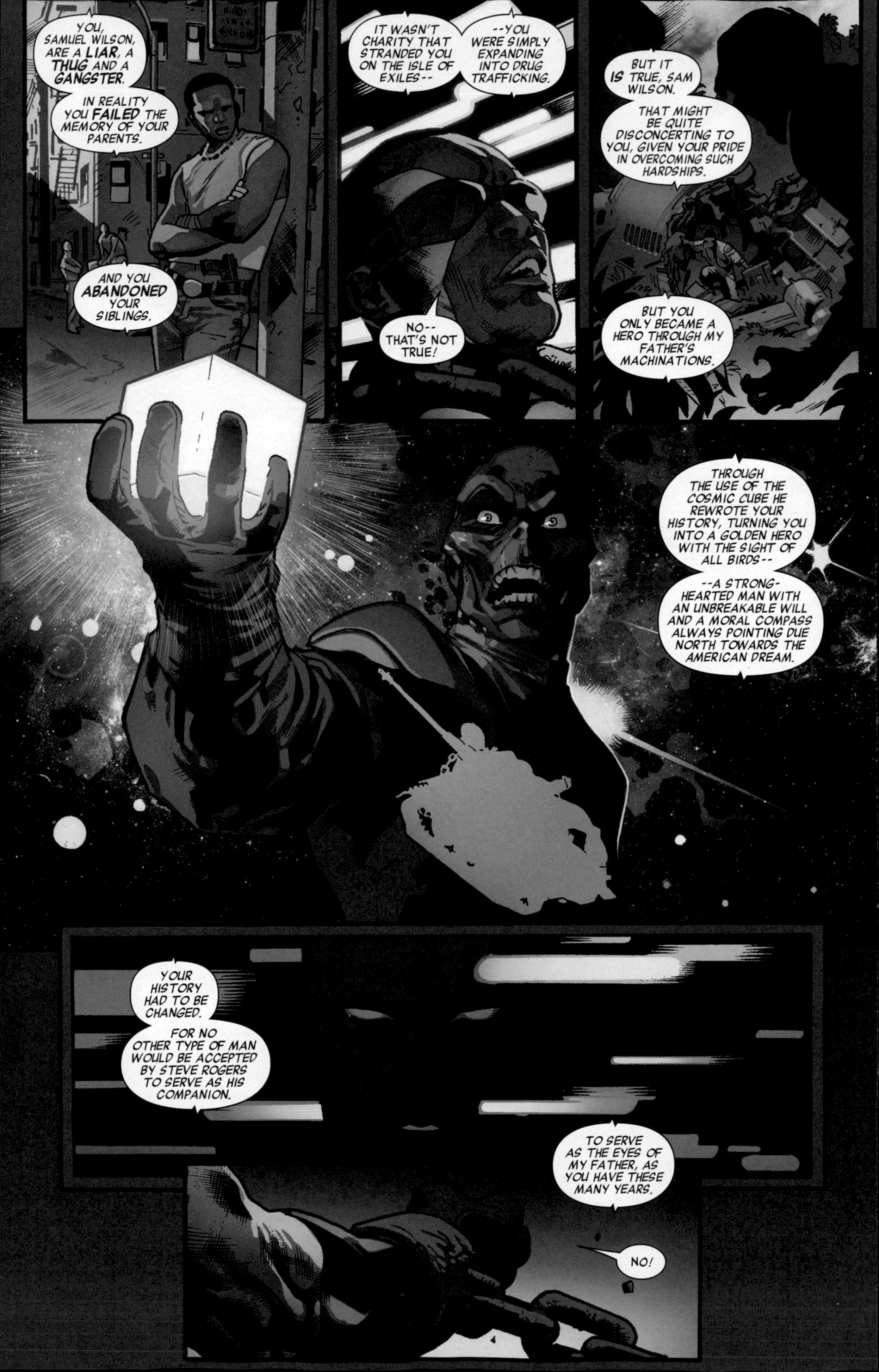
YOU, SAMUEL WILSON, ARE A LIAR, A THUG AND A GANGSTER.
IN REALITY YOU FAILED THE MEMORY OF YOUR PARENTS.
AND YOU ABANDONED YOUR SIBLINGS.
IT WASN'T CHARITY THAT STRANDED YOU ON THE ISLE OF EXILES--
--YOU WERE SIMPLY EXPANDING INTO DRUG TRAFFICKING.
NO-- THAT'S NOT TRUE!
BUT IT IS TRUE, SAM WILSON.
THAT MIGHT BE QUITE DISCONCERTING TO YOU, GIVEN YOUR PRIDE IN OVERCOMING SUCH HARDSHIPS.
BUT YOU ONLY BECAME A HERO THROUGH MY FATHER'S MACHINATIONS.
THROUGH THE USE OF THE COSMIC CUBE HE REWROTE YOUR HISTORY, TURNING YOU INTO A GOLDEN HERO WITH THE SIGHT OF ALL BIRDS--
--A STRONG-HEARTED MAN WITH AN UNBREAKABLE WILL AND A MORAL COMPASS ALWAYS POINTING DUE NORTH TOWARDS THE AMERICAN DREAM.
YOUR HISTORY HAD TO BE CHANGED.
FOR NO OTHER TYPE OF MAN WOULD BE ACCEPTED BY STEVE ROGERS TO SERVE AS HIS COMPANION.
TO SERVE AS THE EYES OF MY FATHER, AS YOU HAVE THESE MANY YEARS.
NO!

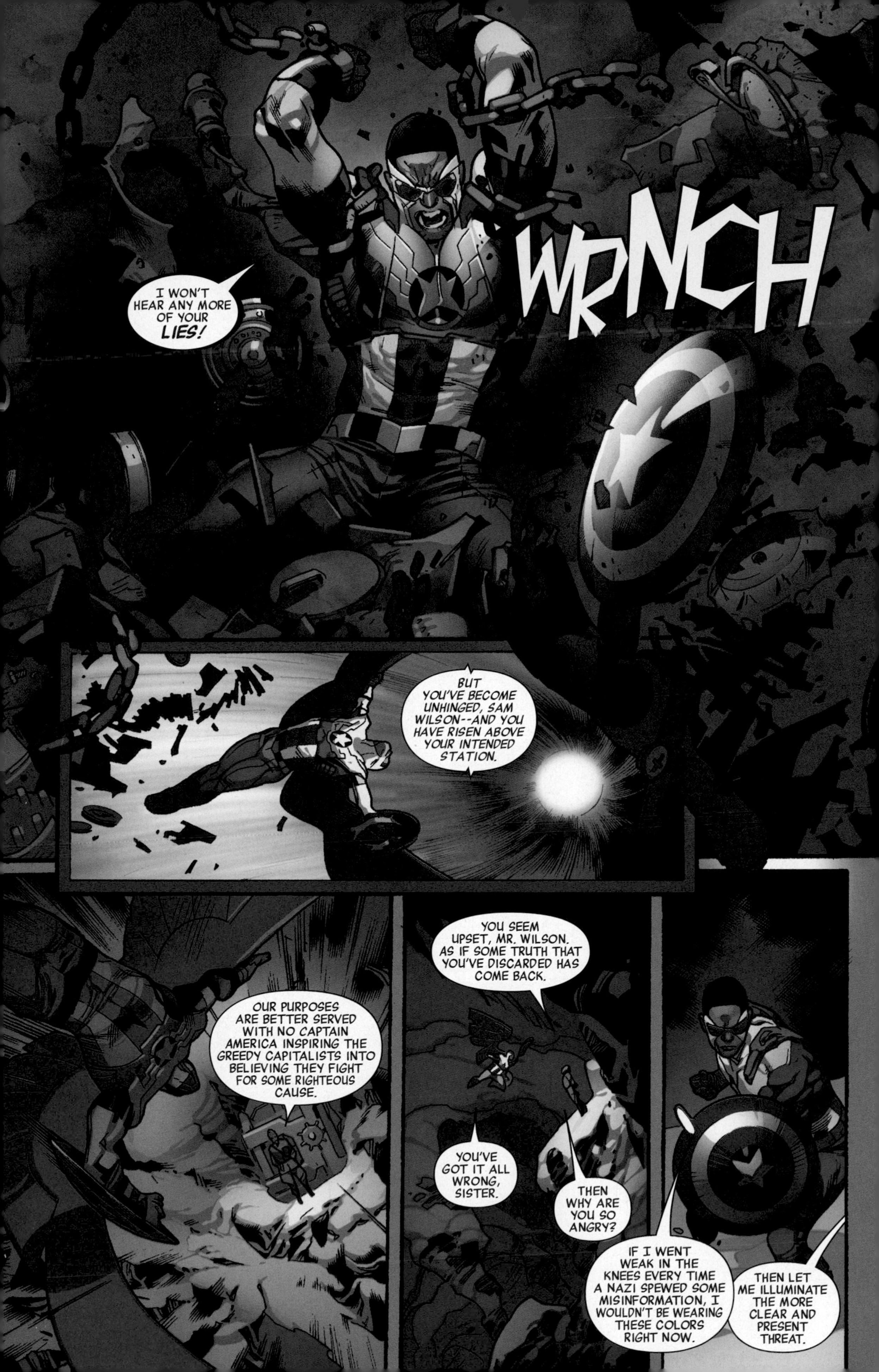
I WON'T HEAR ANY MORE OF YOUR LIES!
WRNCH
BUT YOU'VE BECOME UNHINGED, SAM WILSON--AND YOU HAVE RISEN ABOVE YOUR INTENDED STATION.
OUR PURPOSES ARE BETTER SERVED WITH NO CAPTAIN AMERICA INSPIRING THE GREEDY CAPITALISTS INTO BELIEVING THEY FIGHT FOR SOME RIGHTEOUS CAUSE.
YOU SEEM UPSET, MR. WILSON. AS IF SOME TRUTH THAT YOU'VE DISCARDED HAS COME BACK.
YOU'VE GOT IT ALL WRONG, SISTER.
THEN WHY ARE YOU SO ANGRY?
IF I WENT WEAK IN THE KNEES EVERY TIME A NAZI SPEWED SOME MISINFORMATION, I WOULDN'T BE WEARING THESE COLORS RIGHT NOW.
THEN LET ME ILLUMINATE THE MORE CLEAR AND PRESENT THREAT.

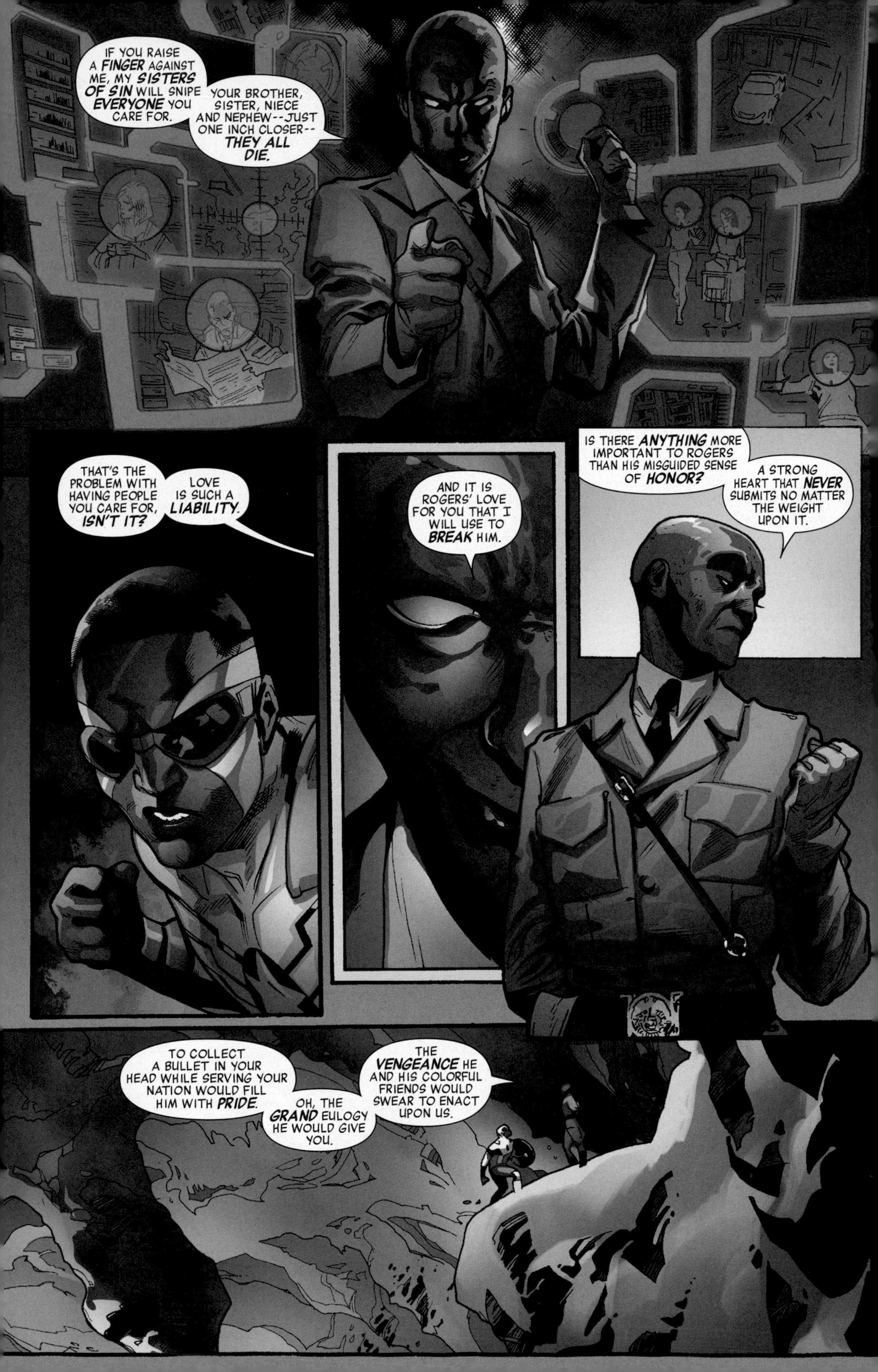
IF YOU RAISE A FINGER AGAINST ME, MY SISTERS OF SIN WILL SNIPE EVERYONE YOU CARE FOR.
YOUR BROTHER, SISTER, NIECE AND NEPHEW--JUST ONE INCH CLOSER--THEY ALL DIE.
THAT'S THE PROBLEM WITH HAVING PEOPLE YOU CARE FOR, ISN'T IT?
LOVE IS SUCH A LIABILITY.
AND IT IS ROGERS' LOVE FOR YOU THAT I WILL USE TO BREAK HIM.
IS THERE ANYTHING MORE IMPORTANT TO ROGERS THAN HIS MISGUIDED SENSE OF HONOR?
A STRONG HEART THAT NEVER SUBMITS NO MATTER THE WEIGHT UPON IT.
TO COLLECT A BULLET IN YOUR HEAD WHILE SERVING YOUR NATION WOULD FILL HIM WITH PRIDE.
OH, THE GRAND EULOGY HE WOULD GIVE YOU.
THE VENGEANCE HE AND HIS COLORFUL FRIENDS WOULD SWEAR TO ENACT UPON US.

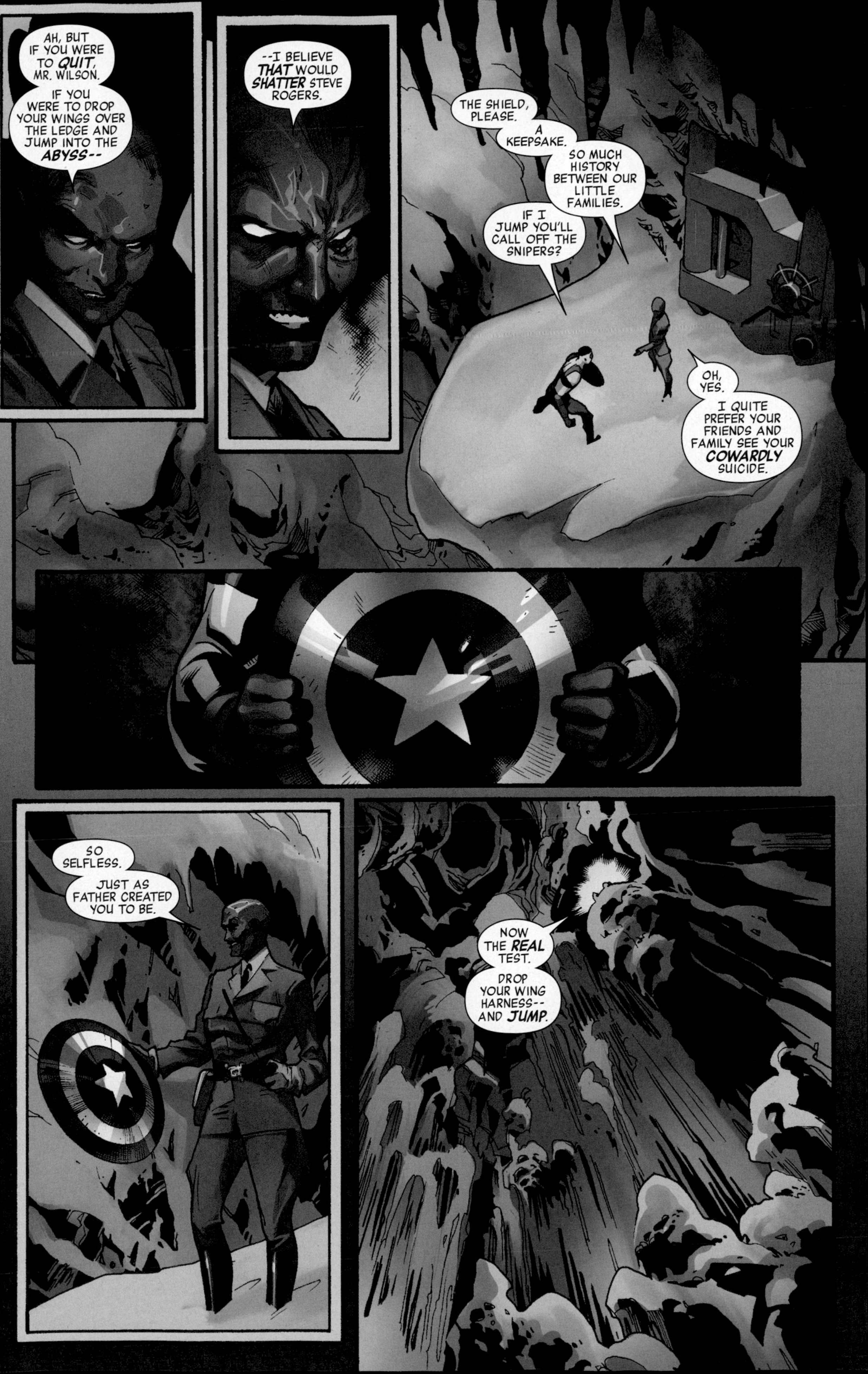
AH, BUT IF YOU WERE TO QUIT, MR. WILSON.
IF YOU WERE TO DROP YOUR WINGS OVER THE LEDGE AND JUMP INTO THE ABYSS--
--I BELIEVE THAT WOULD SHATTER STEVE ROGERS.
THE SHIELD, PLEASE.
A KEEPSAKE.
SO MUCH HISTORY BETWEEN OUR LITTLE FAMILIES.
IF I JUMP YOU'LL CALL OFF THE SNIPERS?
OH, YES.
I QUITE PREFER YOUR FRIENDS AND FAMILY SEE YOUR COWARDLY SUICIDE.
SO SELFLESS.
JUST AS FATHER CREATED YOU TO BE.
NOW THE REAL TEST.
DROP YOUR WING HARNESS-- AND JUMP.

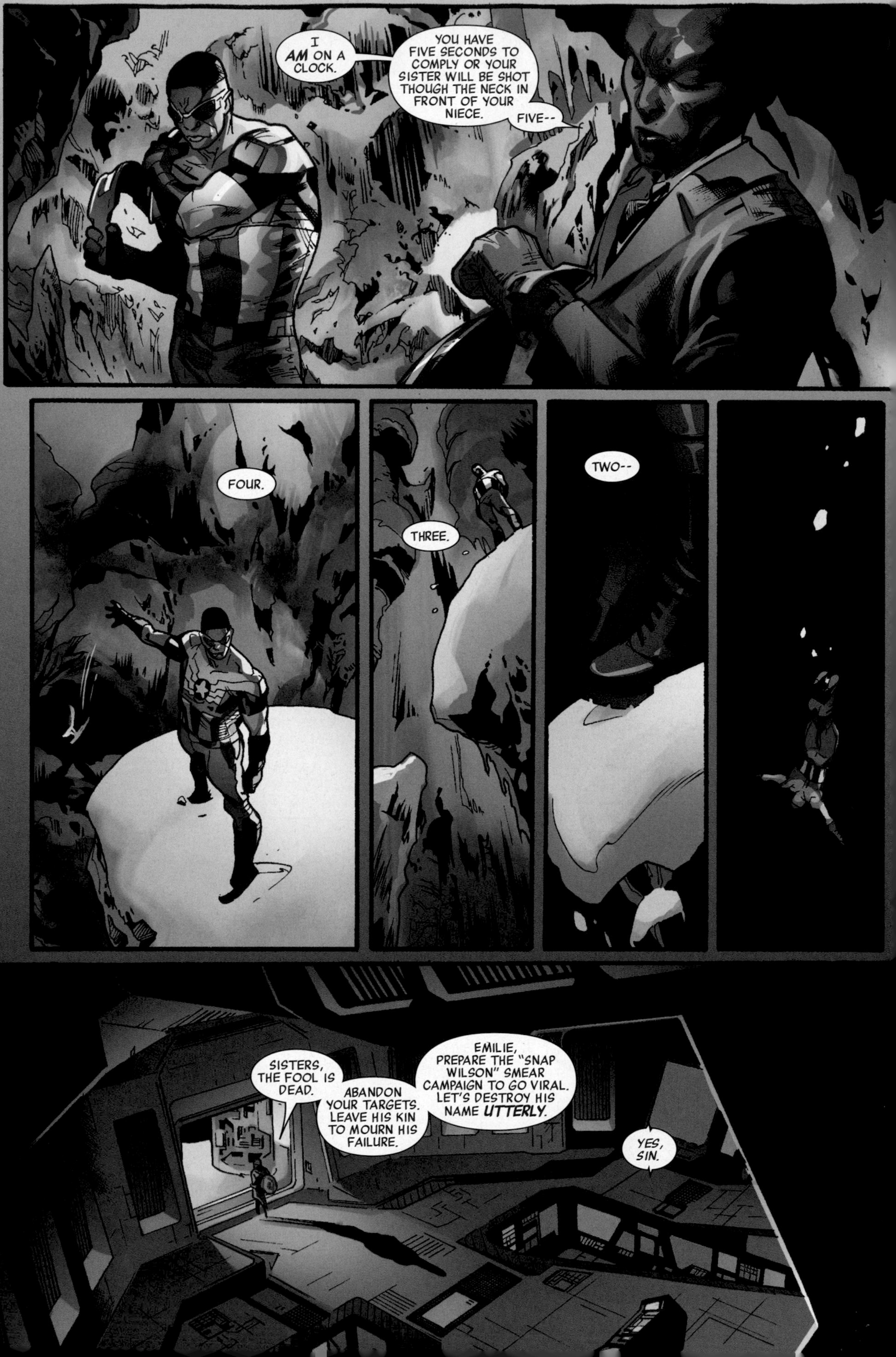
I AM ON A CLOCK.
YOU HAVE FIVE SECONDS TO COMPLY OR YOUR SISTER WILL BE SHOT THOUGH THE NECK IN FRONT OF YOUR NIECE.
FIVE--
FOUR.
THREE.
TWO--
SISTERS, THE FOOL IS DEAD.
ABANDON YOUR TARGETS. LEAVE HIS KIN TO MOURN HIS FAILURE.
EMILIE, PREPARE THE "SNAP WILSON" SMEAR CAMPAIGN TO GO VIRAL. LET'S DESTROY HIS NAME UTTERLY.
YES, SIN.

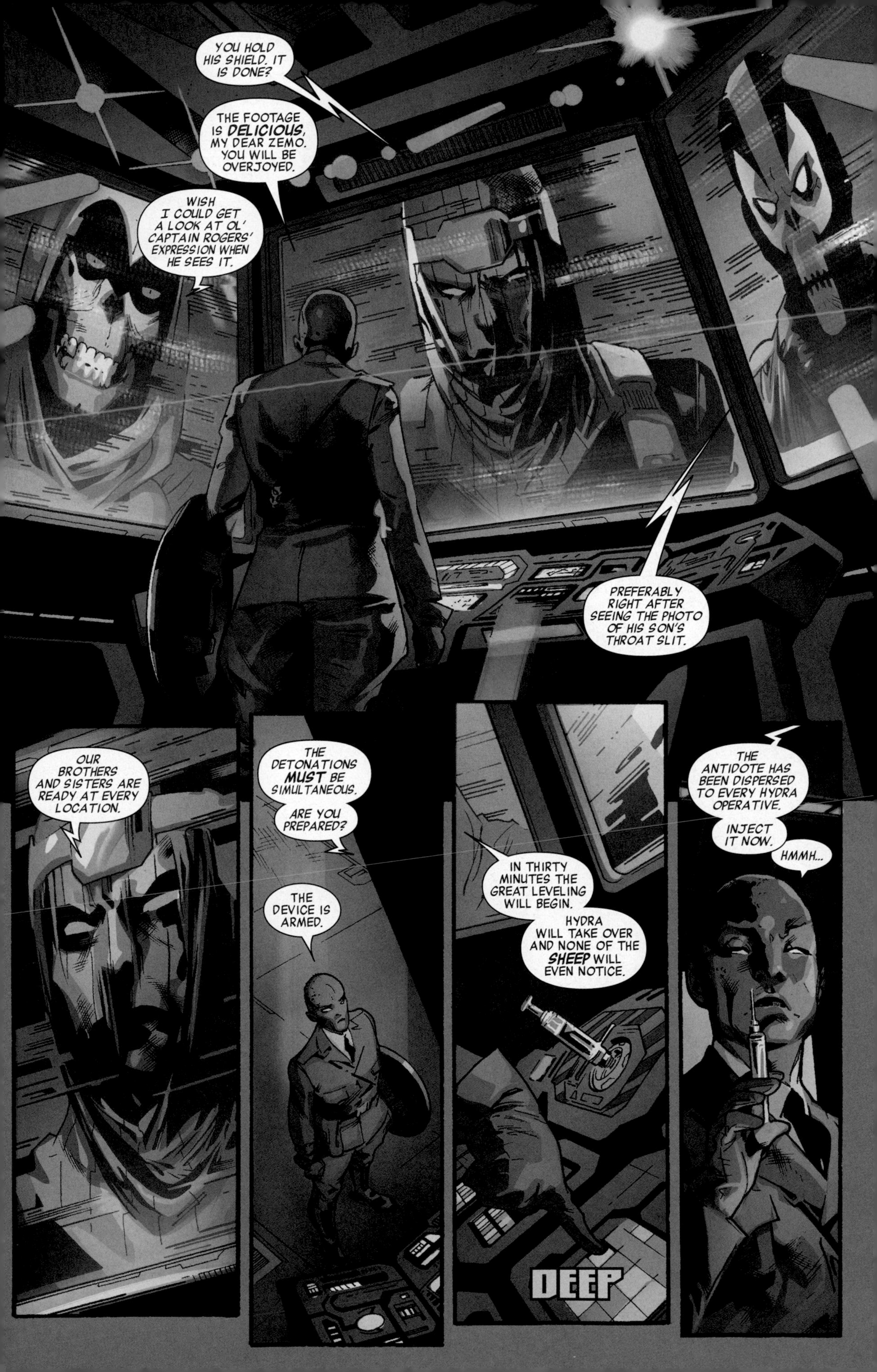
YOU HOLD HIS SHIELD. IT IS DONE?
THE FOOTAGE IS DELICIOUS, MY DEAR ZEMO. YOU WILL BE OVERJOYED.
WISH I COULD GET A LOOK AT OL' CAPTAIN ROGERS' EXPRESSION WHEN HE SEES IT.
PREFERABLY RIGHT AFTER SEEING THE PHOTO OF HIS SON'S THROAT SLIT.
OUR BROTHERS AND SISTERS ARE READY AT EVERY LOCATION.
THE DETONATIONS MUST BE SIMULTANEOUS.
ARE YOU PREPARED?
THE DEVICE IS ARMED.
IN THIRTY MINUTES THE GREAT LEVELING WILL BEGIN.
HYDRA WILL TAKE OVER AND NONE OF THE SHEEP WILL EVEN NOTICE.
DEEP
THE ANTIDOTE HAS BEEN DISPERSED TO EVERY HYDRA OPERATIVE.
INJECT IT NOW.
HMMH...

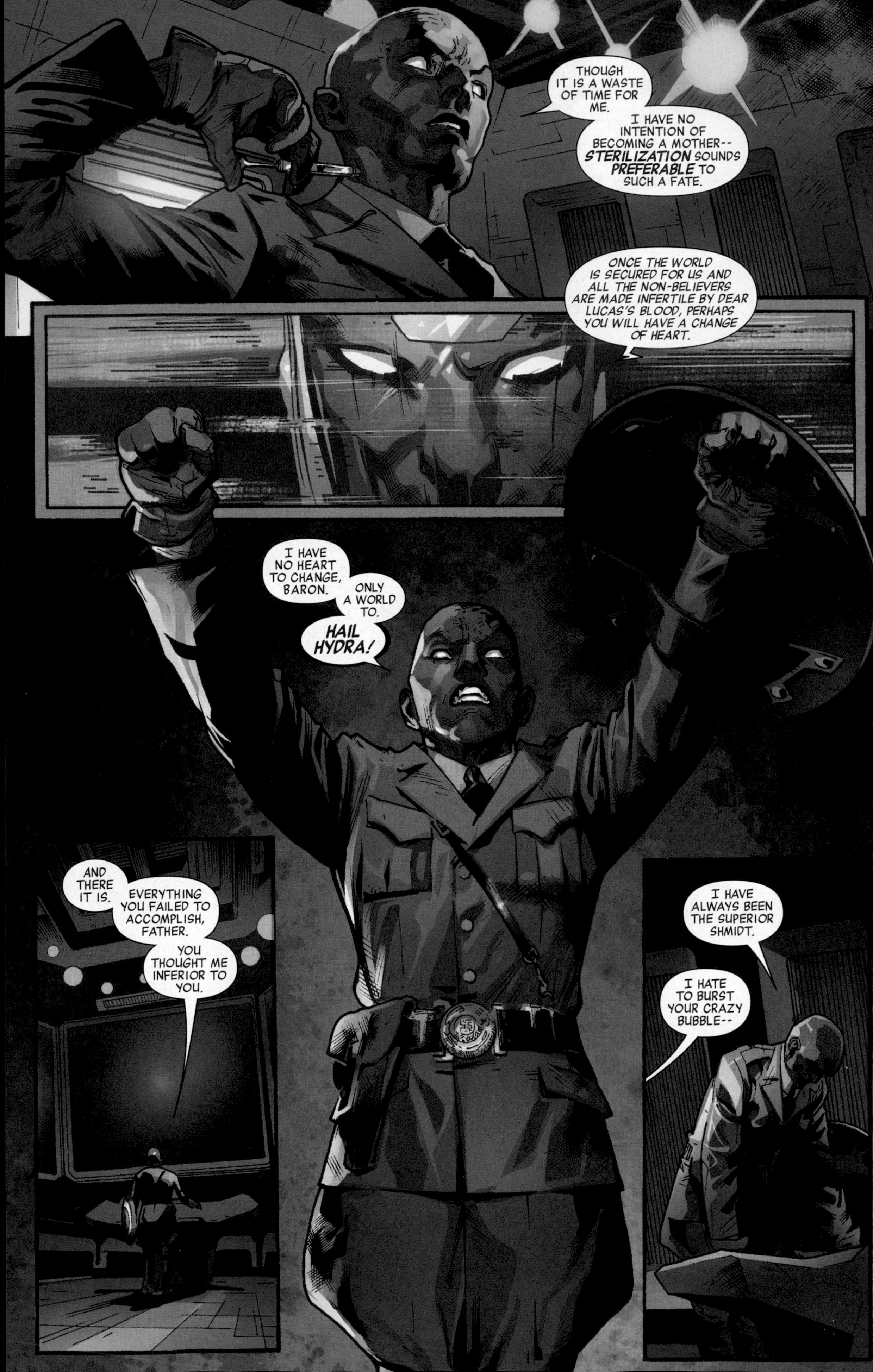
THOUGH IT IS A WASTE OF TIME FOR ME.
I HAVE NO INTENTION OF BECOMING A MOTHER-- STERILIZATION SOUNDS PREFERABLE TO SUCH A FATE.
ONCE THE WORLD IS SECURED FOR US AND ALL THE NON-BELIEVERS ARE MADE INFERTILE BY DEAR LUCAS'S BLOOD, PERHAPS YOU WILL HAVE A CHANGE OF HEART.
I HAVE NO HEART TO CHANGE, BARON.
ONLY A WORLD TO.
HAIL HYDRA!
AND THERE IT IS.
EVERYTHING YOU FAILED TO ACCOMPLISH, FATHER.
YOU THOUGHT ME INFERIOR TO YOU.
I HAVE ALWAYS BEEN THE SUPERIOR SHMIDT.
I HATE TO BURST YOUR CRAZY BUBBLE--

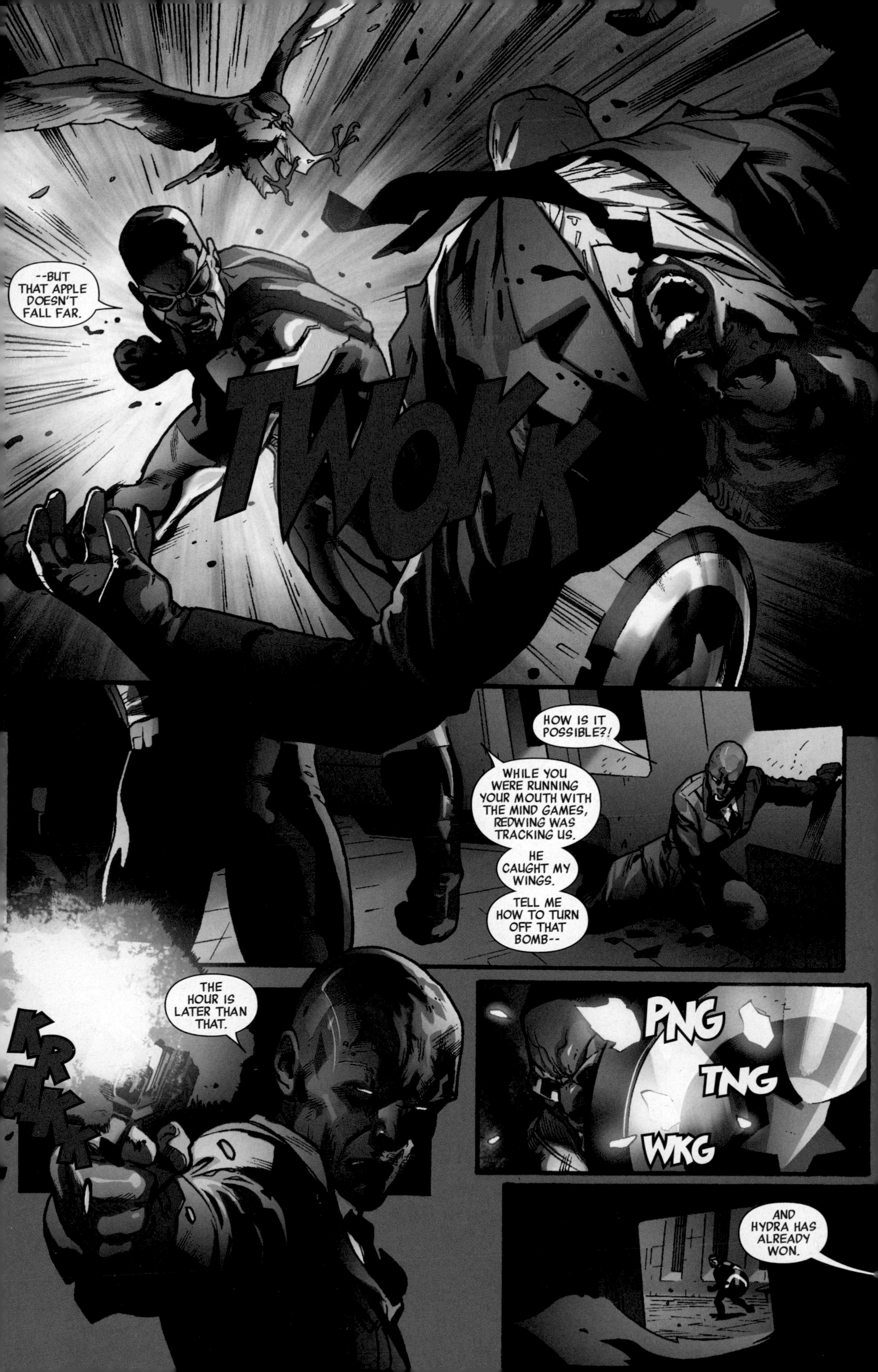
--BUT THAT APPLE DOESN'T FALL FAR.
TWOK
HOW IS IT POSSIBLE?!
WHILE YOU WERE RUNNING YOUR MOUTH WITH THE MIND GAMES, REDWING WAS TRACKING US.
HE CAUGHT MY WINGS.
TELL ME HOW TO TURN OFF THAT BOMB--
THE HOUR IS LATER THAN THAT.
KRAKK
PNG
TNG
WKG
AND HYDRA HAS ALREADY WON.

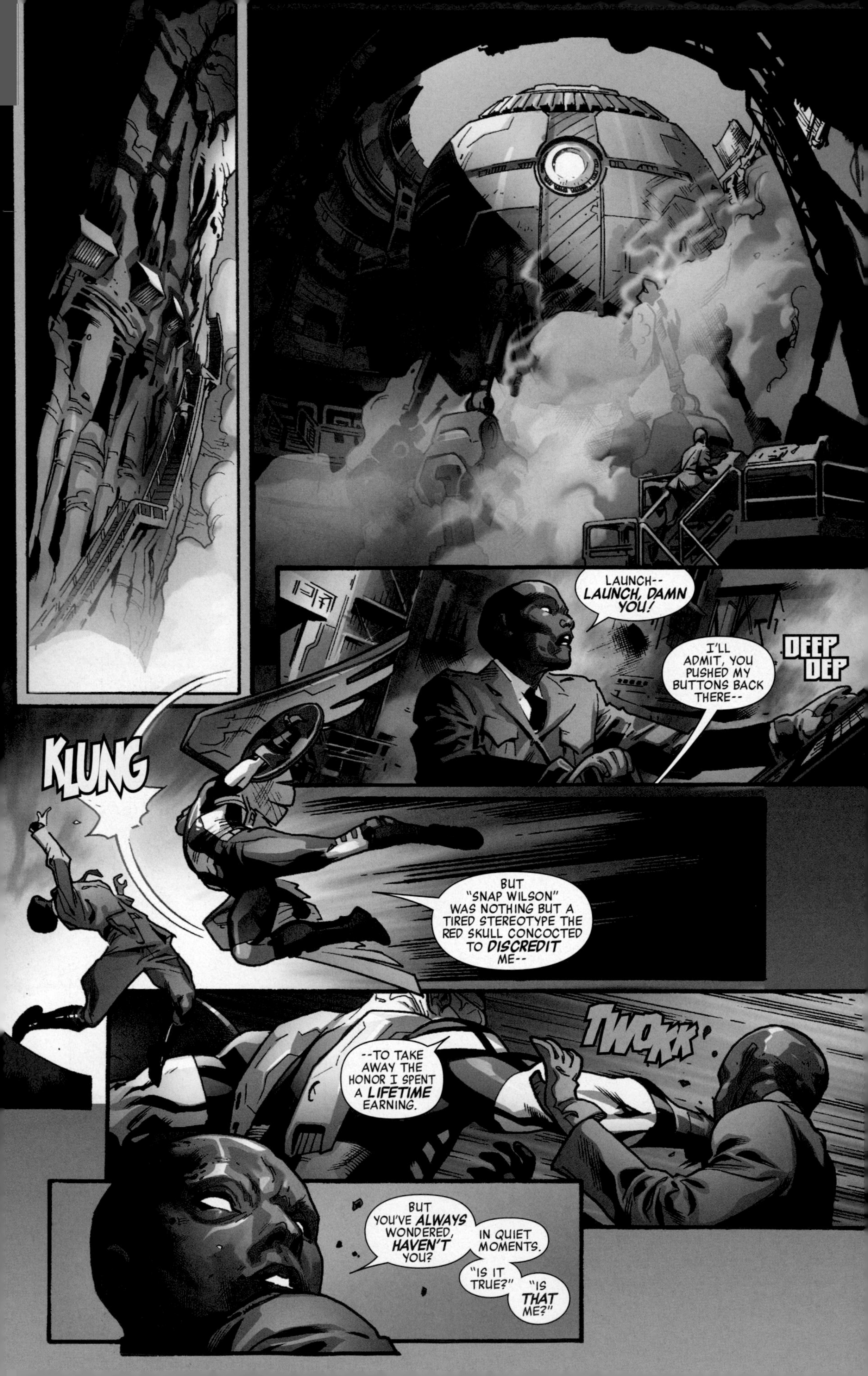

LAUNCH-- LAUNCH, DAMN YOU!
I'LL ADMIT, YOU PUSHED MY BUTTONS BACK THERE--
DEEP DEP
KLUNG
BUT "SNAP WILSON" WAS NOTHING BUT A TIRED STEREOTYPE THE RED SKULL CONCOCTED TO DISCREDIT ME--
--TO TAKE AWAY THE HONOR I SPENT A LIFETIME EARNING.
TWOKK
BUT YOU'VE ALWAYS WONDERED, HAVEN'T YOU?
IN QUIET MOMENTS.
"IS IT TRUE?"
"IS THAT ME?"

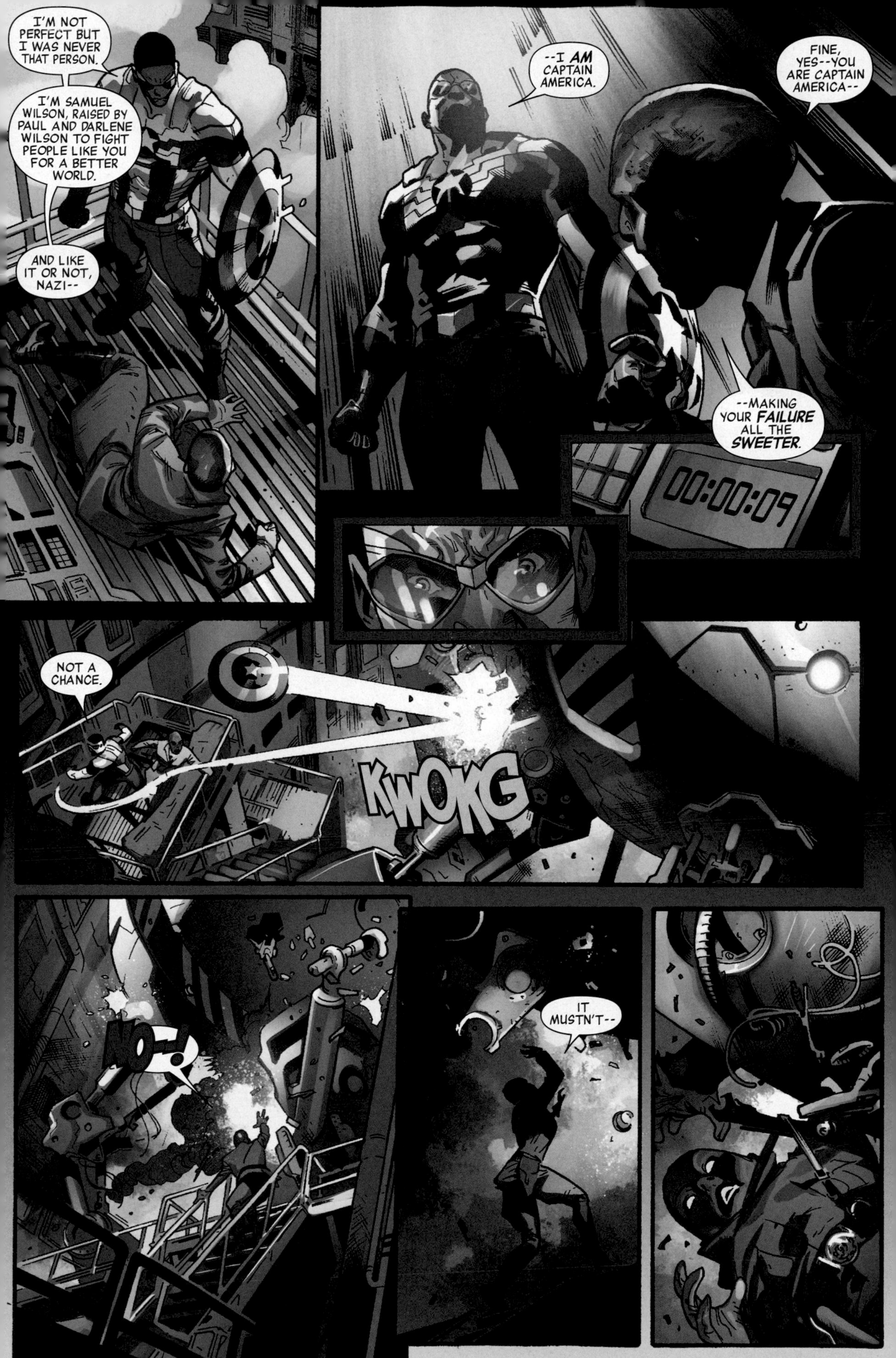
I'M NOT PERFECT BUT I WAS NEVER THAT PERSON.
I'M SAMUEL WILSON, RAISED BY PAUL AND DARLENE WILSON TO FIGHT PEOPLE LIKE YOU FOR A BETTER WORLD.
AND LIKE IT OR NOT, NAZI--
--I AM CAPTAIN AMERICA.
FINE, YES--YOU ARE CAPTAIN AMERICA--
--MAKING YOUR FAILURE ALL THE SWEETER.
00:00:09
NOT A CHANCE.
KWOKG
NO--!
IT MUSTN'T--

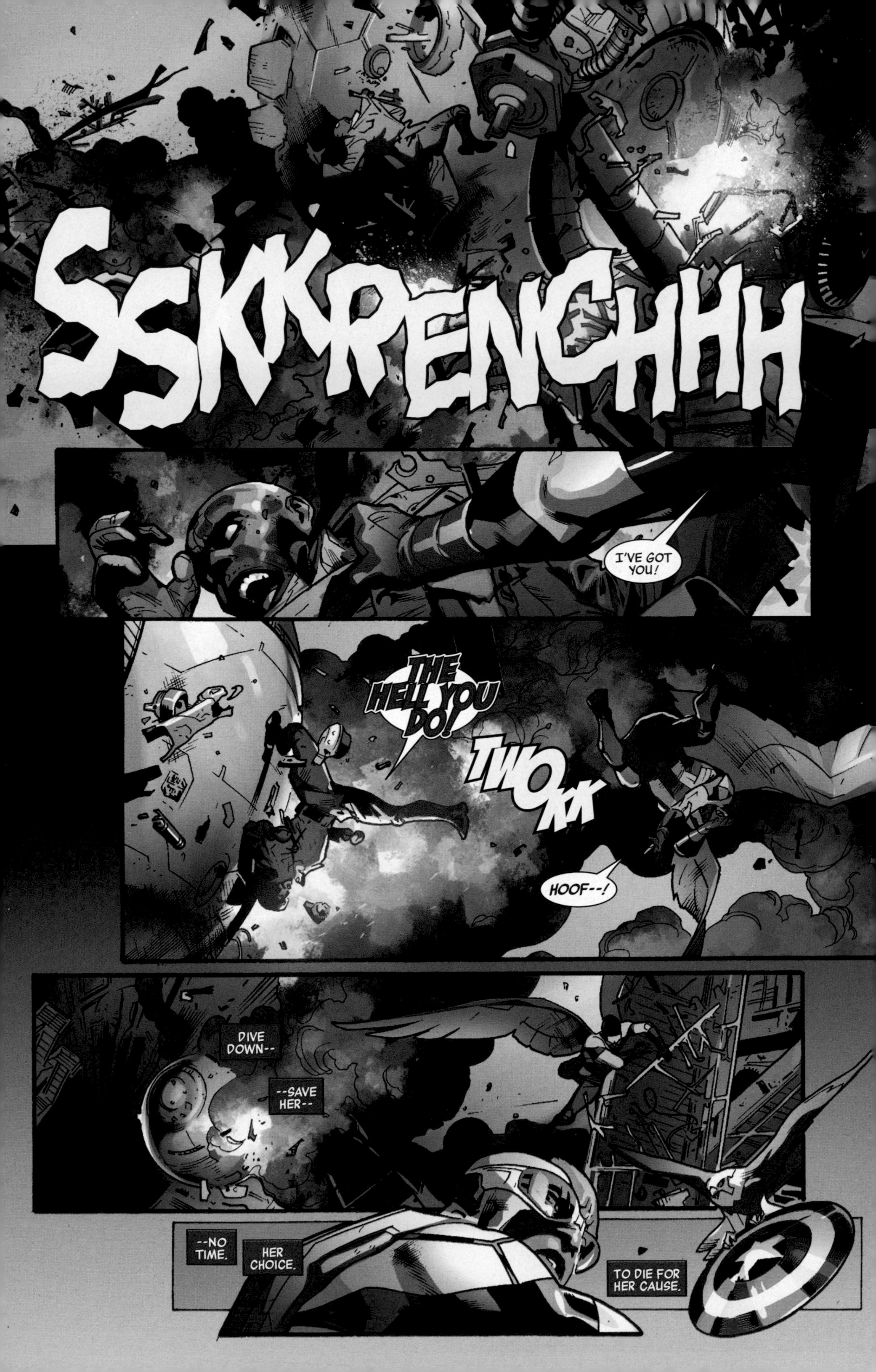
SSKKRENCHHH
I'VE GOT YOU!
THE HELL YOU DO!
TWOKK
HOOF--!
DIVE DOWN--
--SAVE HER--
--NO TIME.
HER CHOICE.
TO DIE FOR HER CAUSE.

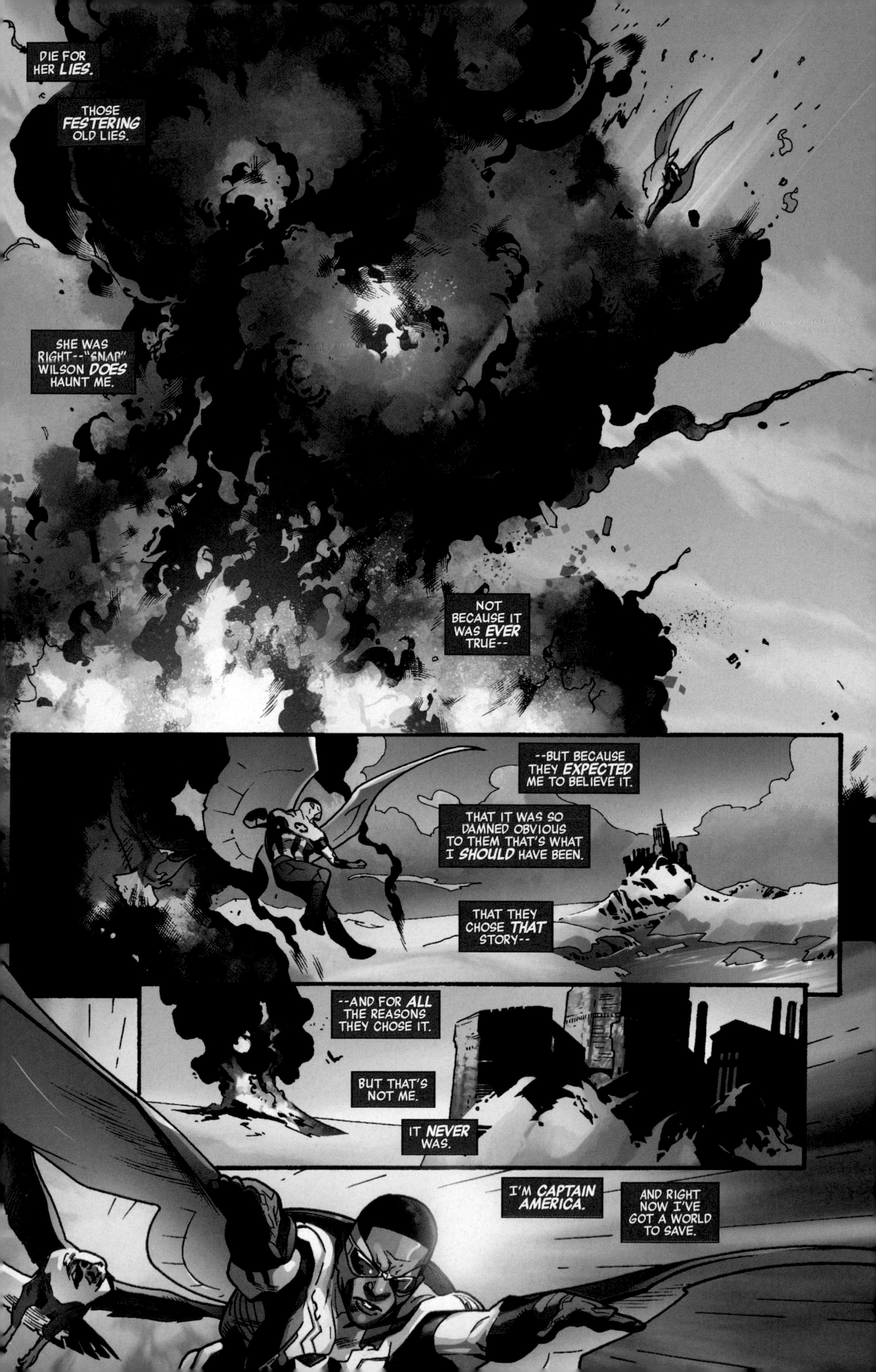
DIE FOR HER LIES.
THOSE FESTERING OLD LIES.
SHE WAS RIGHT--"SNAP" WILSON DOES HAUNT ME.
NOT BECAUSE IT WAS EVER TRUE--
--BUT BECAUSE THEY EXPECTED ME TO BELIEVE IT.
THAT IT WAS SO DAMNED OBVIOUS TO THEM THAT'S WHAT I SHOULD HAVE BEEN.
THAT THEY CHOSE THAT STORY--
--AND FOR ALL THE REASONS THEY CHOSE IT.
BUT THAT'S NOT ME.
IT NEVER WAS.
I'M CAPTAIN AMERICA.
AND RIGHT NOW I'VE GOT A WORLD TO SAVE.

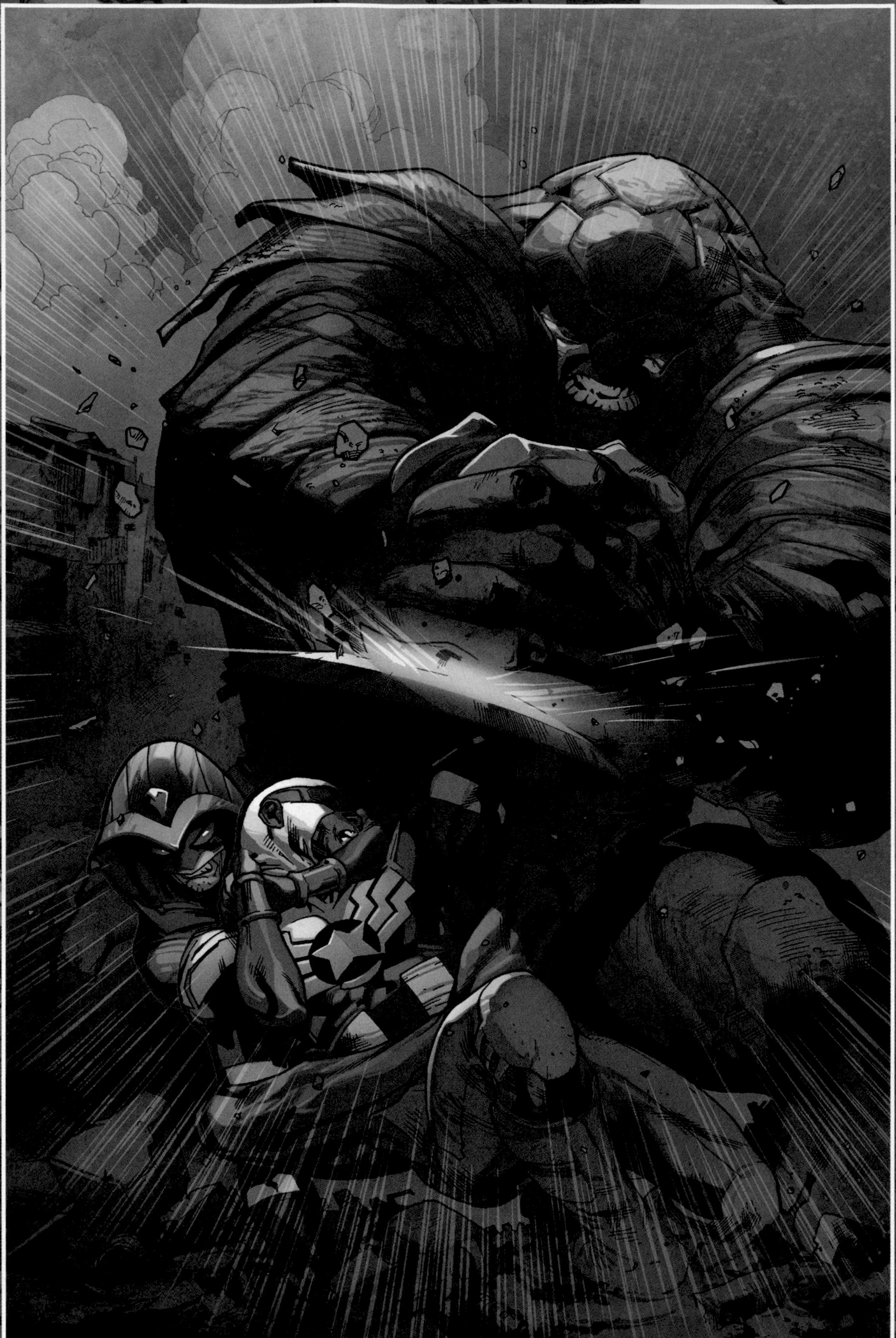

FOUR

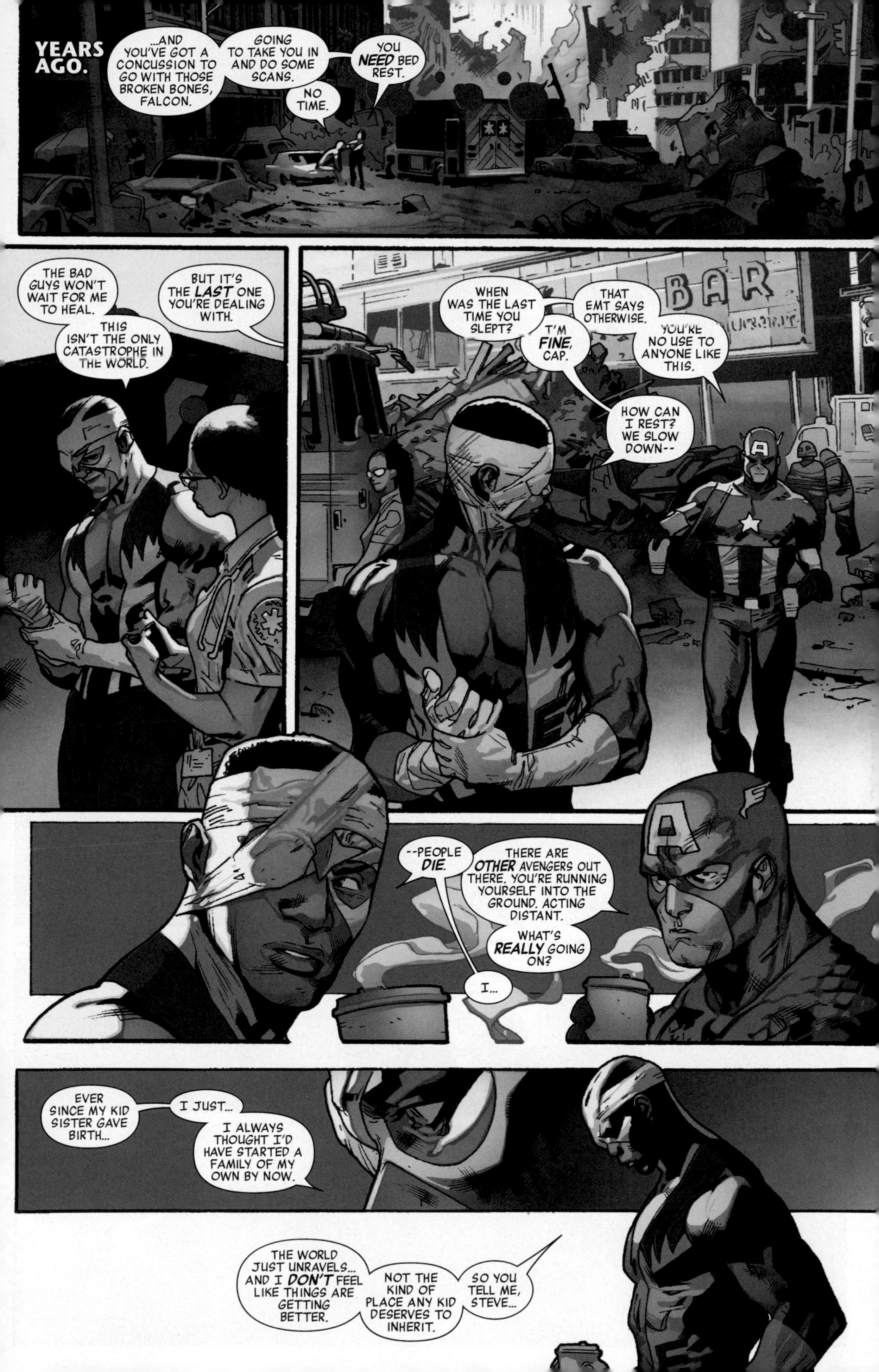
YEARS AGO.
...AND YOU'VE GOT A CONCUSSION TO GO WITH THOSE BROKEN BONES, FALCON.
GOING TO TAKE YOU IN AND DO SOME SCANS.
YOU NEED BED REST.
NO TIME.
THE BAD GUYS WON'T WAIT FOR ME TO HEAL.
THIS ISN'T THE ONLY CATASTROPHE IN THE WORLD.
BUT IT'S THE LAST ONE YOU'RE DEALING WITH.
BAR
WHEN WAS THE LAST TIME YOU SLEPT?
I'M FINE, CAP.
THAT EMT SAYS OTHERWISE.
YOU'RE NO USE TO ANYONE LIKE THIS.
HOW CAN I REST? WE SLOW DOWN--
--PEOPLE DIE.
THERE ARE OTHER AVENGERS OUT THERE. YOU'RE RUNNING YOURSELF INTO THE GROUND. ACTING DISTANT.
WHAT'S REALLY GOING ON?
I...
EVER SINCE MY KID SISTER GAVE BIRTH...
I JUST...
I ALWAYS THOUGHT I'D HAVE STARTED A FAMILY OF MY OWN BY NOW.
THE WORLD JUST UNRAVELS... AND I DON'T FEEL LIKE THINGS ARE GETTING BETTER.
NOT THE KIND OF PLACE ANY KID DESERVES TO INHERIT.
SO YOU TELL ME, STEVE...

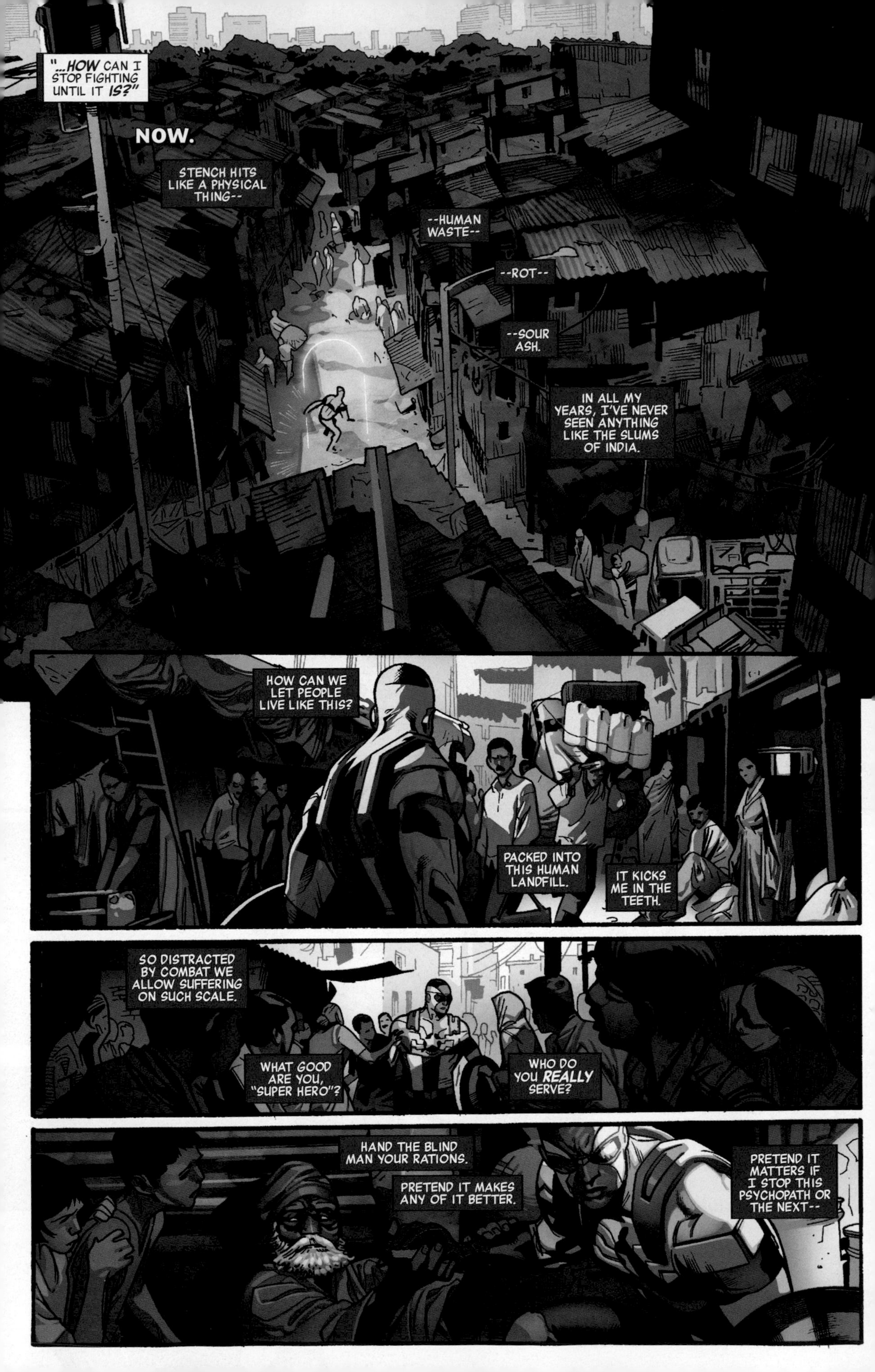
"...HOW CAN I STOP FIGHTING UNTIL IT IS?"
NOW.
STENCH HITS LIKE A PHYSICAL THING--
--HUMAN WASTE--
--ROT--
--SOUR ASH.
IN ALL MY YEARS, I'VE NEVER SEEN ANYTHING LIKE THE SLUMS OF INDIA.
HOW CAN WE LET PEOPLE LIVE LIKE THIS?
PACKED INTO THIS HUMAN LANDFILL.
IT KICKS ME IN THE TEETH.
SO DISTRACTED BY COMBAT WE ALLOW SUFFERING ON SUCH SCALE.
WHAT GOOD ARE YOU, "SUPER HERO"?
WHO DO YOU REALLY SERVE?
HAND THE BLIND MAN YOUR RATIONS.
PRETEND IT MAKES ANY OF IT BETTER.
PRETEND IT MATTERS IF I STOP THIS PSYCHOPATH OR THE NEXT--

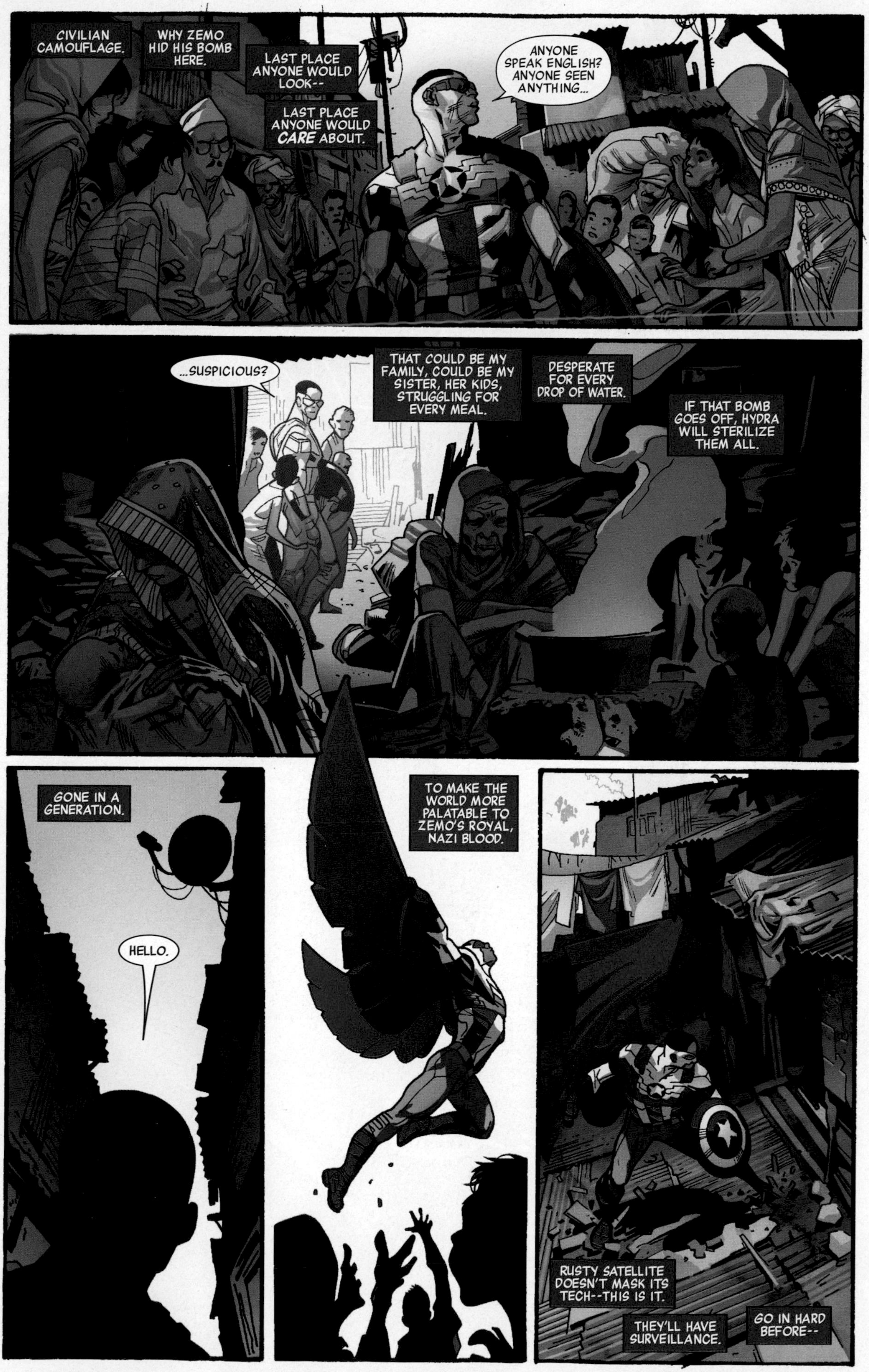
CIVILIAN CAMOUFLAGE.
WHY ZEMO HID HIS BOMB HERE.
LAST PLACE ANYONE WOULD LOOK--
LAST PLACE ANYONE WOULD CARE ABOUT.
ANYONE SPEAK ENGLISH? ANYONE SEEN ANYTHING...
...SUSPICIOUS?
THAT COULD BE MY FAMILY, COULD BE MY SISTER, HER KIDS, STRUGGLING FOR EVERY MEAL.
DESPERATE FOR EVERY DROP OF WATER.
IF THAT BOMB GOES OFF, HYDRA WILL STERILIZE THEM ALL.
GONE IN A GENERATION.
HELLO.
TO MAKE THE WORLD MORE PALATABLE TO ZEMO'S ROYAL, NAZI BLOOD.
RUSTY SATELLITE DOESN'T MASK ITS TECH--THIS IS IT.
THEY'LL HAVE SURVEILLANCE.
GO IN HARD BEFORE--

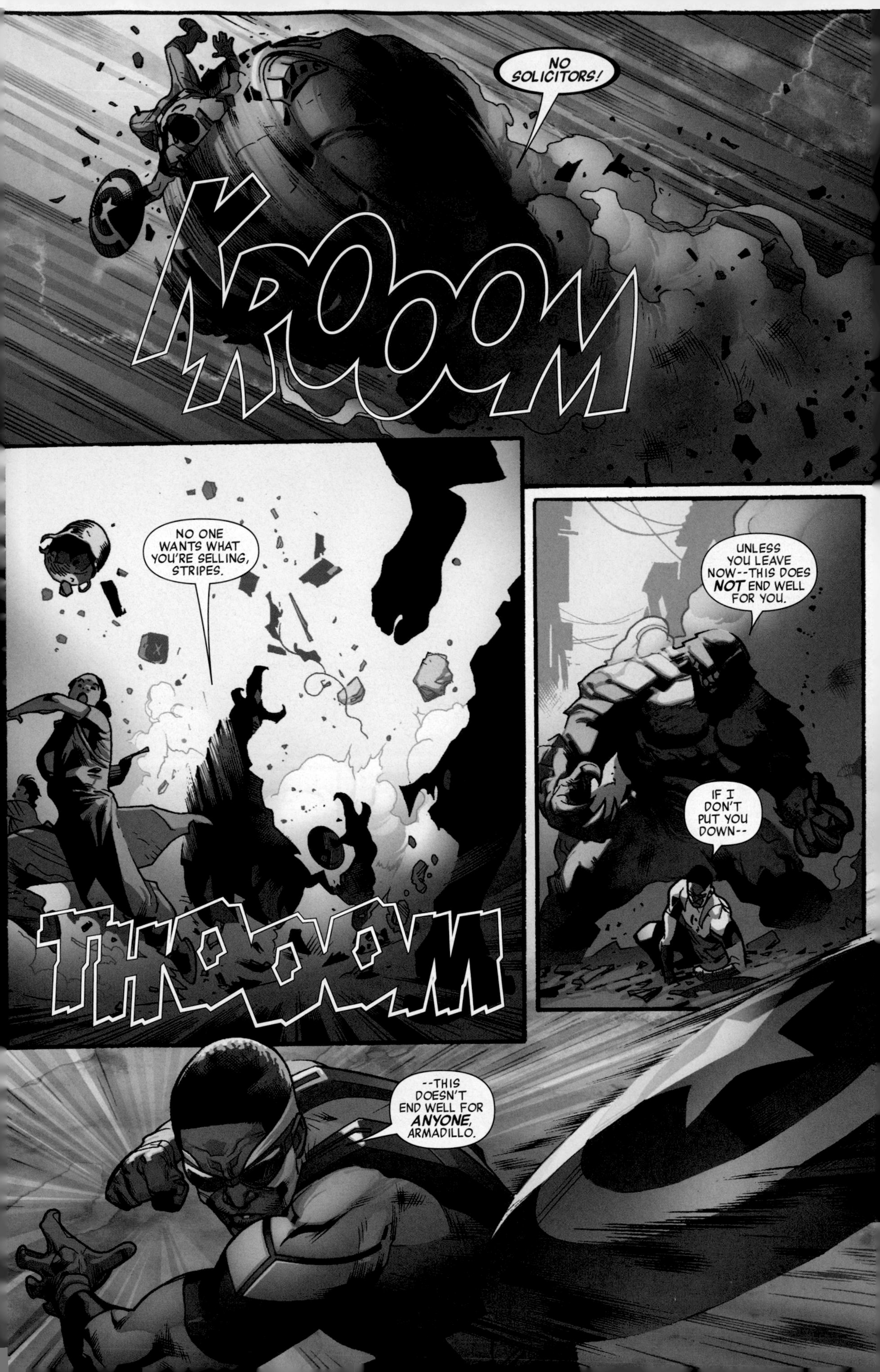
NO SOLICITORS!
KROOOM
NO ONE WANTS WHAT YOU'RE SELLING, STRIPES.
THOOOM
UNLESS YOU LEAVE NOW--THIS DOES NOT END WELL FOR YOU.
IF I DON'T PUT YOU DOWN--
--THIS DOESN'T END WELL FOR ANYONE, ARMADILLO.

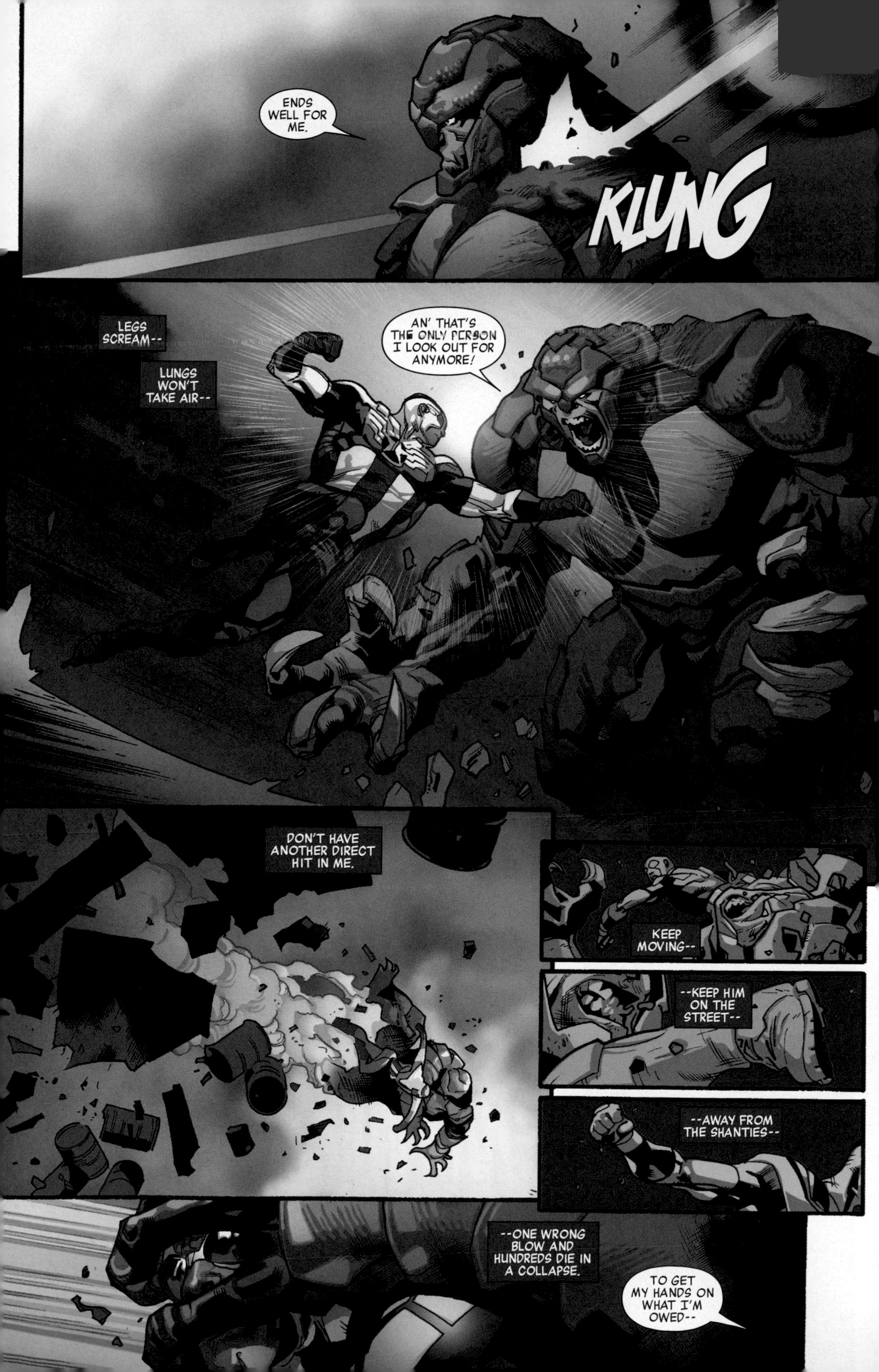
ENDS WELL FOR ME.
KLUNG
LEGS SCREAM--
LUNGS WON'T TAKE AIR--
AN' THAT'S THE ONLY PERSON I LOOK OUT FOR ANYMORE!
DON'T HAVE ANOTHER DIRECT HIT IN ME.
KEEP MOVING--
--KEEP HIM ON THE STREET--
--AWAY FROM THE SHANTIES--
--ONE WRONG BLOW AND HUNDREDS DIE IN A COLLAPSE.
TO GET MY HANDS ON WHAT I'M OWED--

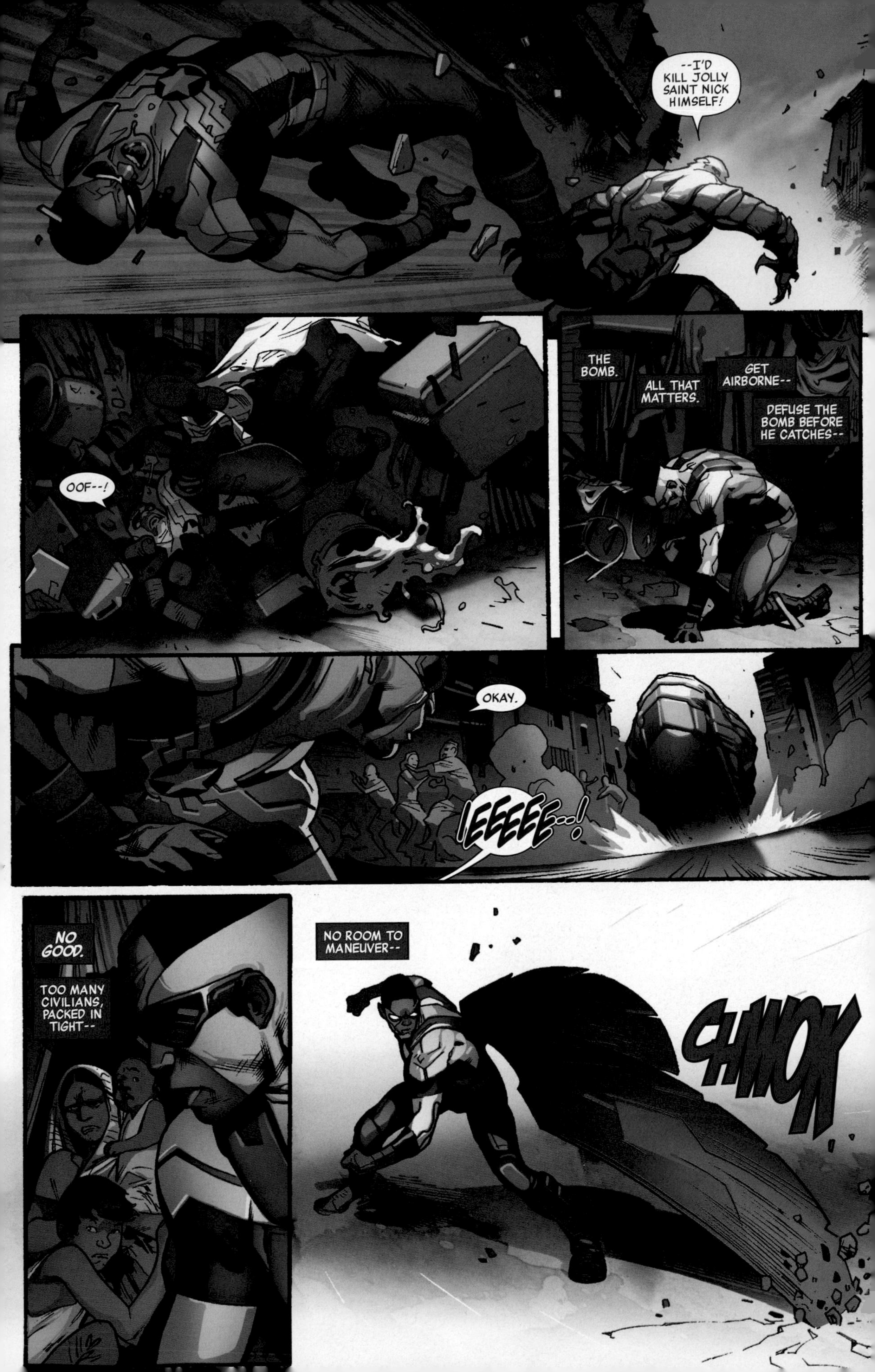
--I'D KILL JOLLY SAINT NICK HIMSELF!
OOF--!
THE BOMB.
ALL THAT MATTERS.
GET AIRBORNE--
DEFUSE THE BOMB BEFORE HE CATCHES--
OKAY.
IEEEEE--!
NO GOOD.
TOO MANY CIVILIANS, PACKED IN TIGHT--
NO ROOM TO MANEUVER--
CHNOK

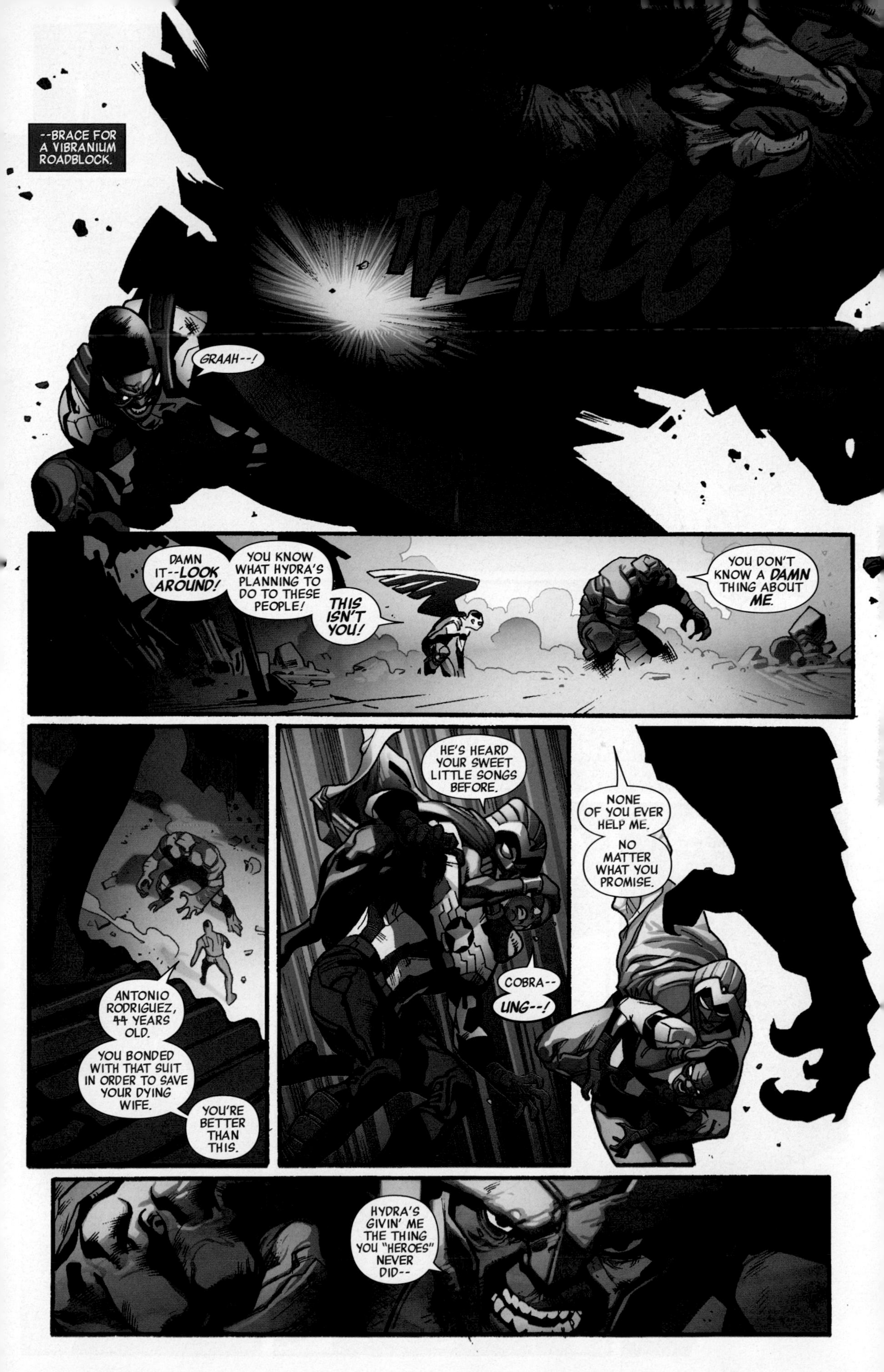
--BRACE FOR A VIBRANIUM ROADBLOCK.
TWANGG
GRAAH--!
DAMN IT--LOOK AROUND!
YOU KNOW WHAT HYDRA'S PLANNING TO DO TO THESE PEOPLE!
THIS ISN'T YOU!
YOU DON'T KNOW A DAMN THING ABOUT ME.
ANTONIO RODRIGUEZ, 44 YEARS OLD.
YOU BONDED WITH THAT SUIT IN ORDER TO SAVE YOUR DYING WIFE.
YOU'RE BETTER THAN THIS.
HE'S HEARD YOUR SWEET LITTLE SONGS BEFORE.
COBRA--
UNG--!
NONE OF YOU EVER HELP ME.
NO MATTER WHAT YOU PROMISE.
HYDRA'S GIVIN' ME THE THING YOU "HEROES" NEVER DID--

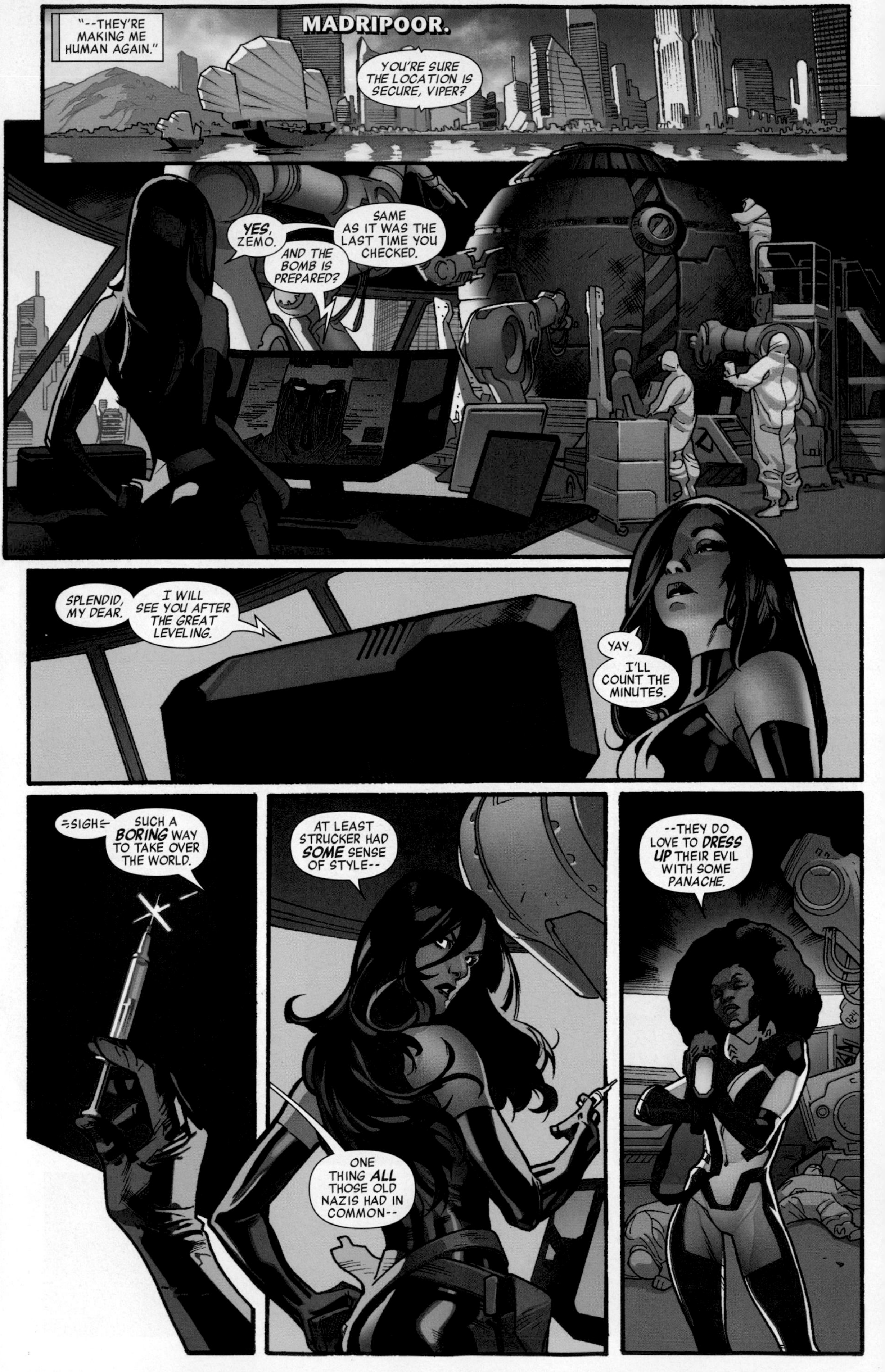
"--THEY'RE MAKING ME HUMAN AGAIN."
MADRIPOOR.
YOU'RE SURE THE LOCATION IS SECURE, VIPER?
YES, ZEMO.
SAME AS IT WAS THE LAST TIME YOU CHECKED.
AND THE BOMB IS PREPARED?
SPLENDID, MY DEAR.
I WILL SEE YOU AFTER THE GREAT LEVELING.
YAY.
I'LL COUNT THE MINUTES.
=SIGH=
SUCH A BORING WAY TO TAKE OVER THE WORLD.
AT LEAST STRUCKER HAD SOME SENSE OF STYLE--
ONE THING ALL THOSE OLD NAZIS HAD IN COMMON--
--THEY DO LOVE TO DRESS UP THEIR EVIL WITH SOME PANACHE.

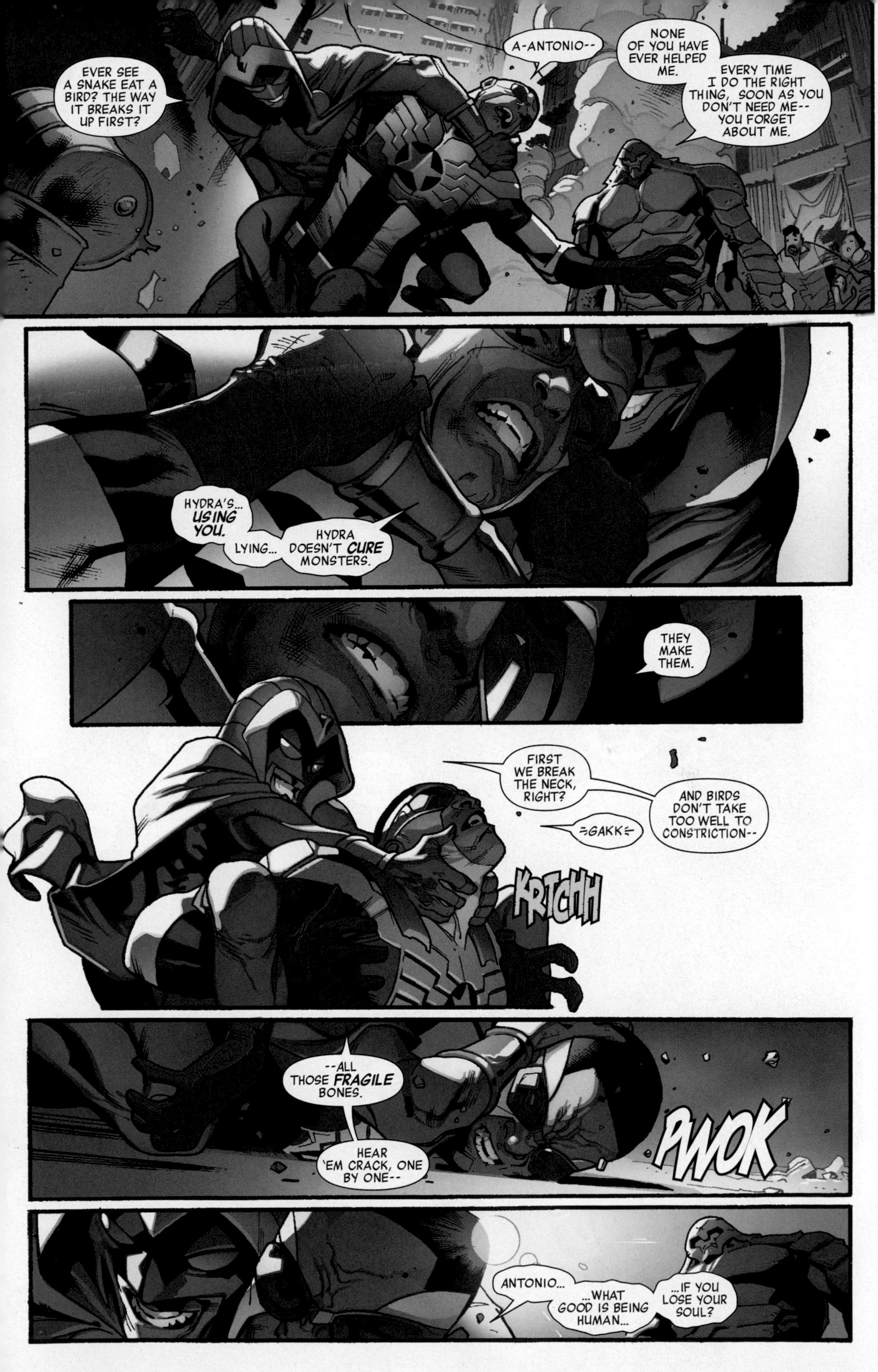
EVER SEE A SNAKE EAT A BIRD? THE WAY IT BREAKS IT UP FIRST?
A-ANTONIO--
NONE OF YOU HAVE EVER HELPED ME.
EVERY TIME I DO THE RIGHT THING, SOON AS YOU DON'T NEED ME-- YOU FORGET ABOUT ME.
HYDRA'S... USING YOU.
LYING...
HYDRA DOESN'T CURE MONSTERS.
THEY MAKE THEM.
FIRST WE BREAK THE NECK, RIGHT?
AND BIRDS DON'T TAKE TOO WELL TO CONSTRICTION--
GAKK
KRTCHH
--ALL THOSE FRAGILE BONES.
HEAR 'EM CRACK, ONE BY ONE--
PWOK
ANTONIO...
...WHAT GOOD IS BEING HUMAN...
...IF YOU LOSE YOUR SOUL?

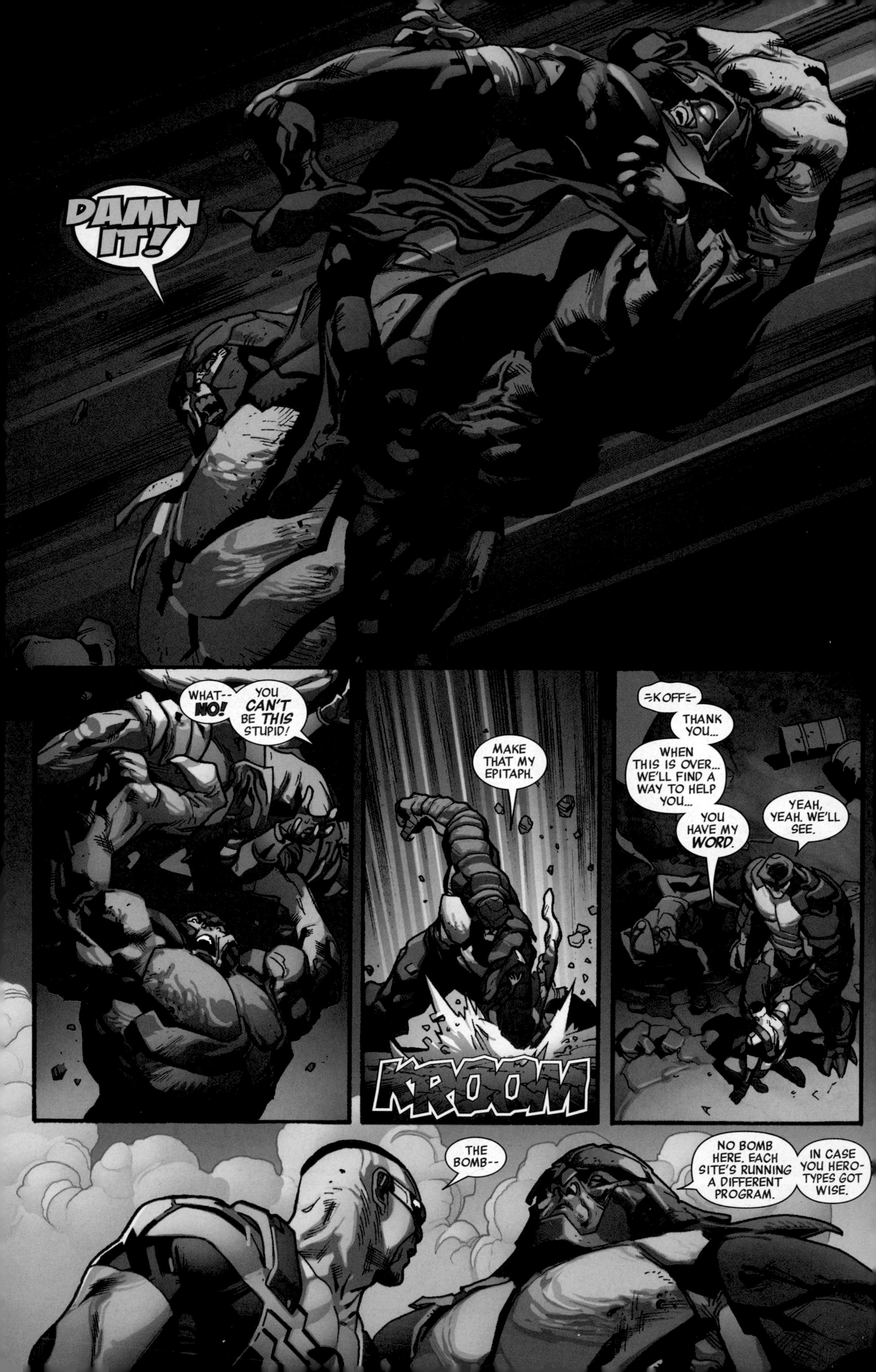
DAMN IT!
WHAT-- NO!
YOU CAN'T BE THIS STUPID!
MAKE THAT MY EPITAPH.
KROOM
=KOFF=
THANK YOU...
WHEN THIS IS OVER... WE'LL FIND A WAY TO HELP YOU...
YOU HAVE MY WORD.
YEAH, YEAH. WE'LL SEE.
THE BOMB--
NO BOMB HERE. EACH SITE'S RUNNING A DIFFERENT PROGRAM.
IN CASE YOU HERO-TYPES GOT WISE.

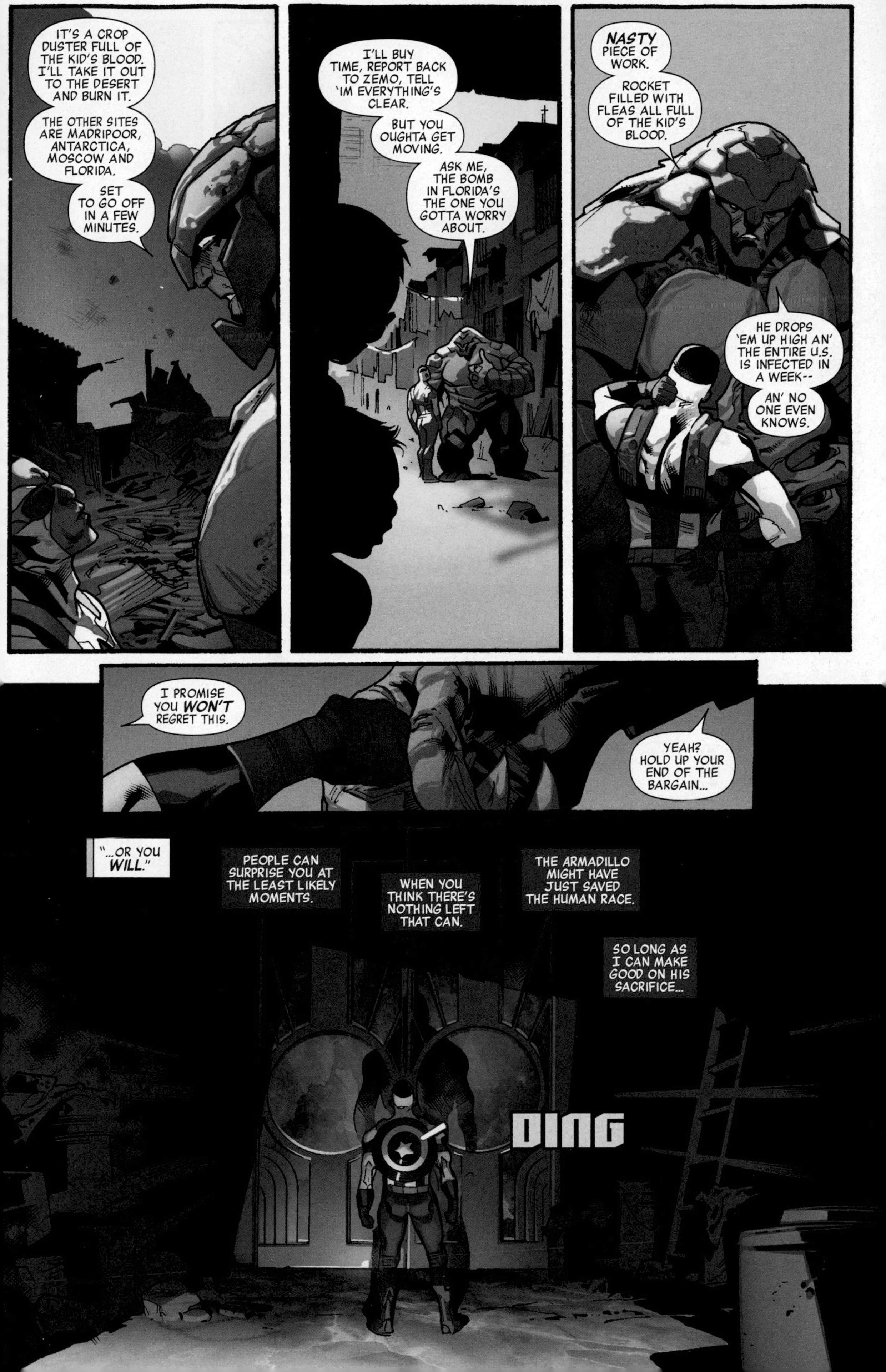
IT'S A CROP DUSTER FULL OF THE KID'S BLOOD. I'LL TAKE IT OUT TO THE DESERT AND BURN IT.
THE OTHER SITES ARE MADRIPOOR, ANTARCTICA, MOSCOW AND FLORIDA.
SET TO GO OFF IN A FEW MINUTES.
I'LL BUY TIME, REPORT BACK TO ZEMO, TELL 'IM EVERYTHING'S CLEAR.
BUT YOU OUGHTA GET MOVING.
ASK ME, THE BOMB IN FLORIDA'S THE ONE YOU GOTTA WORRY ABOUT.
NASTY PIECE OF WORK.
ROCKET FILLED WITH FLEAS ALL FULL OF THE KID'S BLOOD.
HE DROPS 'EM UP HIGH AN' THE ENTIRE U.S. IS INFECTED IN A WEEK--
AN' NO ONE EVEN KNOWS.
I PROMISE YOU WON'T REGRET THIS.
YEAH? HOLD UP YOUR END OF THE BARGAIN...
"...OR YOU WILL."
PEOPLE CAN SURPRISE YOU AT THE LEAST LIKELY MOMENTS.
WHEN YOU THINK THERE'S NOTHING LEFT THAT CAN.
THE ARMADILLO MIGHT HAVE JUST SAVED THE HUMAN RACE.
SO LONG AS I CAN MAKE GOOD ON HIS SACRIFICE...
DING

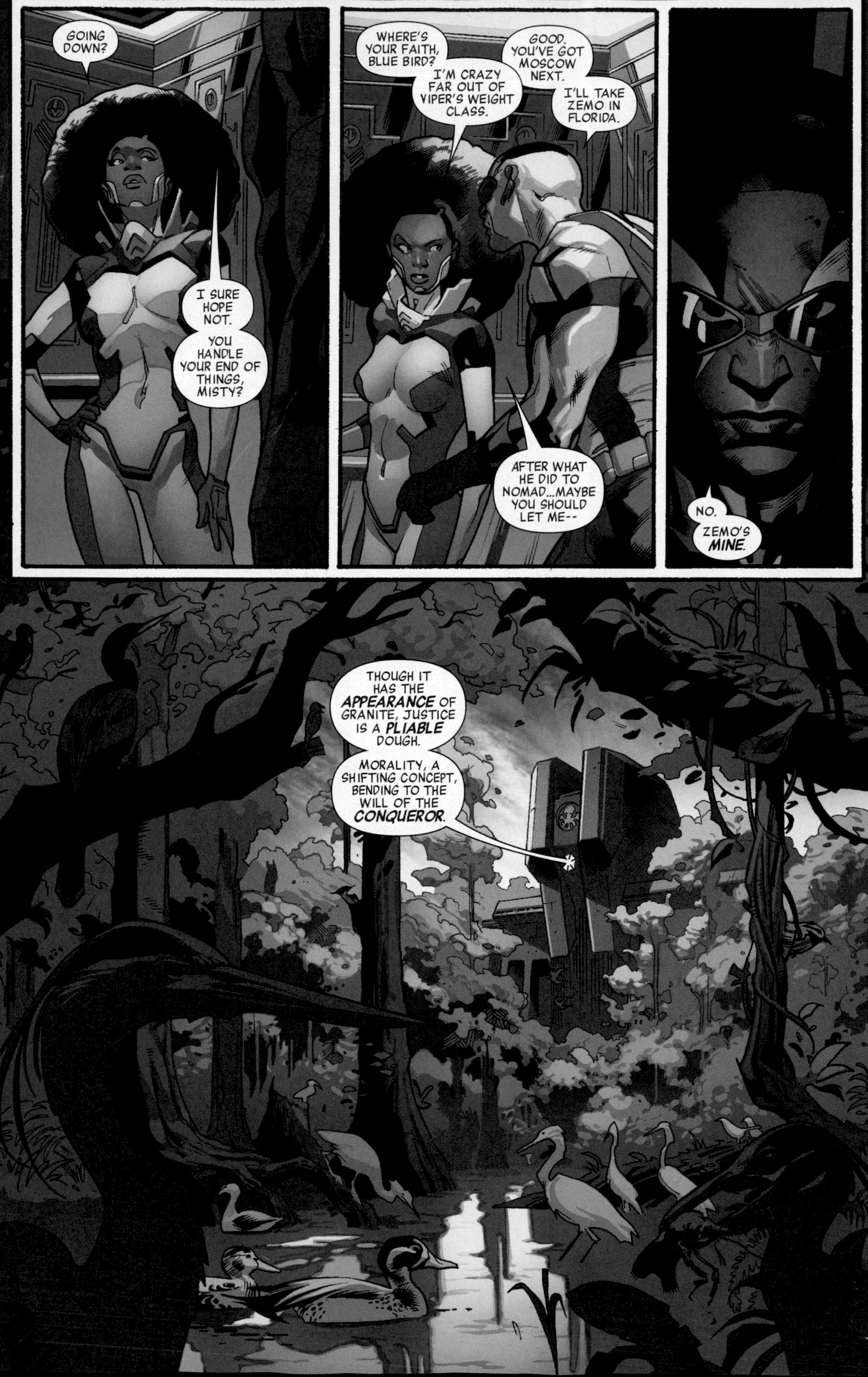
GOING DOWN?
I SURE HOPE NOT.
YOU HANDLE YOUR END OF THINGS, MISTY?
WHERE'S YOUR FAITH, BLUE BIRD?
I'M CRAZY FAR OUT OF VIPER'S WEIGHT CLASS.
GOOD. YOU'VE GOT MOSCOW NEXT.
I'LL TAKE ZEMO IN FLORIDA.
AFTER WHAT HE DID TO NOMAD...MAYBE YOU SHOULD LET ME--
NO.
ZEMO'S MINE.
THOUGH IT HAS THE APPEARANCE OF GRANITE, JUSTICE IS A PLIABLE DOUGH.
MORALITY, A SHIFTING CONCEPT, BENDING TO THE WILL OF THE CONQUEROR.

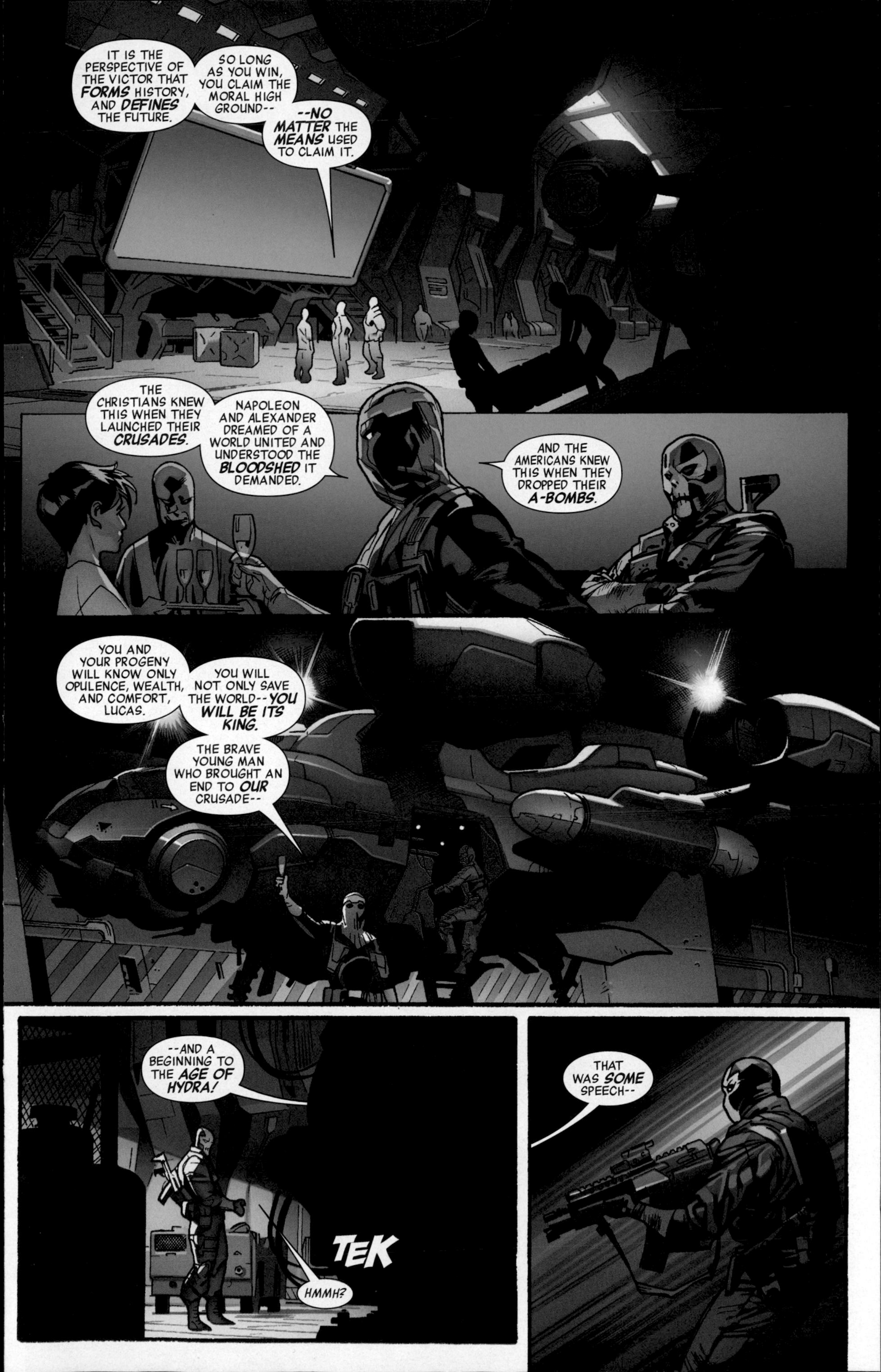
IT IS THE PERSPECTIVE OF THE VICTOR THAT FORMS HISTORY, AND DEFINES THE FUTURE.
SO LONG AS YOU WIN, YOU CLAIM THE MORAL HIGH GROUND--
--NO MATTER THE MEANS USED TO CLAIM IT.
THE CHRISTIANS KNEW THIS WHEN THEY LAUNCHED THEIR CRUSADES.
NAPOLEON AND ALEXANDER DREAMED OF A WORLD UNITED AND UNDERSTOOD THE BLOODSHED IT DEMANDED.
AND THE AMERICANS KNEW THIS WHEN THEY DROPPED THEIR A-BOMBS.
YOU AND YOUR PROGENY WILL KNOW ONLY OPULENCE, WEALTH, AND COMFORT, LUCAS.
YOU WILL NOT ONLY SAVE THE WORLD--YOU WILL BE ITS KING.
THE BRAVE YOUNG MAN WHO BROUGHT AN END TO OUR CRUSADE--
--AND A BEGINNING TO THE AGE OF HYDRA!
TEK
HMMH?
THAT WAS SOME SPEECH--

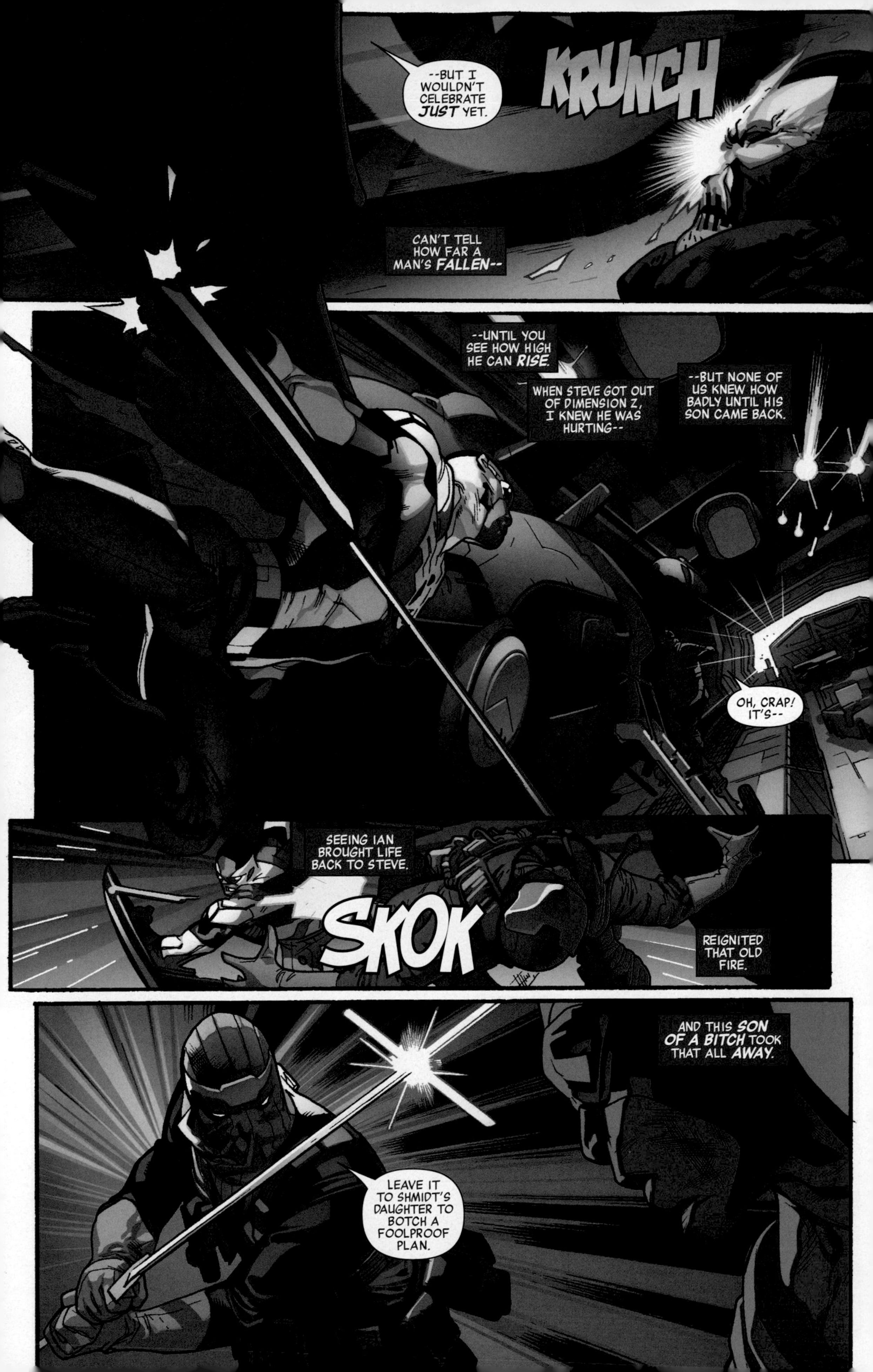
--BUT I WOULDN'T CELEBRATE JUST YET.
KRUNCH
CAN'T TELL HOW FAR A MAN'S FALLEN--
--UNTIL YOU SEE HOW HIGH HE CAN RISE.
WHEN STEVE GOT OUT OF DIMENSION Z, I KNEW HE WAS HURTING--
--BUT NONE OF US KNEW HOW BADLY UNTIL HIS SON CAME BACK.
OH, CRAP! IT'S--
SEEING IAN BROUGHT LIFE BACK TO STEVE.
SKOK
REIGNITED THAT OLD FIRE.
AND THIS SON OF A BITCH TOOK THAT ALL AWAY.
LEAVE IT TO SHMIDT'S DAUGHTER TO BOTCH A FOOLPROOF PLAN.

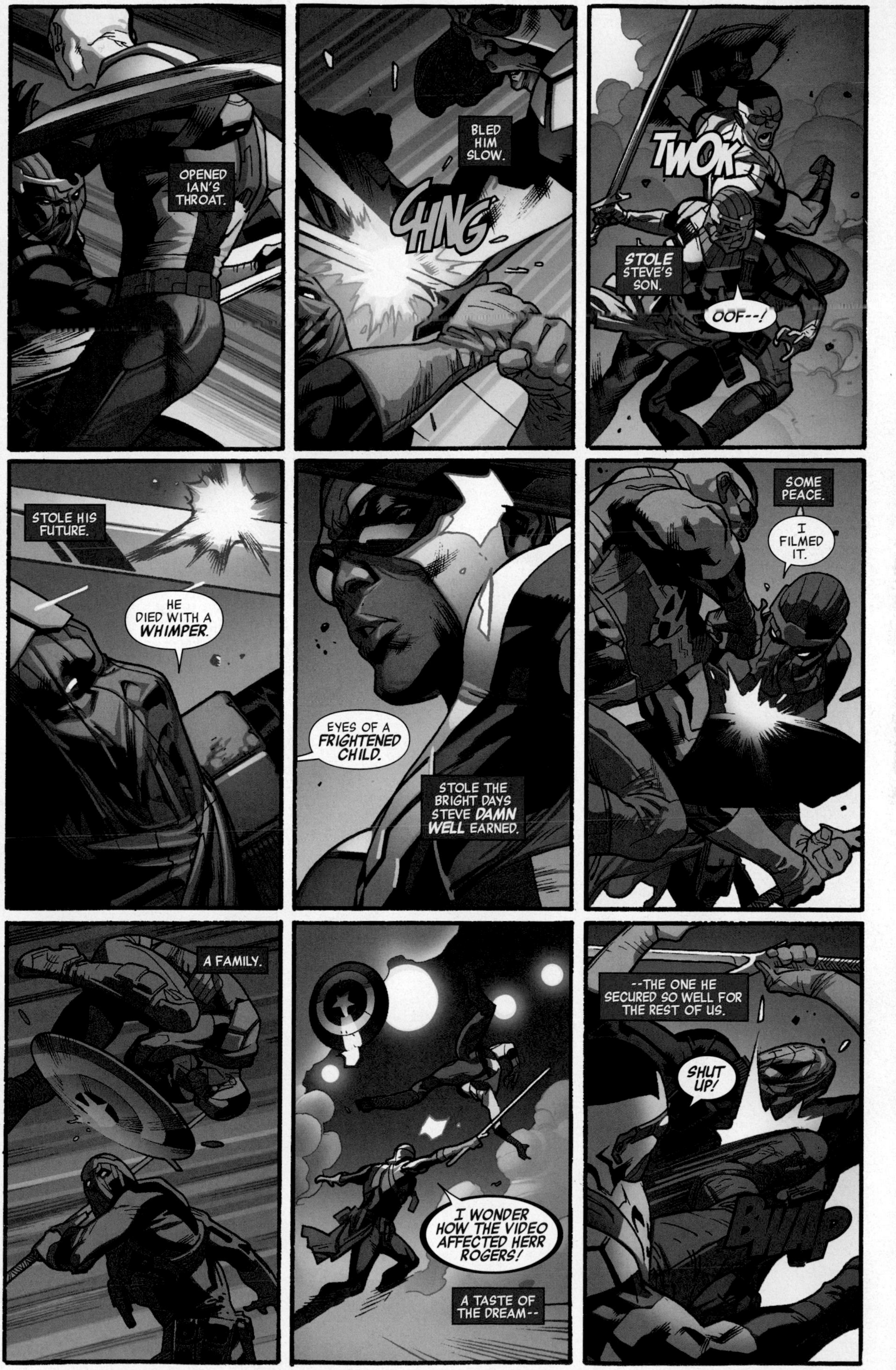
OPENED IAN'S THROAT.
BLED HIM SLOW.
CHNG
TWOK
STOLE STEVE'S SON.
OOF--!
STOLE HIS FUTURE.
HE DIED WITH A WHIMPER.
EYES OF A FRIGHTENED CHILD.
STOLE THE BRIGHT DAYS STEVE DAMN WELL EARNED.
SOME PEACE.
I FILMED IT.
A FAMILY.
I WONDER HOW THE VIDEO AFFECTED HERR ROGERS!
A TASTE OF THE DREAM--
--THE ONE HE SECURED SO WELL FOR THE REST OF US.
SHUT UP!

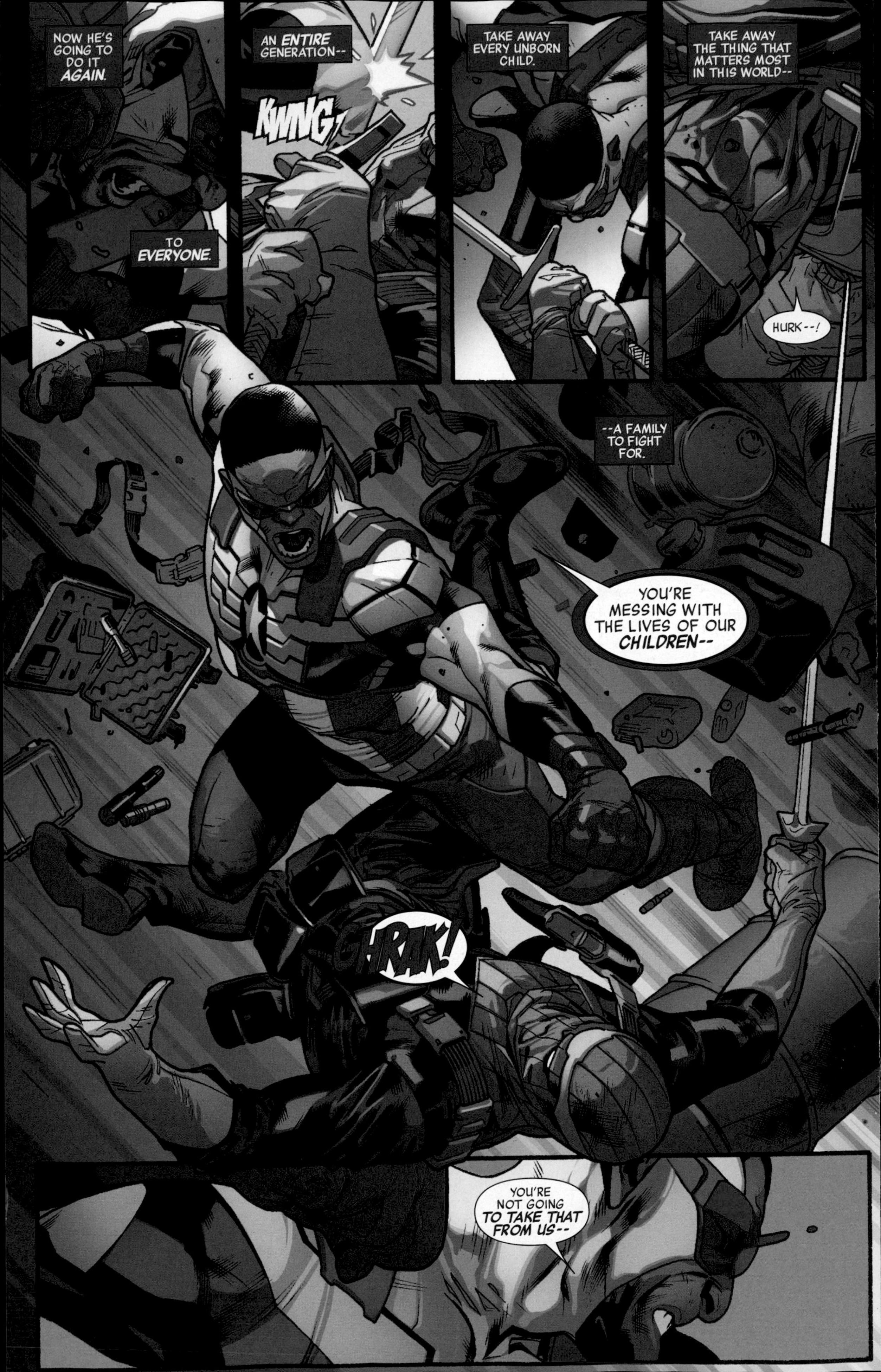
NOW HE'S GOING TO DO IT AGAIN.
TO EVERYONE.
AN ENTIRE GENERATION--
KWING
TAKE AWAY EVERY UNBORN CHILD.
TAKE AWAY THE THING THAT MATTERS MOST IN THIS WORLD--
HURK--!
--A FAMILY TO FIGHT FOR.
YOU'RE MESSING WITH THE LIVES OF OUR CHILDREN--
GHRAK!
YOU'RE NOT GOING TO TAKE THAT FROM US--

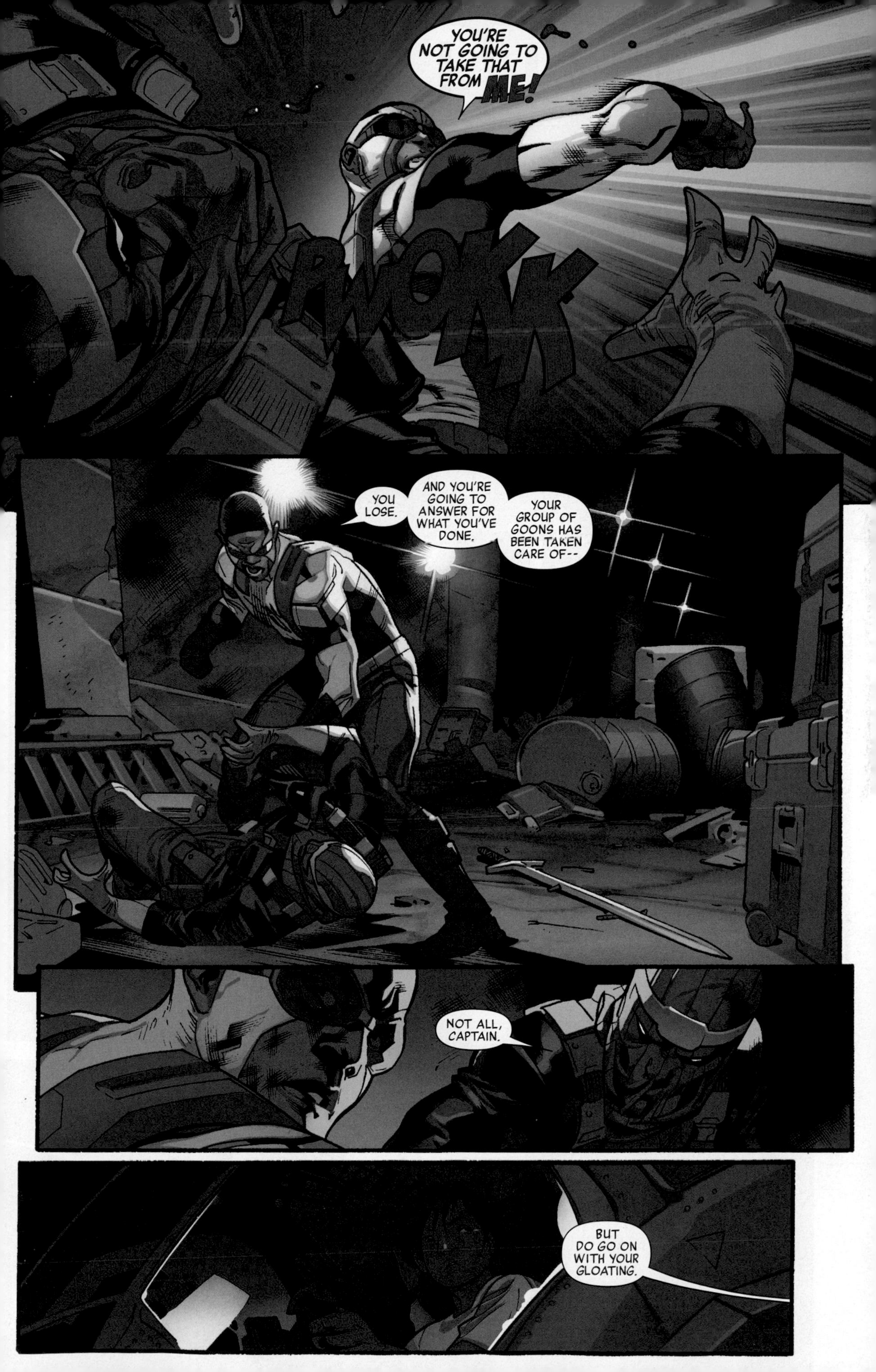
YOU'RE NOT GOING TO TAKE THAT FROM ME!
KWOK
YOU LOSE.
AND YOU'RE GOING TO ANSWER FOR WHAT YOU'VE DONE.
YOUR GROUP OF GOONS HAS BEEN TAKEN CARE OF--
NOT ALL, CAPTAIN.
BUT DO GO ON WITH YOUR GLOATING.

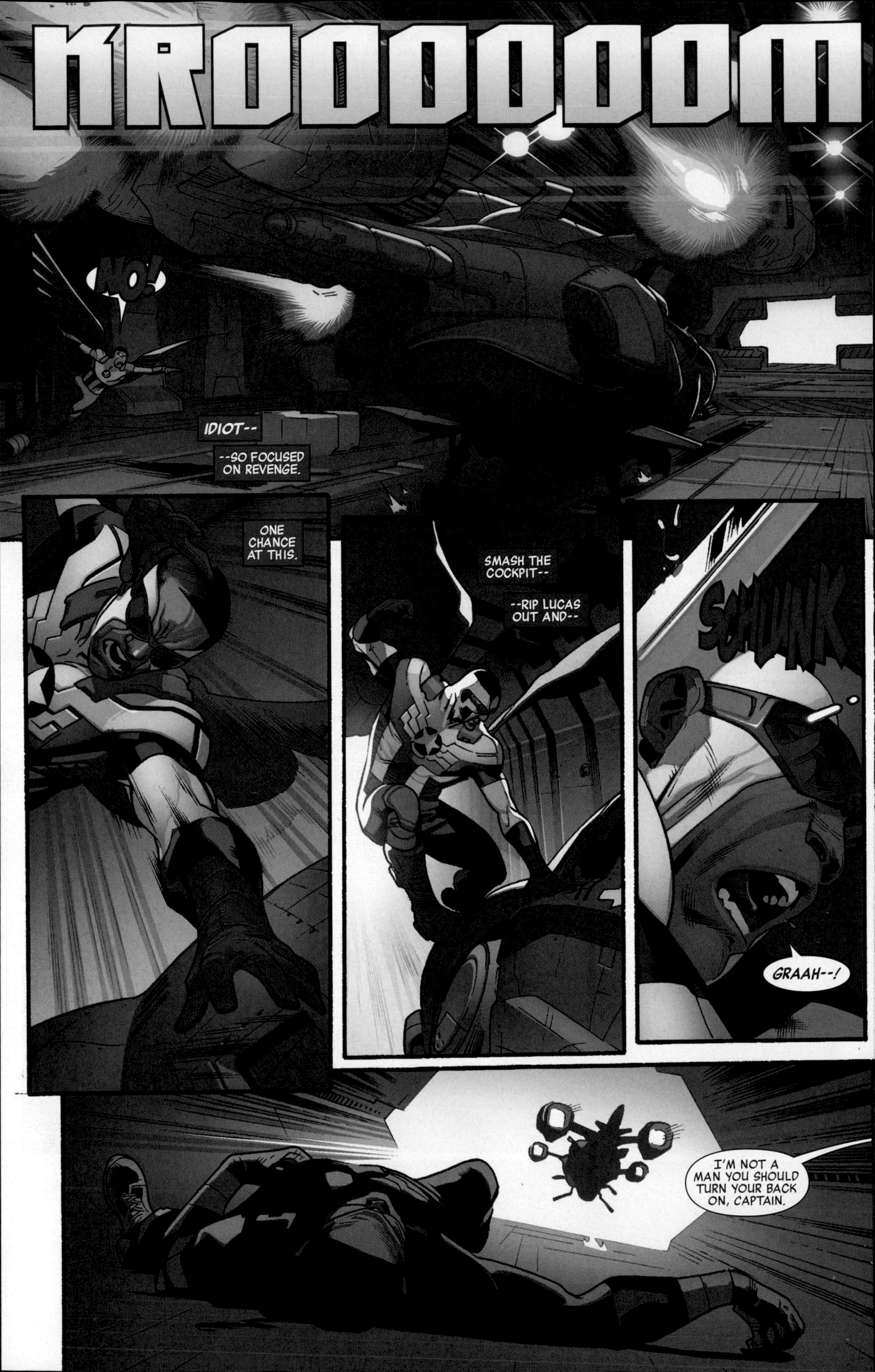
KROOOOOOM
NO!
IDIOT--
--SO FOCUSED ON REVENGE.
ONE CHANCE AT THIS.
SMASH THE COCKPIT--
--RIP LUCAS OUT AND--
SCHUNK
GRAAH--!
I'M NOT A MAN YOU SHOULD TURN YOUR BACK ON, CAPTAIN.

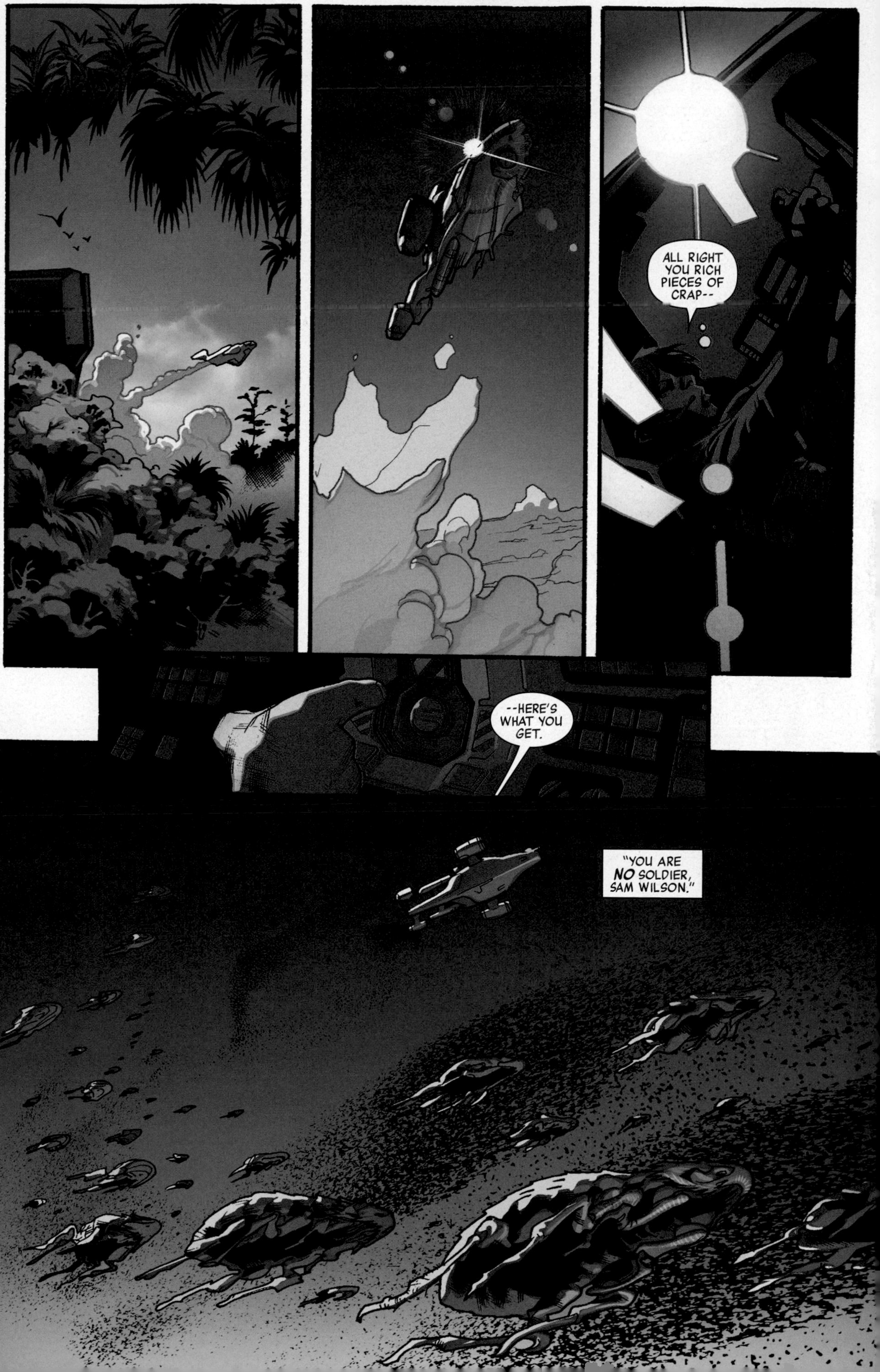
ALL RIGHT YOU RICH PIECES OF CRAP--
--HERE'S WHAT YOU GET.
"YOU ARE NO SOLDIER, SAM WILSON."

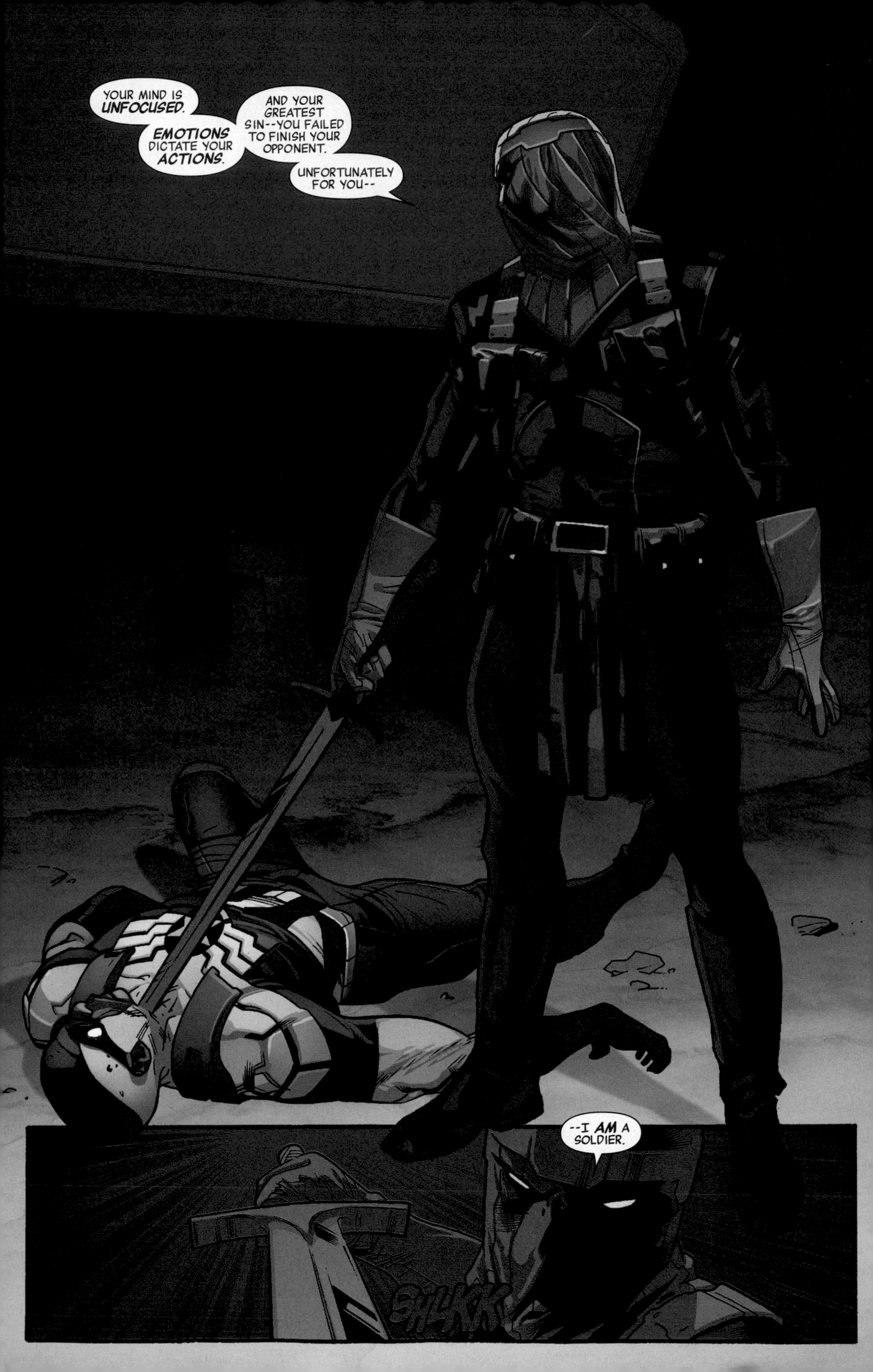

YOUR MIND IS UNFOCUSED.
EMOTIONS DICTATE YOUR ACTIONS.
AND YOUR GREATEST SIN--YOU FAILED TO FINISH YOUR OPPONENT.
UNFORTUNATELY FOR YOU--
--I AM A SOLDIER.
SHLKKK

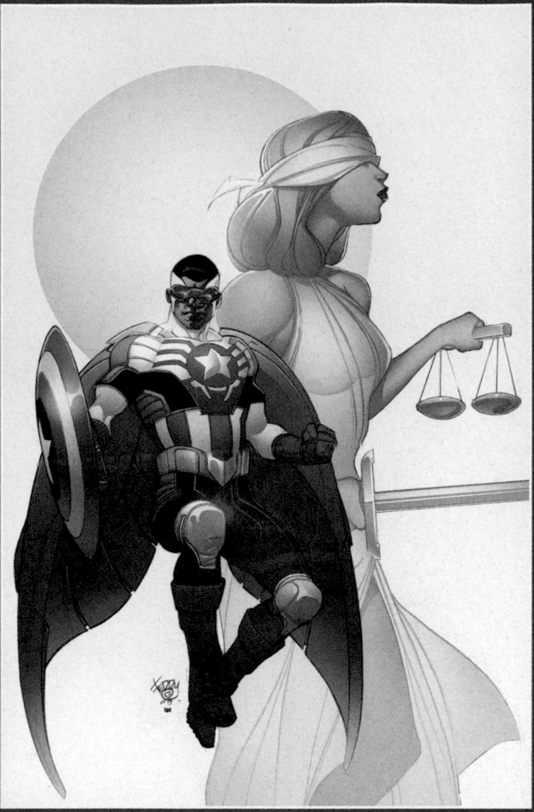

#1 VARIANT
BY PASQUAL FERRY & FRANK D'ARMATA

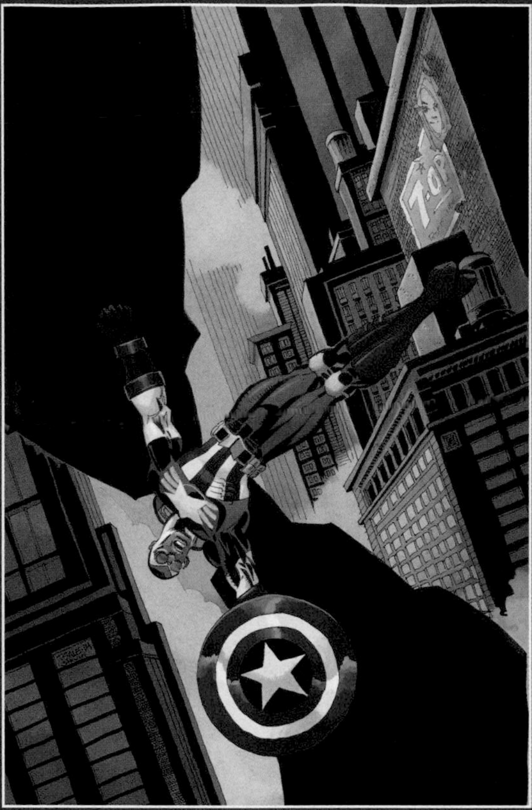

#2 VARIANT BY TIM SALE

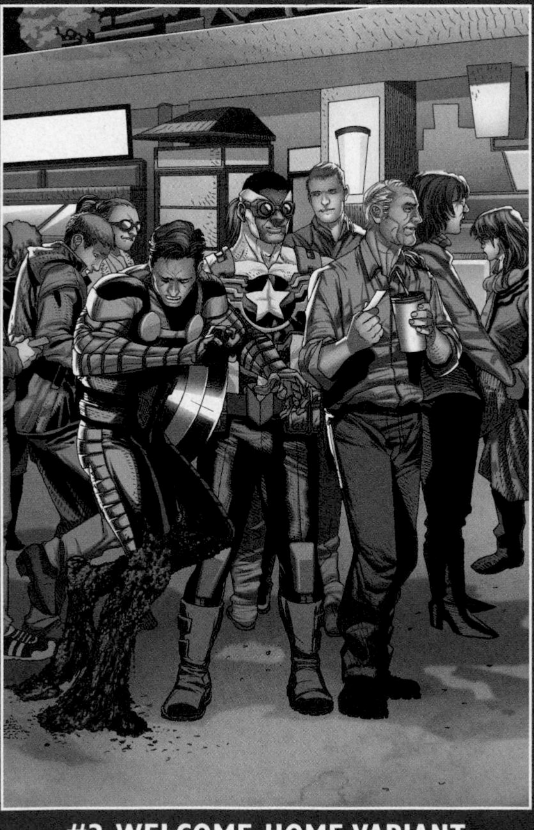

#3 WELCOME HOME VARIANT
BY SALVADOR LARROCA & ISRAEL SILVA

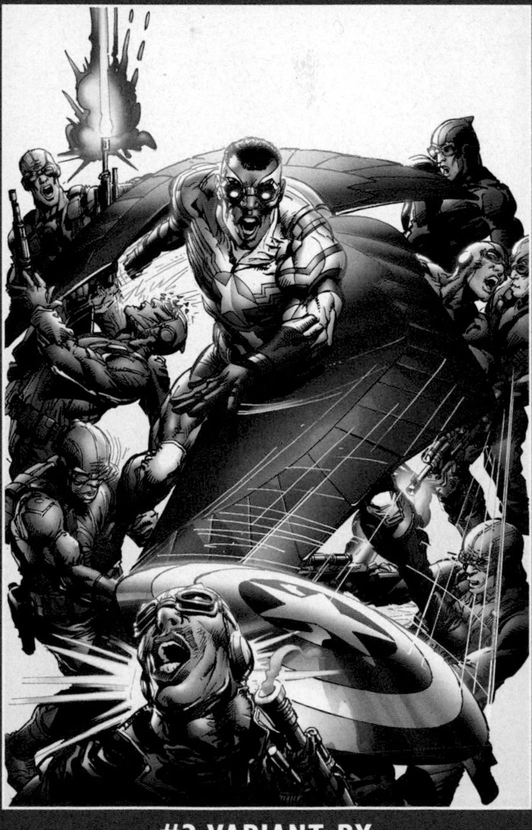

#3 VARIANT BY
NEAL ADAMS & WILLIAM BAUMANN

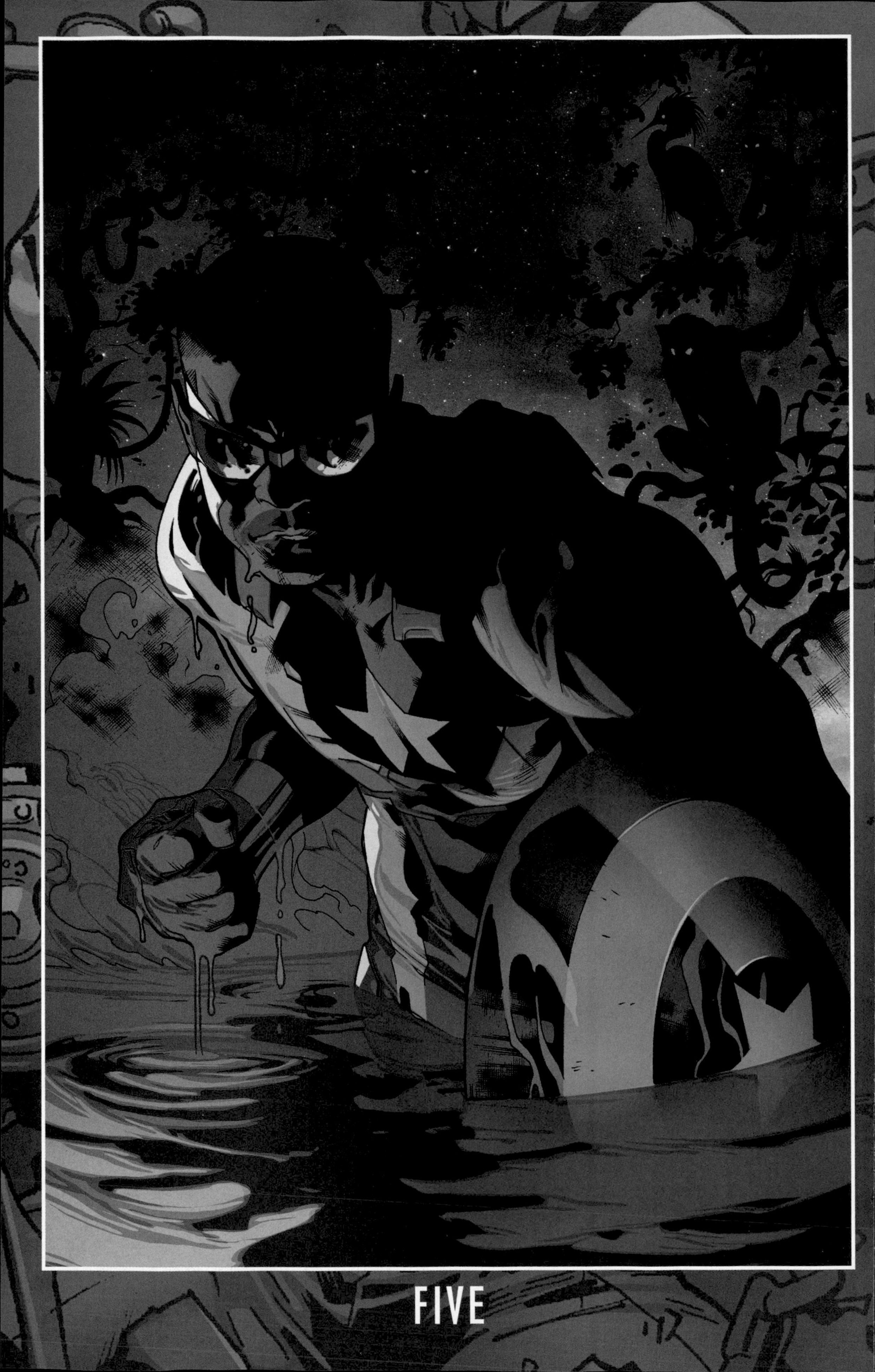

FIVE

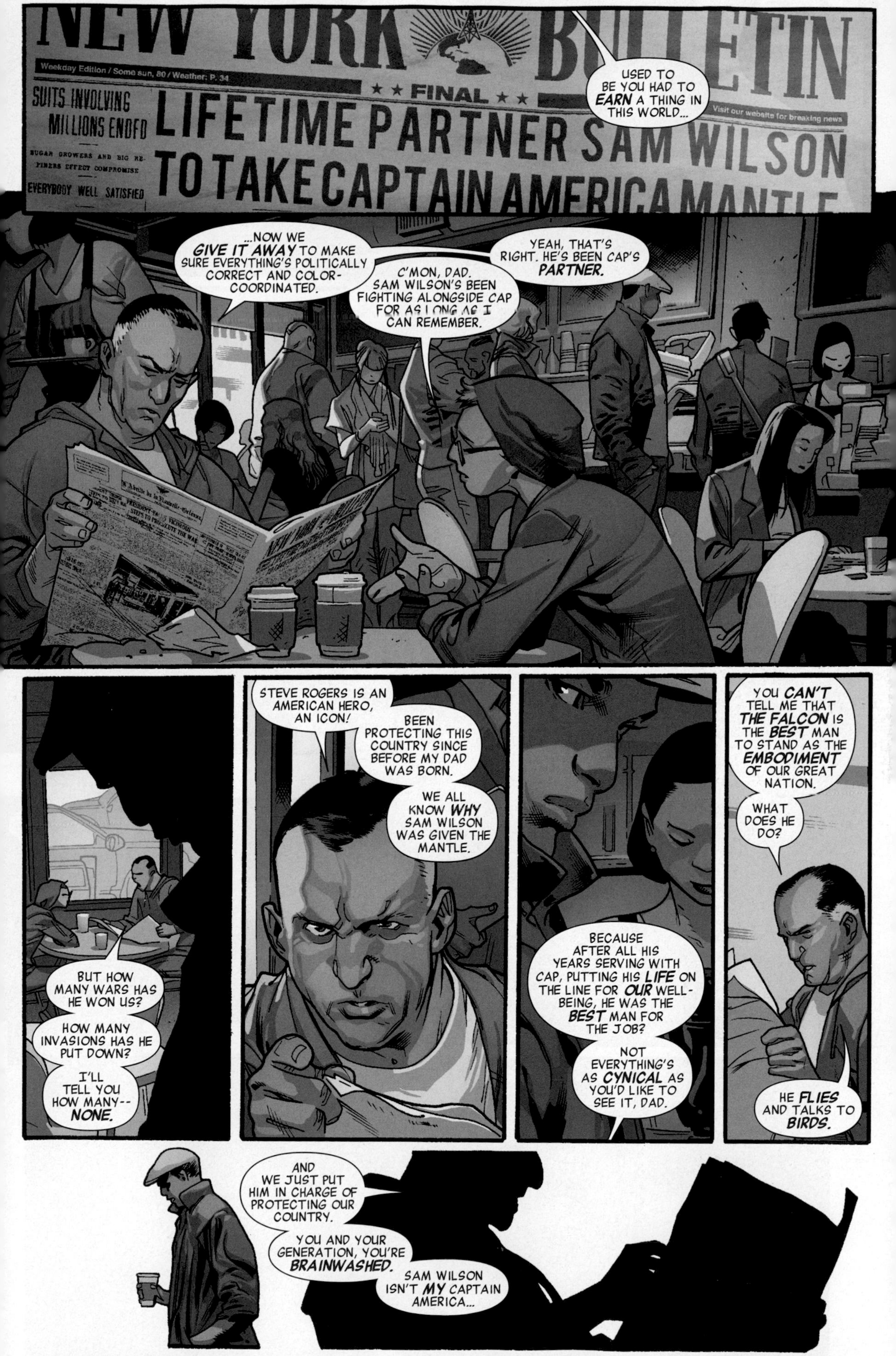
NEW YORK BULLETIN
Weekday Edition / Some sun, 80 / Weather: P. 34
FINAL
Visit our website for breaking news
SUITS INVOLVING MILLIONS ENDED
SUGAR GROWERS AND BIG REFINERS EFFECT COMPROMISE
EVERYBODY WELL SATISFIED
LIFETIME PARTNER SAM WILSON TO TAKE CAPTAIN AMERICA MANTLE
USED TO BE YOU HAD TO EARN A THING IN THIS WORLD...
...NOW WE GIVE IT AWAY TO MAKE SURE EVERYTHING'S POLITICALLY CORRECT AND COLOR-COORDINATED.
C'MON, DAD. SAM WILSON'S BEEN FIGHTING ALONGSIDE CAP FOR AS LONG AS I CAN REMEMBER.
YEAH, THAT'S RIGHT. HE'S BEEN CAP'S PARTNER.
BUT HOW MANY WARS HAS HE WON US?
HOW MANY INVASIONS HAS HE PUT DOWN?
I'LL TELL YOU HOW MANY-- NONE.
STEVE ROGERS IS AN AMERICAN HERO, AN ICON!
BEEN PROTECTING THIS COUNTRY SINCE BEFORE MY DAD WAS BORN.
WE ALL KNOW WHY SAM WILSON WAS GIVEN THE MANTLE.
BECAUSE AFTER ALL HIS YEARS SERVING WITH CAP, PUTTING HIS LIFE ON THE LINE FOR OUR WELL-BEING, HE WAS THE BEST MAN FOR THE JOB?
NOT EVERYTHING'S AS CYNICAL AS YOU'D LIKE TO SEE IT, DAD.
YOU CAN'T TELL ME THAT THE FALCON IS THE BEST MAN TO STAND AS THE EMBODIMENT OF OUR GREAT NATION.
WHAT DOES HE DO?
HE FLIES AND TALKS TO BIRDS.
AND WE JUST PUT HIM IN CHARGE OF PROTECTING OUR COUNTRY.
YOU AND YOUR GENERATION, YOU'RE BRAINWASHED.
SAM WILSON ISN'T MY CAPTAIN AMERICA...

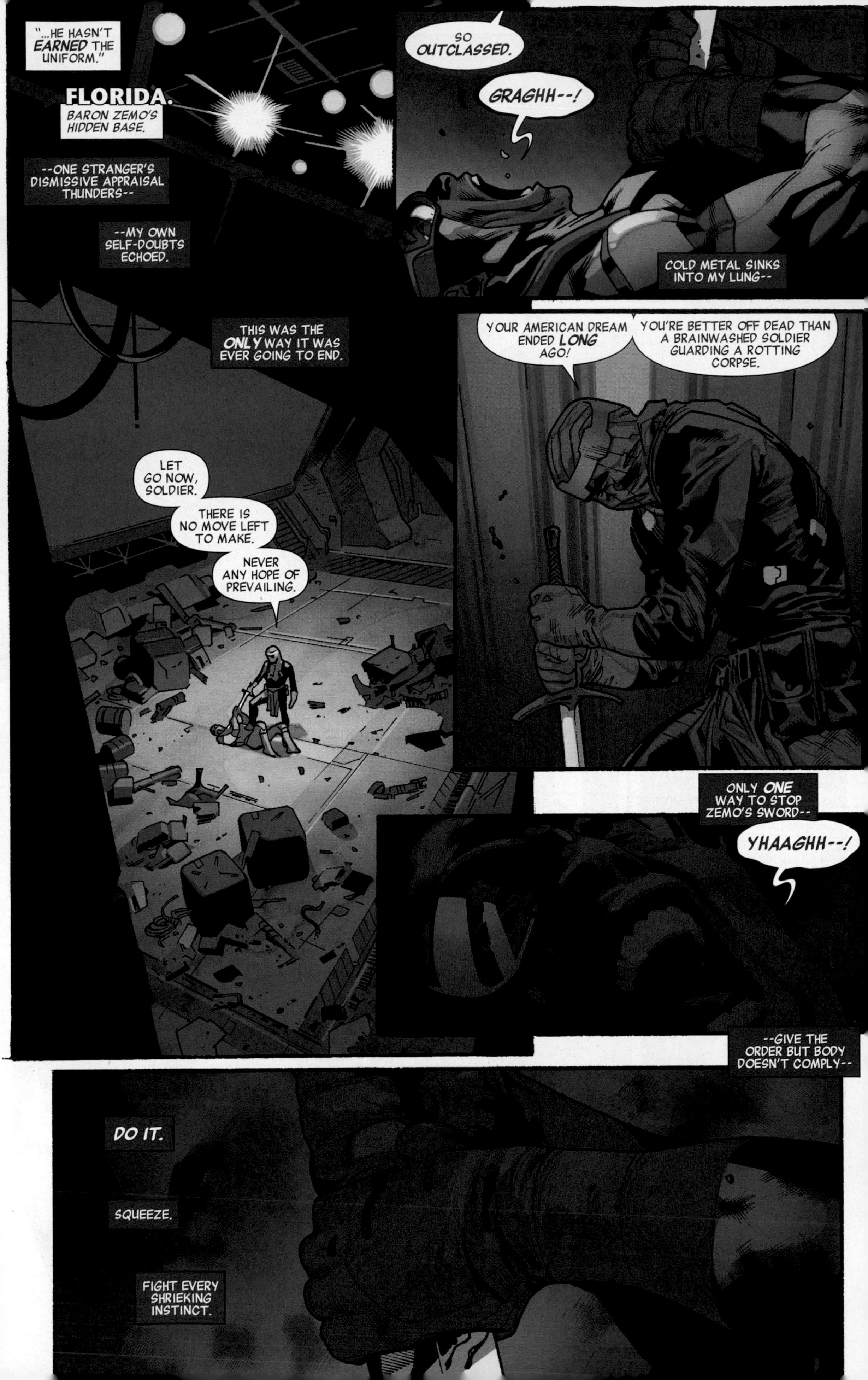
"...HE HASN'T EARNED THE UNIFORM."
FLORIDA.
BARON ZEMO'S HIDDEN BASE.
--ONE STRANGER'S DISMISSIVE APPRAISAL THUNDERS--
--MY OWN SELF-DOUBTS ECHOED.
SO OUTCLASSED.
GRAGHH--!
COLD METAL SINKS INTO MY LUNG--
THIS WAS THE ONLY WAY IT WAS EVER GOING TO END.
LET GO NOW, SOLDIER.
THERE IS NO MOVE LEFT TO MAKE.
NEVER ANY HOPE OF PREVAILING.
YOUR AMERICAN DREAM ENDED LONG AGO!
YOU'RE BETTER OFF DEAD THAN A BRAINWASHED SOLDIER GUARDING A ROTTING CORPSE.
ONLY ONE WAY TO STOP ZEMO'S SWORD--
YHAAGHH--!
--GIVE THE ORDER BUT BODY DOESN'T COMPLY--
DO IT.
SQUEEZE.
FIGHT EVERY SHRIEKING INSTINCT.

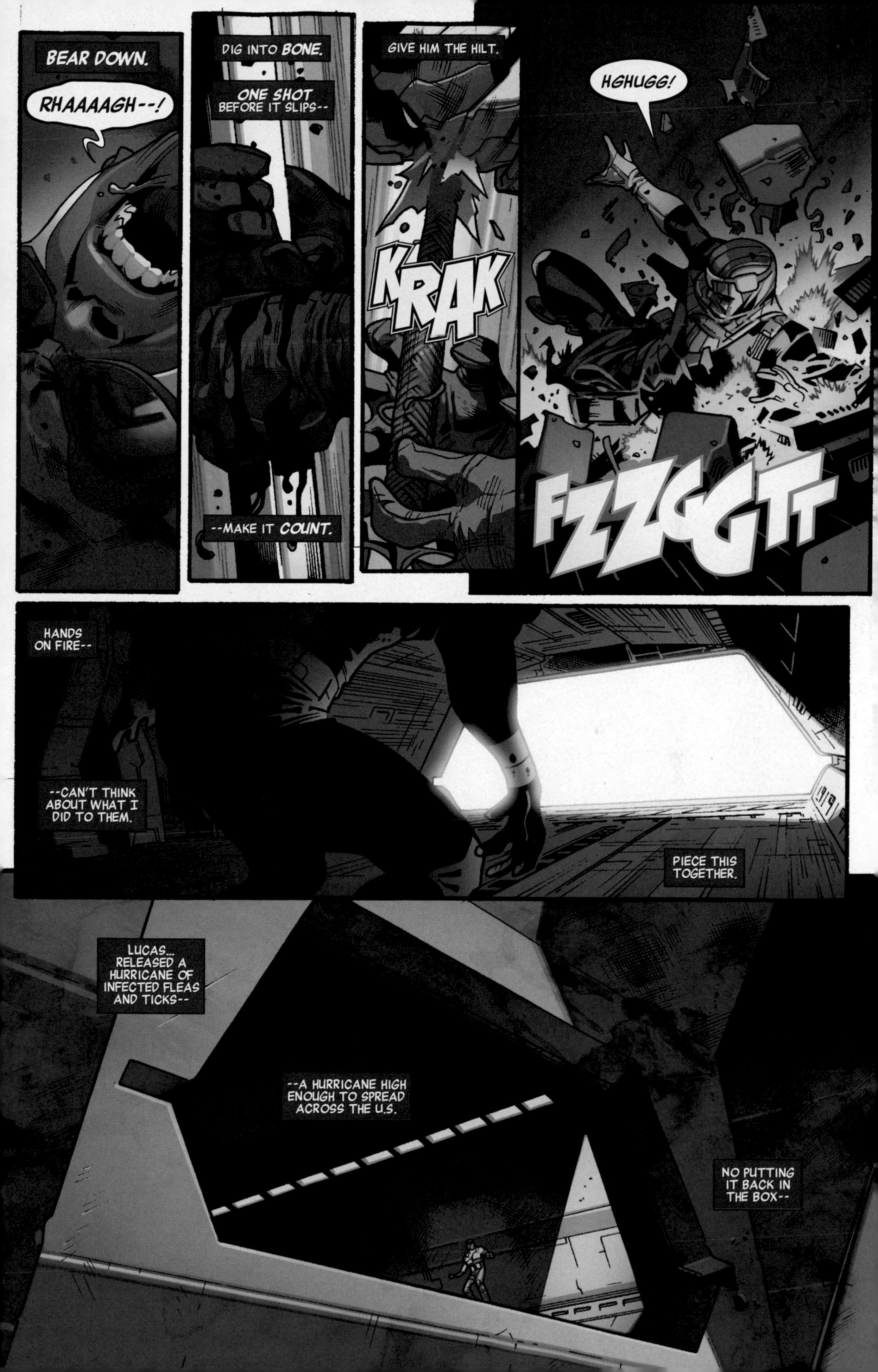
BEAR DOWN.
RHAAAAGH--!
DIG INTO BONE.
ONE SHOT BEFORE IT SLIPS--
--MAKE IT COUNT.
GIVE HIM THE HILT.
KRAK
HGHUGG!
FZZGTT
HANDS ON FIRE--
--CAN'T THINK ABOUT WHAT I DID TO THEM.
PIECE THIS TOGETHER.
LUCAS... RELEASED A HURRICANE OF INFECTED FLEAS AND TICKS--
--A HURRICANE HIGH ENOUGH TO SPREAD ACROSS THE U.S.
NO PUTTING IT BACK IN THE BOX--

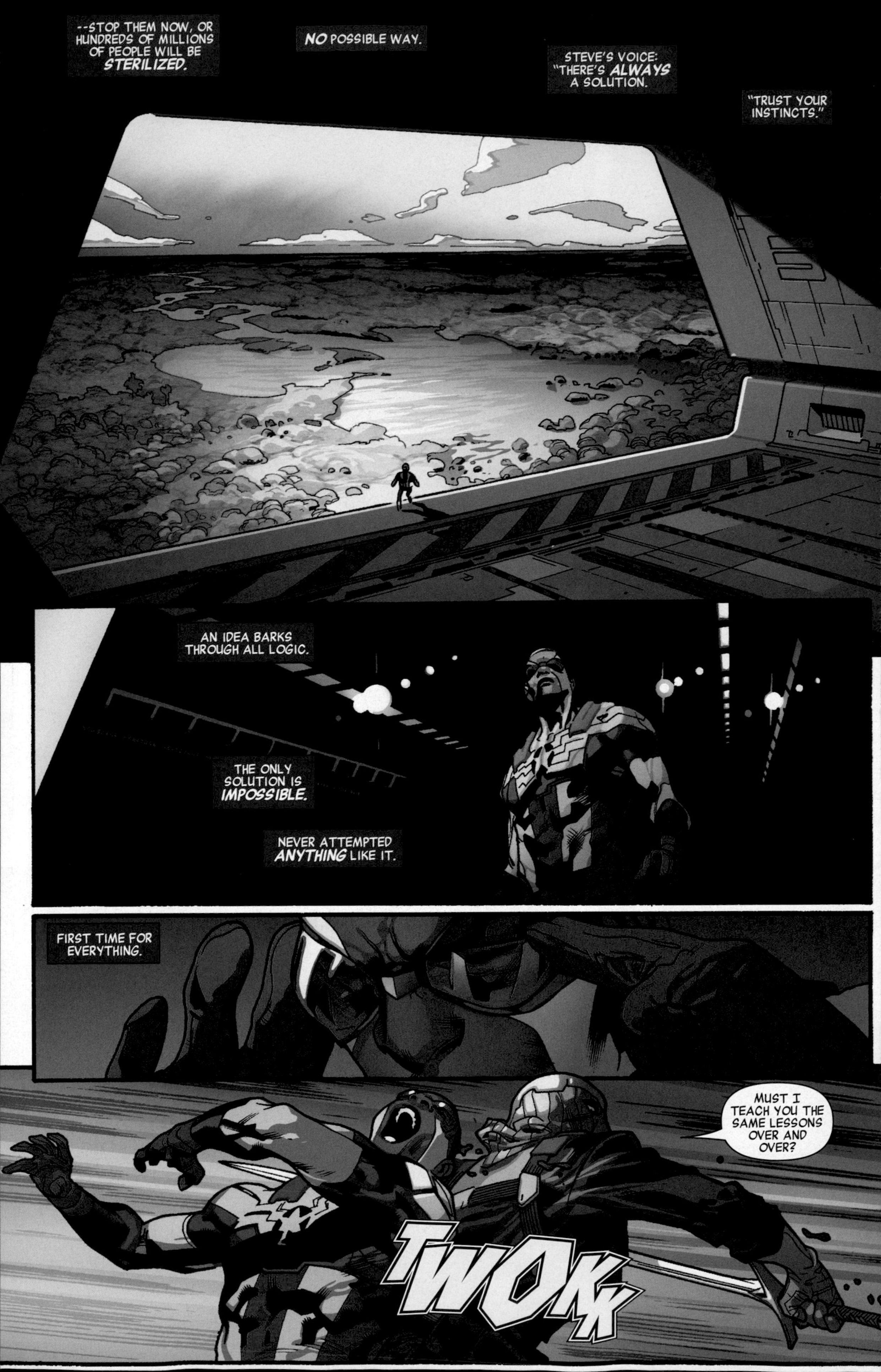
--STOP THEM NOW, OR HUNDREDS OF MILLIONS OF PEOPLE WILL BE STERILIZED.
NO POSSIBLE WAY.
STEVE'S VOICE: "THERE'S ALWAYS A SOLUTION.
"TRUST YOUR INSTINCTS."
AN IDEA BARKS THROUGH ALL LOGIC.
THE ONLY SOLUTION IS IMPOSSIBLE.
NEVER ATTEMPTED ANYTHING LIKE IT.
FIRST TIME FOR EVERYTHING.
MUST I TEACH YOU THE SAME LESSONS OVER AND OVER?
TWOKK

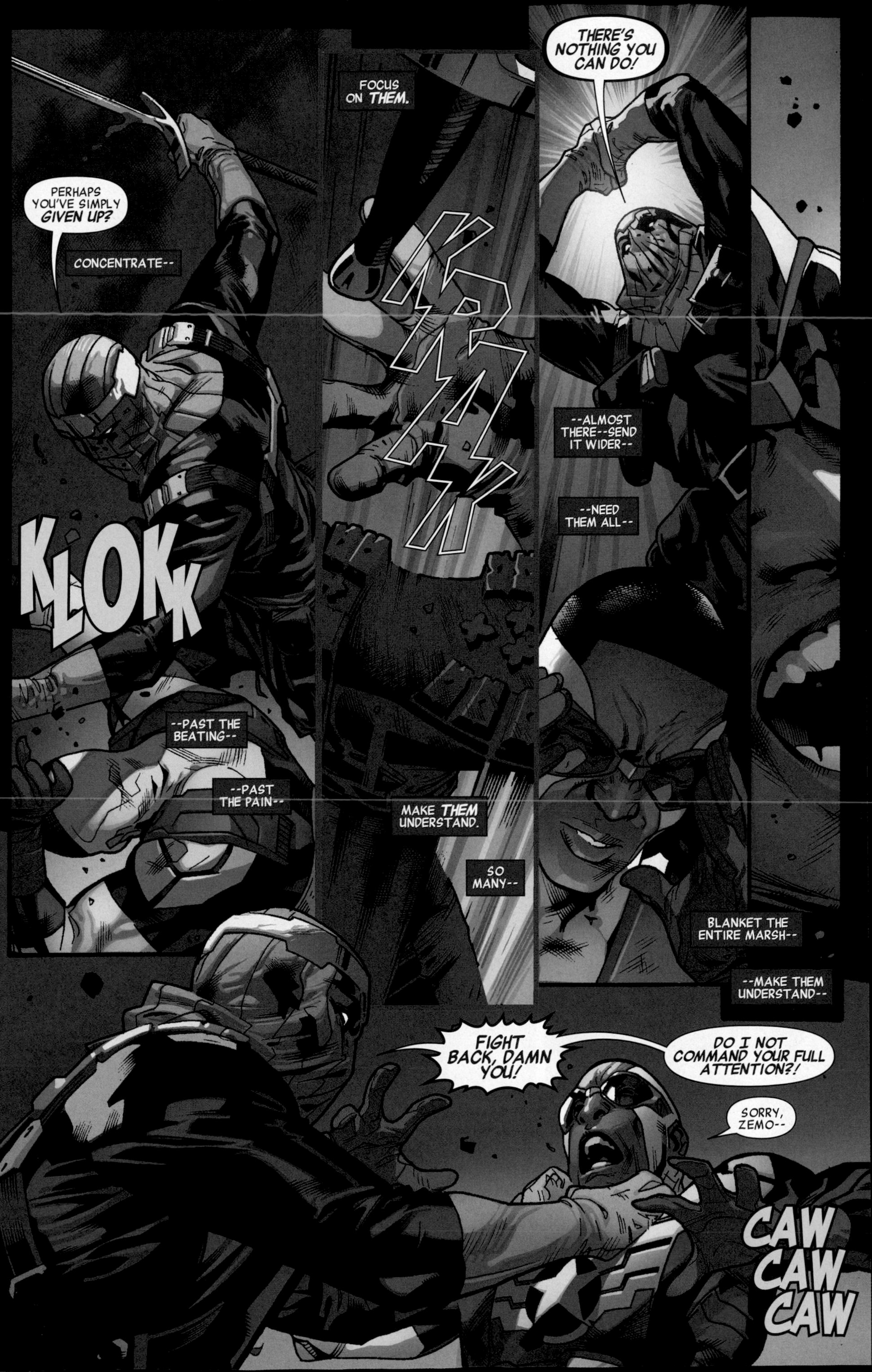
PERHAPS YOU'VE SIMPLY GIVEN UP?
CONCENTRATE--
KLOKK
--PAST THE BEATING--
--PAST THE PAIN--
FOCUS ON THEM.
KRAKK
MAKE THEM UNDERSTAND.
SO MANY--
THERE'S NOTHING YOU CAN DO!
--ALMOST THERE--SEND IT WIDER--
--NEED THEM ALL--
BLANKET THE ENTIRE MARSH--
--MAKE THEM UNDERSTAND--
FIGHT BACK, DAMN YOU!
DO I NOT COMMAND YOUR FULL ATTENTION?!
SORRY, ZEMO--
CAW CAW CAW

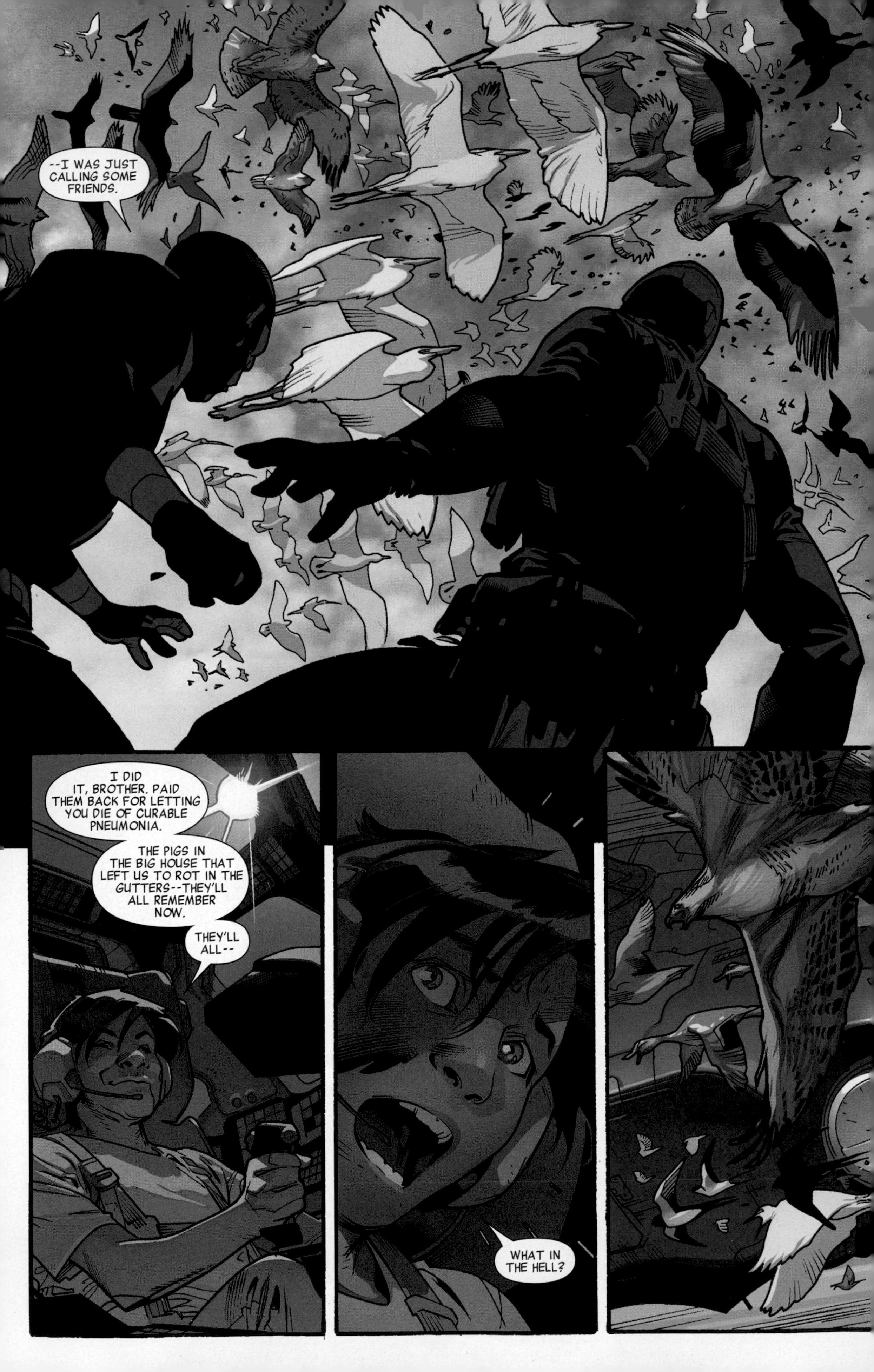
--I WAS JUST CALLING SOME FRIENDS.
I DID IT, BROTHER. PAID THEM BACK FOR LETTING YOU DIE OF CURABLE PNEUMONIA.
THE PIGS IN THE BIG HOUSE THAT LEFT US TO ROT IN THE GUTTERS--THEY'LL ALL REMEMBER NOW.
THEY'LL ALL--
WHAT IN THE HELL?

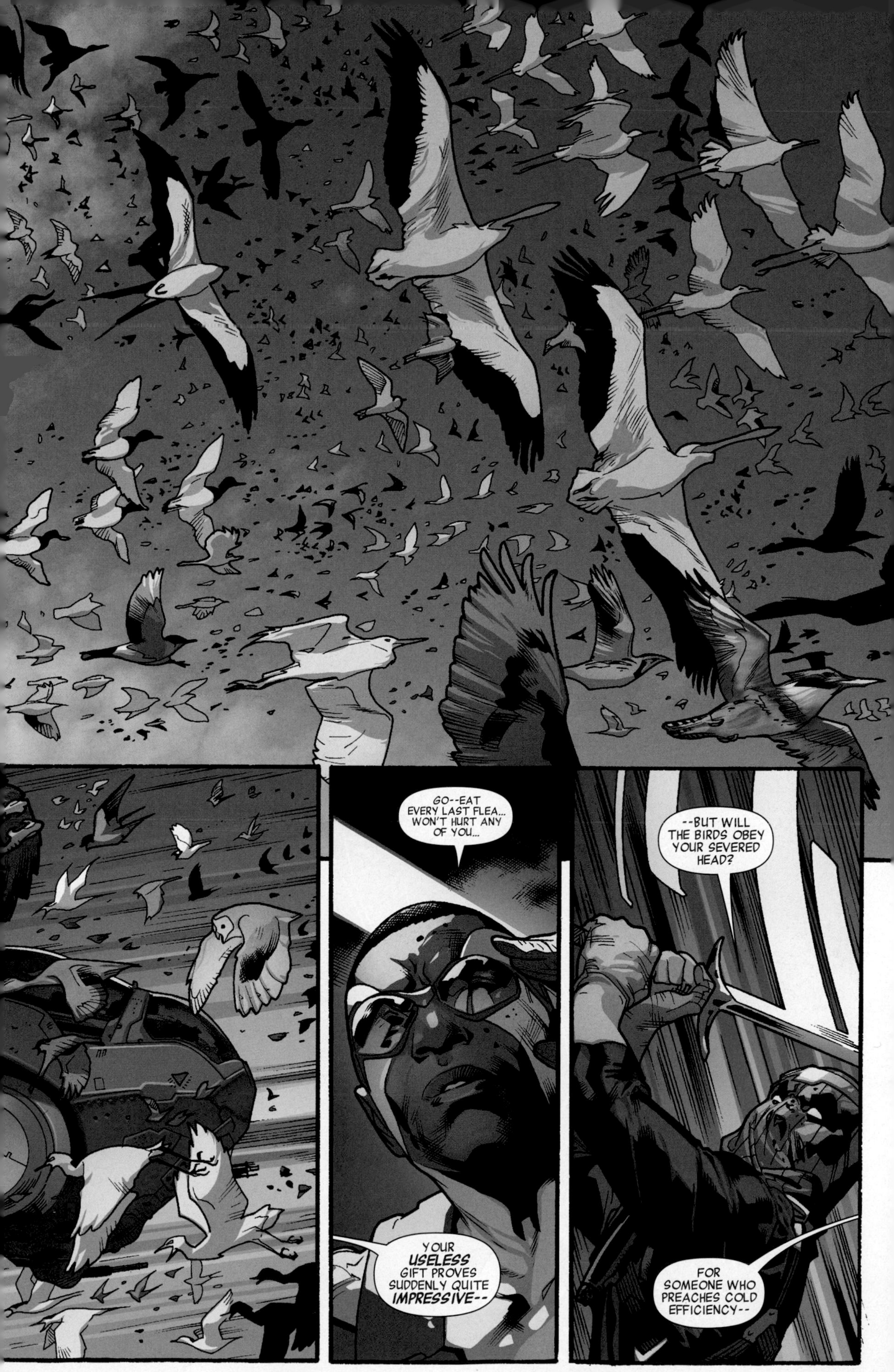
GO--EAT EVERY LAST FLEA... WON'T HURT ANY OF YOU...
YOUR USELESS GIFT PROVES SUDDENLY QUITE IMPRESSIVE--
--BUT WILL THE BIRDS OBEY YOUR SEVERED HEAD?
FOR SOMEONE WHO PREACHES COLD EFFICIENCY--

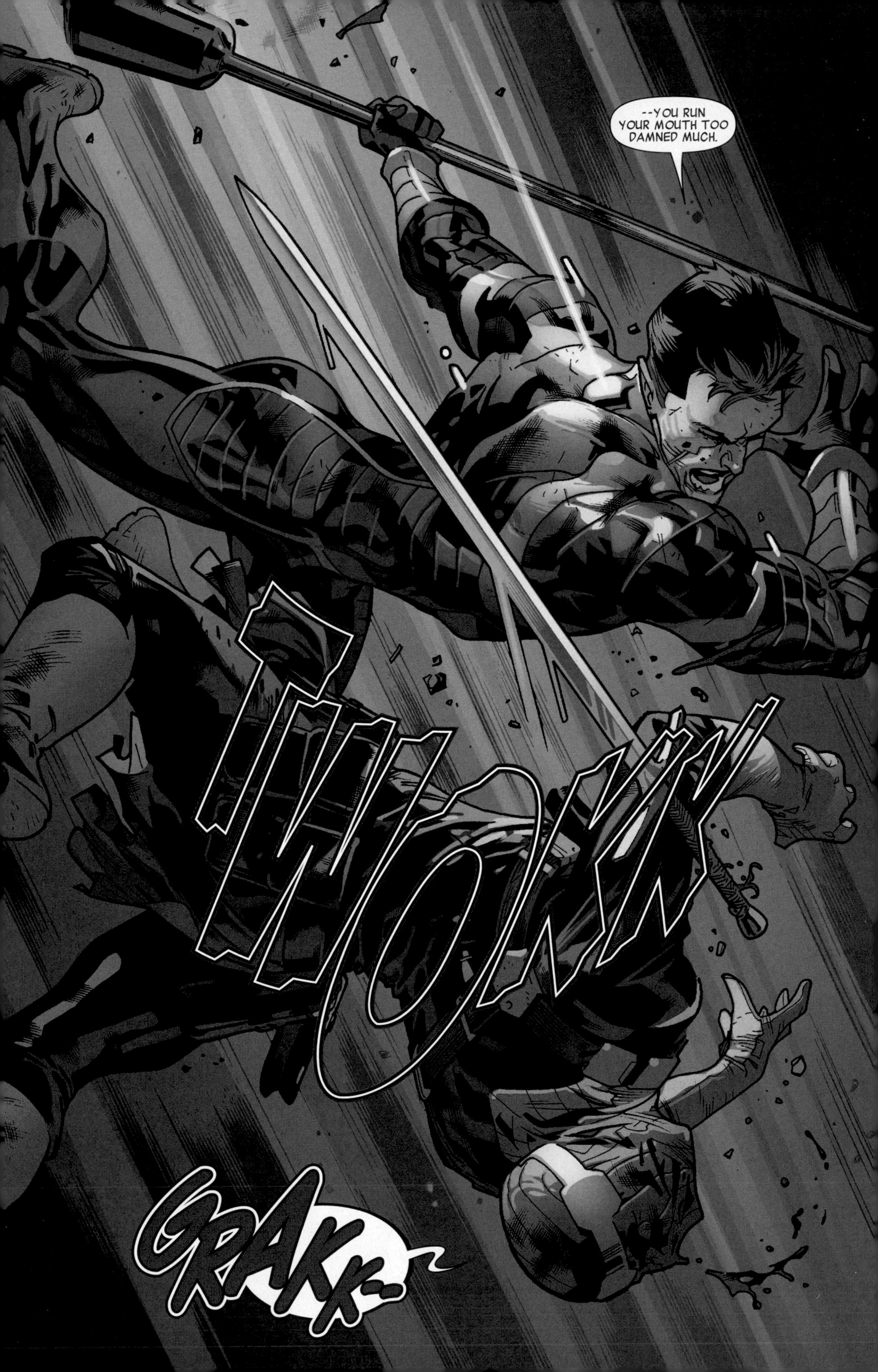
--YOU RUN YOUR MOUTH TOO DAMNED MUCH.
THWOKK
GRAKK--

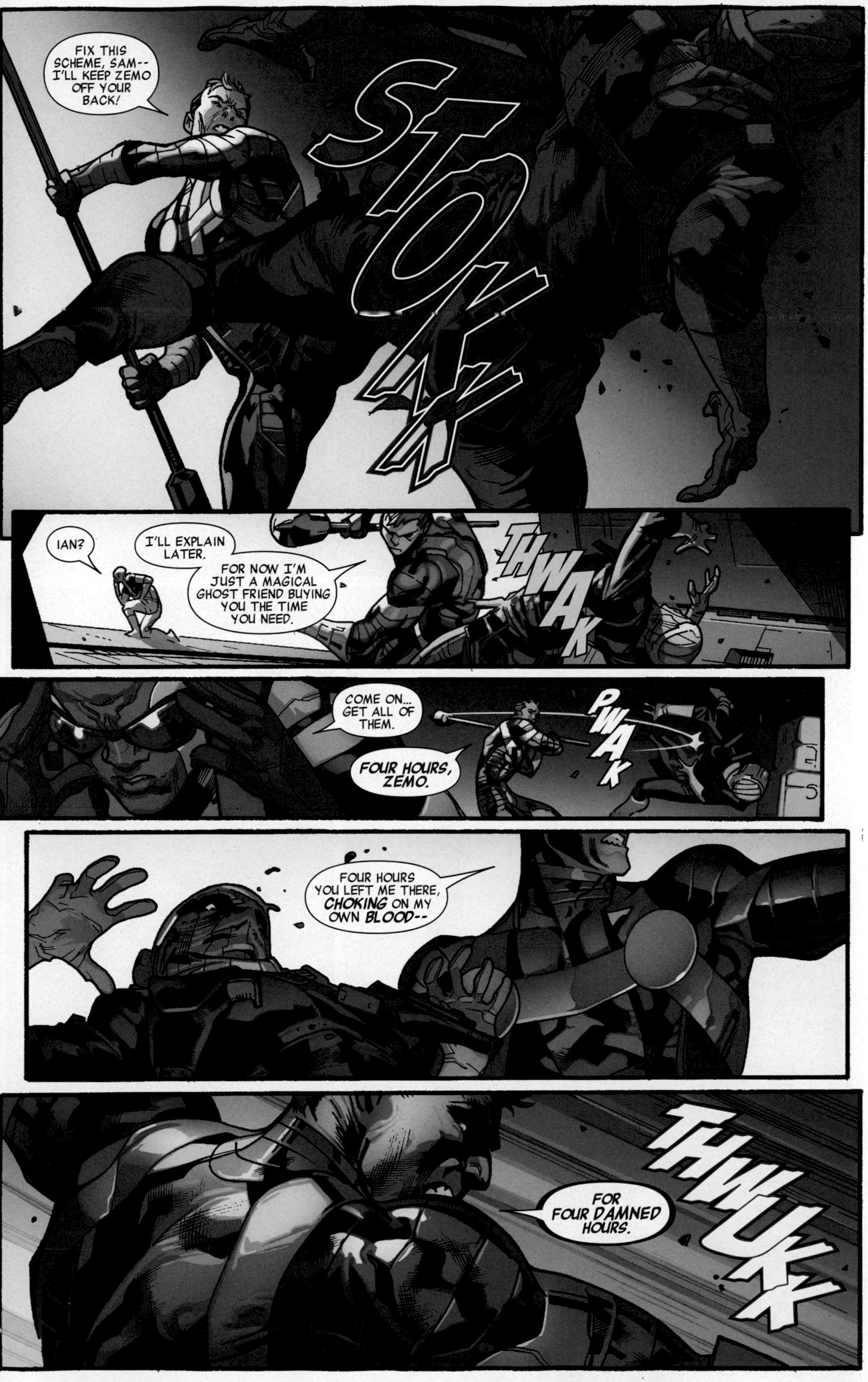
FIX THIS SCHEME, SAM-- I'LL KEEP ZEMO OFF YOUR BACK!
STOKK
IAN?
I'LL EXPLAIN LATER.
FOR NOW I'M JUST A MAGICAL GHOST FRIEND BUYING YOU THE TIME YOU NEED.
THWAK
COME ON... GET ALL OF THEM.
PWAK
FOUR HOURS, ZEMO.
FOUR HOURS YOU LEFT ME THERE, CHOKING ON MY OWN BLOOD--
THWUKK
FOR FOUR DAMNED HOURS.

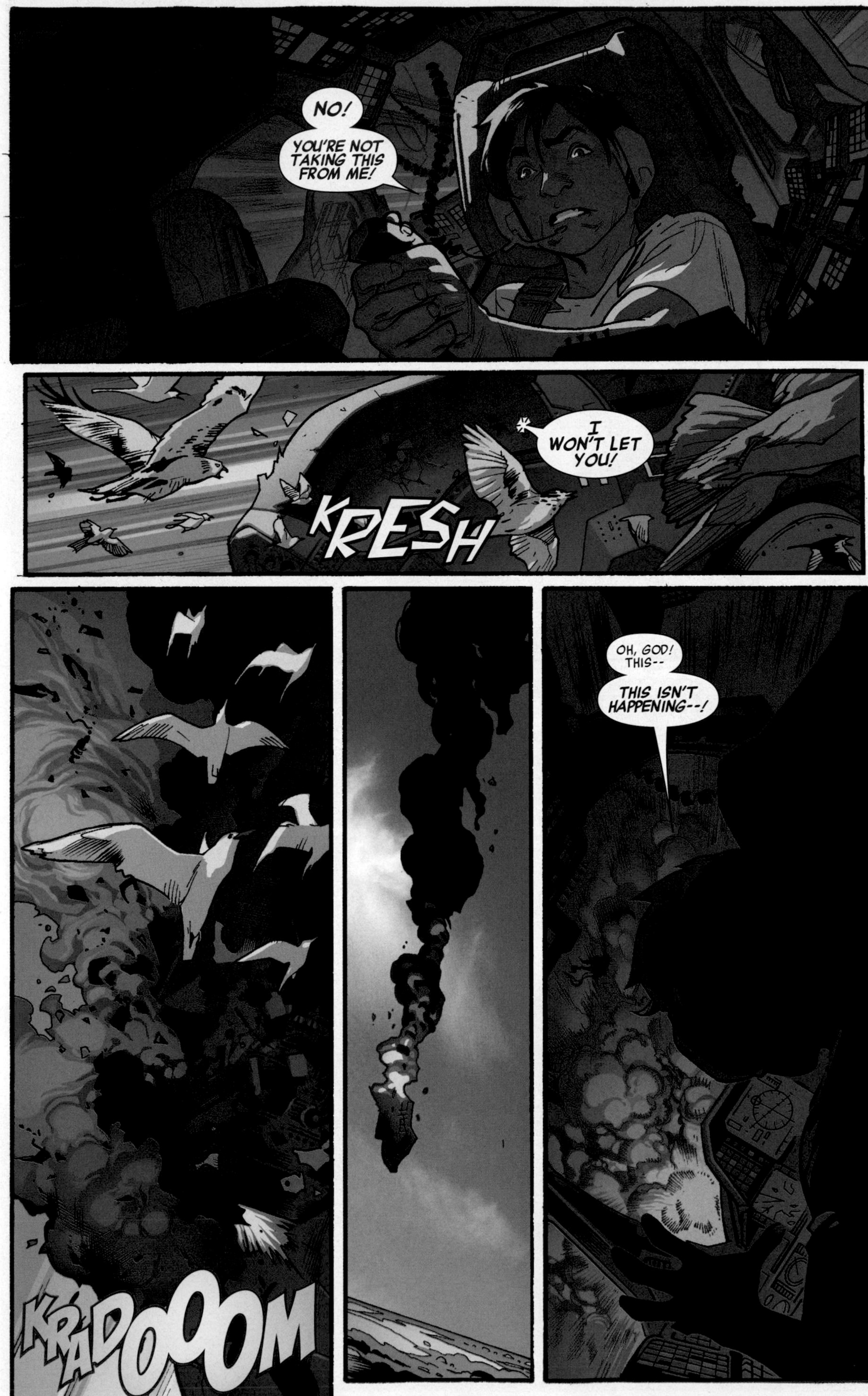
NO!
YOU'RE NOT TAKING THIS FROM ME!
I WON'T LET YOU!
KRESH
KRADOOOOM
OH, GOD! THIS--
THIS ISN'T HAPPENING--!

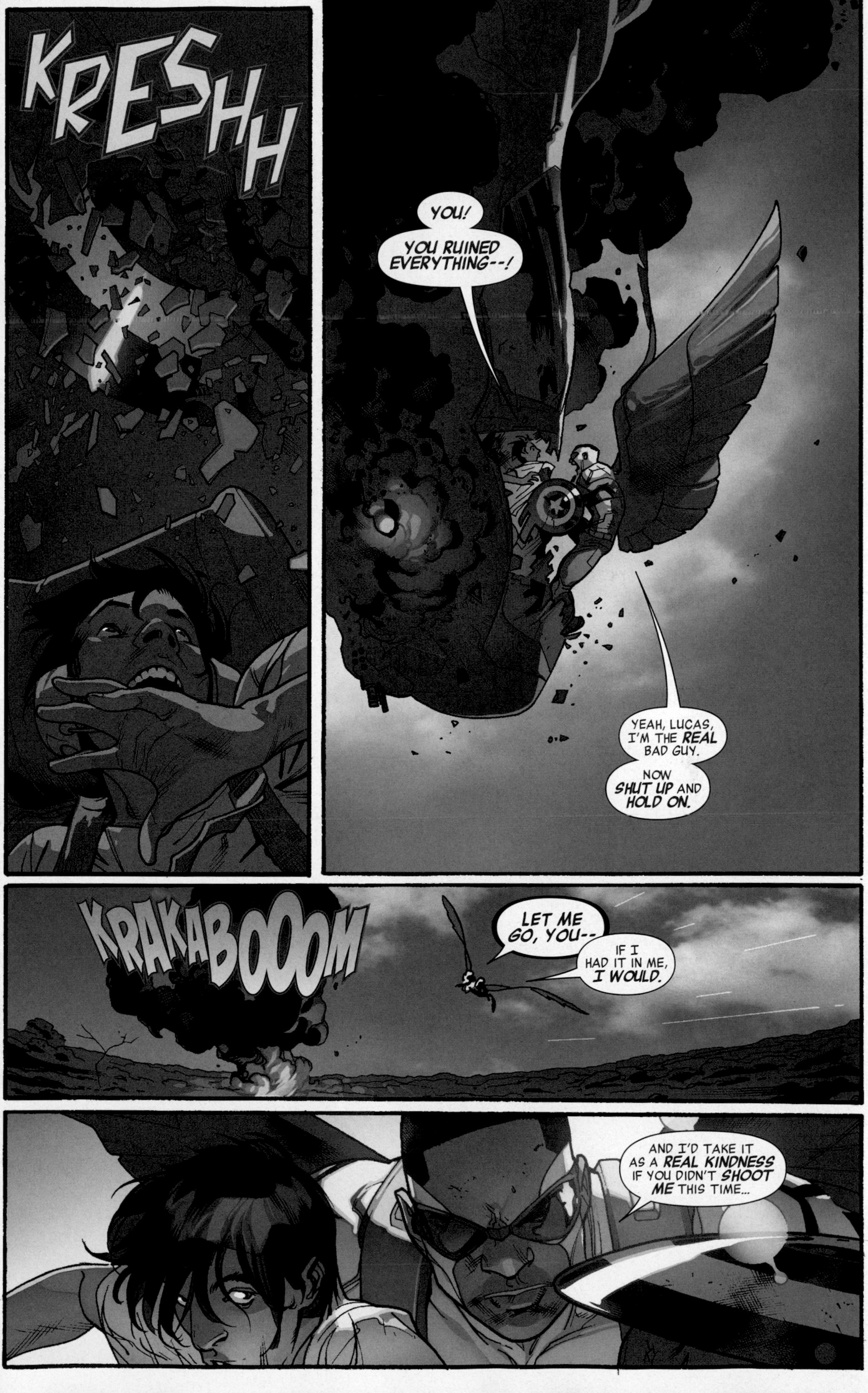
KRESHH
YOU! YOU RUINED EVERYTHING--!
YEAH, LUCAS, I'M THE REAL BAD GUY.
NOW SHUT UP AND HOLD ON.
KRAKABOOOM
LET ME GO, YOU--
IF I HAD IT IN ME, I WOULD.
AND I'D TAKE IT AS A REAL KINDNESS IF YOU DIDN'T SHOOT ME THIS TIME...

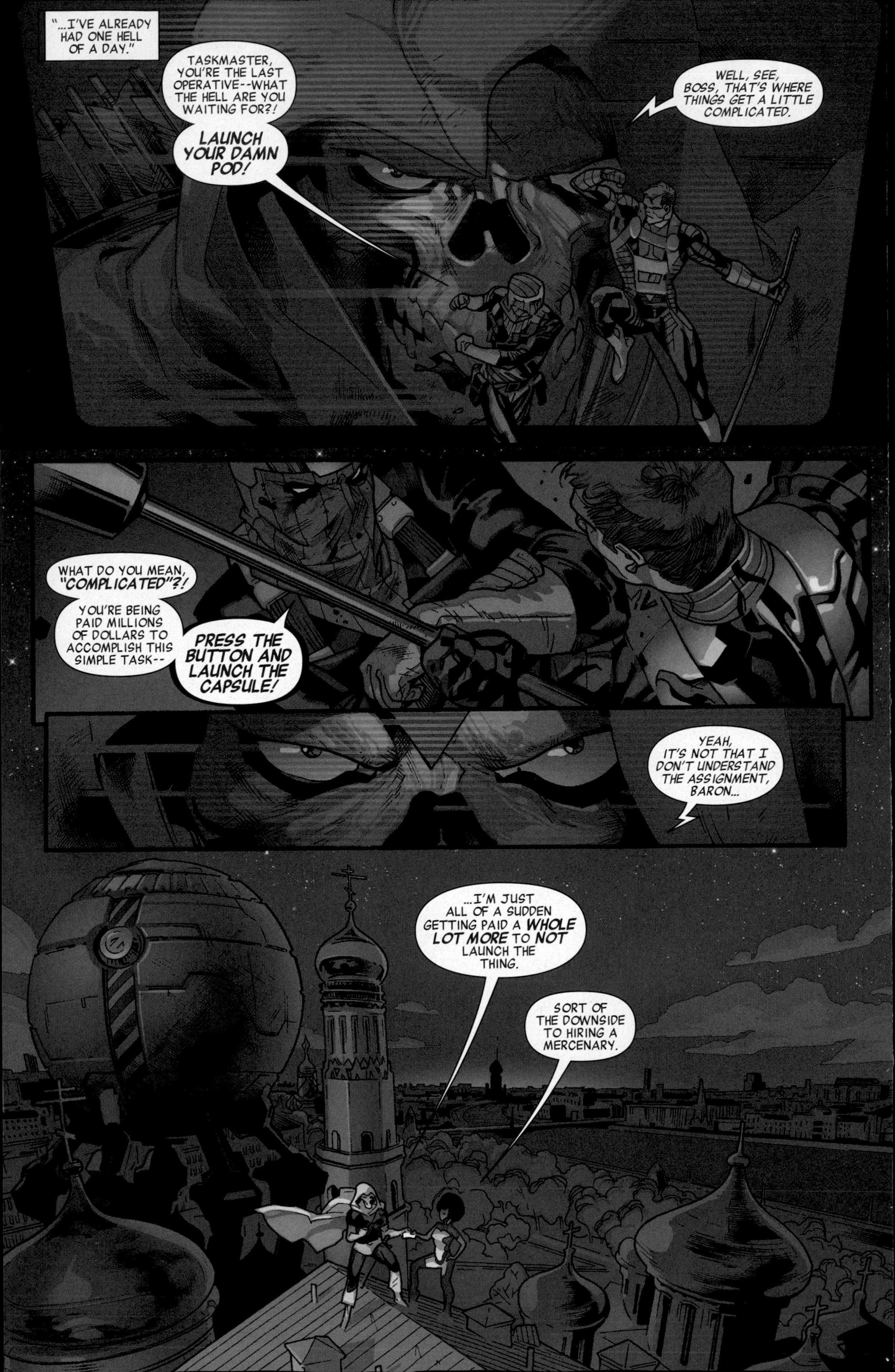
"...I'VE ALREADY HAD ONE HELL OF A DAY."
TASKMASTER, YOU'RE THE LAST OPERATIVE--WHAT THE HELL ARE YOU WAITING FOR?!
LAUNCH YOUR DAMN POD!
WELL, SEE, BOSS, THAT'S WHERE THINGS GET A LITTLE COMPLICATED.
WHAT DO YOU MEAN, "COMPLICATED"?!
YOU'RE BEING PAID MILLIONS OF DOLLARS TO ACCOMPLISH THIS SIMPLE TASK--
PRESS THE BUTTON AND LAUNCH THE CAPSULE!
YEAH, IT'S NOT THAT I DON'T UNDERSTAND THE ASSIGNMENT, BARON...
...I'M JUST ALL OF A SUDDEN GETTING PAID A WHOLE LOT MORE TO NOT LAUNCH THE THING.
SORT OF THE DOWNSIDE TO HIRING A MERCENARY.

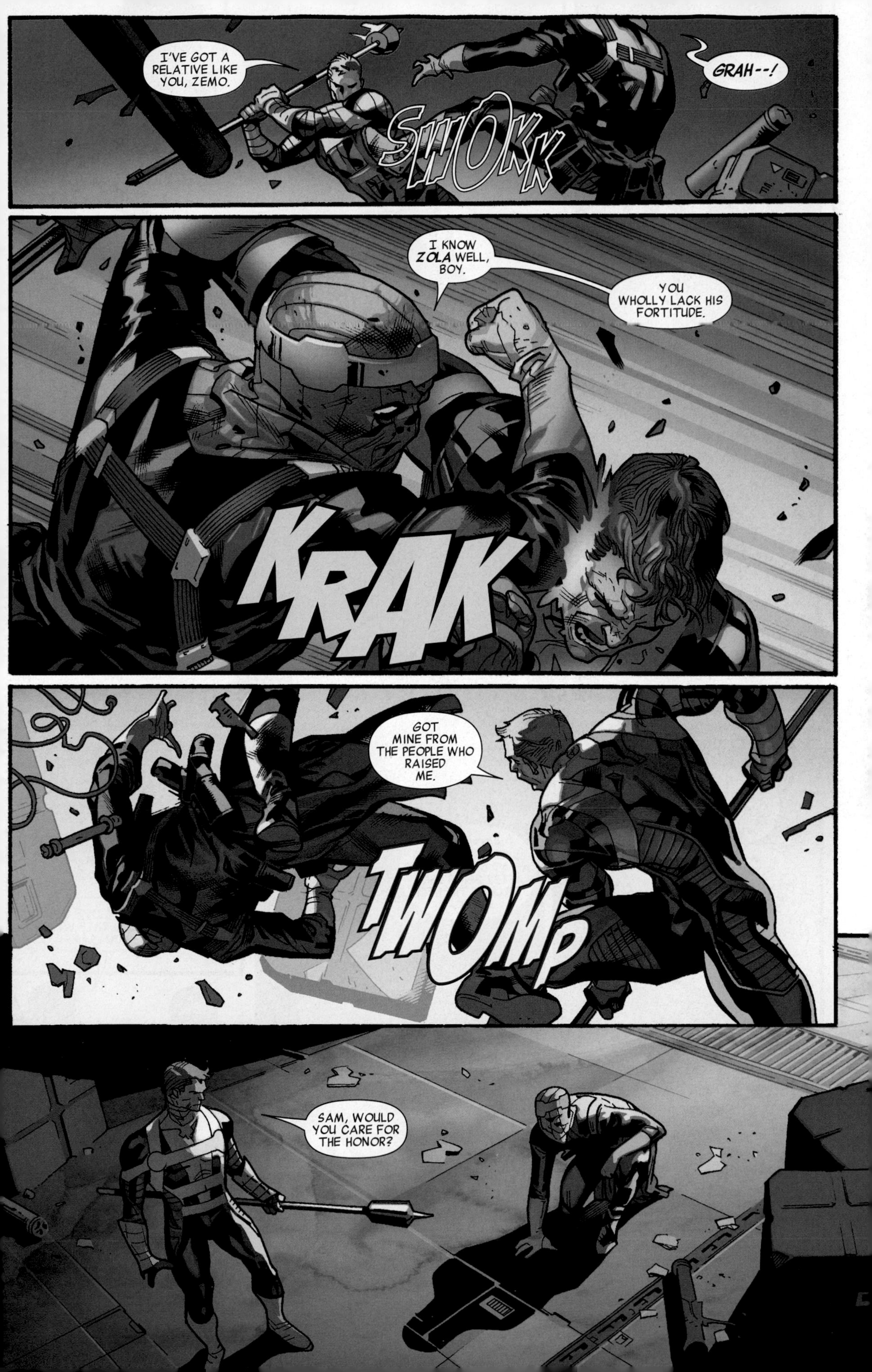
I'VE GOT A RELATIVE LIKE YOU, ZEMO.
GRAH--!
SWOKK
I KNOW ZOLA WELL, BOY.
YOU WHOLLY LACK HIS FORTITUDE.
KRAK
GOT MINE FROM THE PEOPLE WHO RAISED ME.
TWOMP
SAM, WOULD YOU CARE FOR THE HONOR?

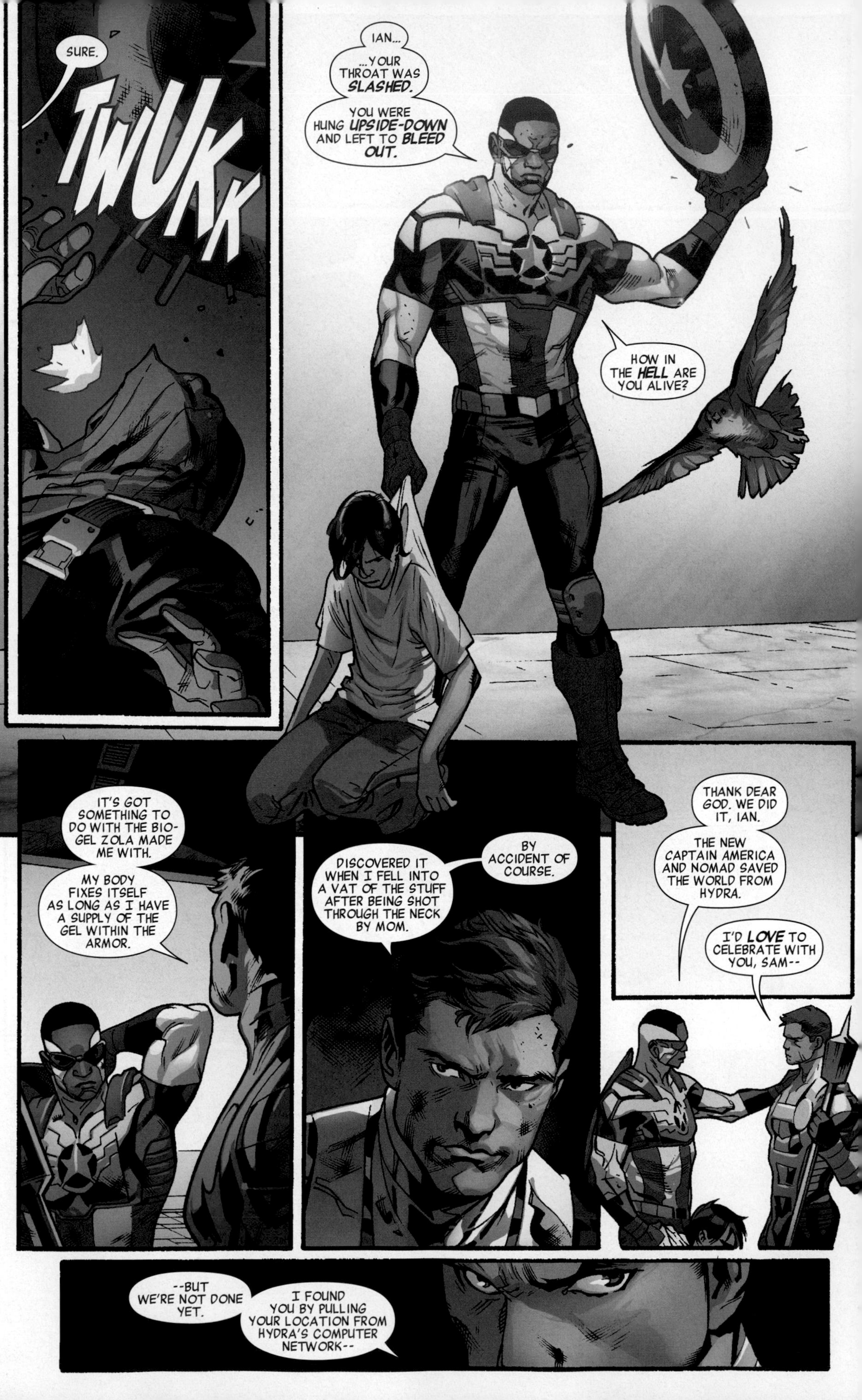
SURE.
TWUKK
IAN...
...YOUR THROAT WAS SLASHED.
YOU WERE HUNG UPSIDE-DOWN AND LEFT TO BLEED OUT.
HOW IN THE HELL ARE YOU ALIVE?
IT'S GOT SOMETHING TO DO WITH THE BIO-GEL ZOLA MADE ME WITH.
MY BODY FIXES ITSELF AS LONG AS I HAVE A SUPPLY OF THE GEL WITHIN THE ARMOR.
DISCOVERED IT WHEN I FELL INTO A VAT OF THE STUFF AFTER BEING SHOT THROUGH THE NECK BY MOM.
BY ACCIDENT OF COURSE.
THANK DEAR GOD. WE DID IT, IAN.
THE NEW CAPTAIN AMERICA AND NOMAD SAVED THE WORLD FROM HYDRA.
I'D LOVE TO CELEBRATE WITH YOU, SAM--
--BUT WE'RE NOT DONE YET.
I FOUND YOU BY PULLING YOUR LOCATION FROM HYDRA'S COMPUTER NETWORK--

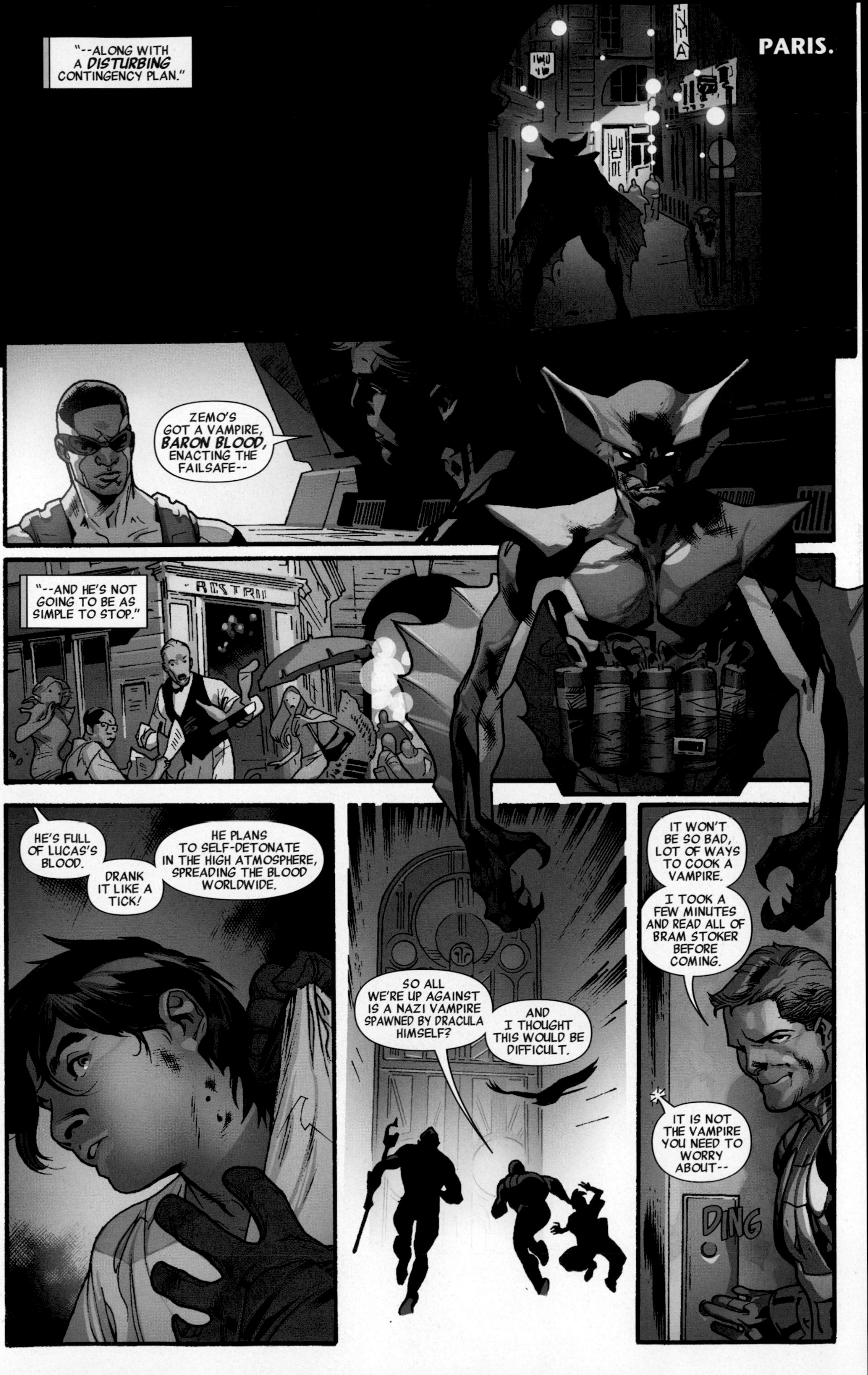
"--ALONG WITH A DISTURBING CONTINGENCY PLAN."
PARIS.
ZEMO'S GOT A VAMPIRE, BARON BLOOD, ENACTING THE FAILSAFE--
"--AND HE'S NOT GOING TO BE AS SIMPLE TO STOP."
HE'S FULL OF LUCAS'S BLOOD.
DRANK IT LIKE A TICK!
HE PLANS TO SELF-DETONATE IN THE HIGH ATMOSPHERE, SPREADING THE BLOOD WORLDWIDE.
SO ALL WE'RE UP AGAINST IS A NAZI VAMPIRE SPAWNED BY DRACULA HIMSELF?
AND I THOUGHT THIS WOULD BE DIFFICULT.
IT WON'T BE SO BAD, LOT OF WAYS TO COOK A VAMPIRE.
I TOOK A FEW MINUTES AND READ ALL OF BRAM STOKER BEFORE COMING.
IT IS NOT THE VAMPIRE YOU NEED TO WORRY ABOUT--
DING

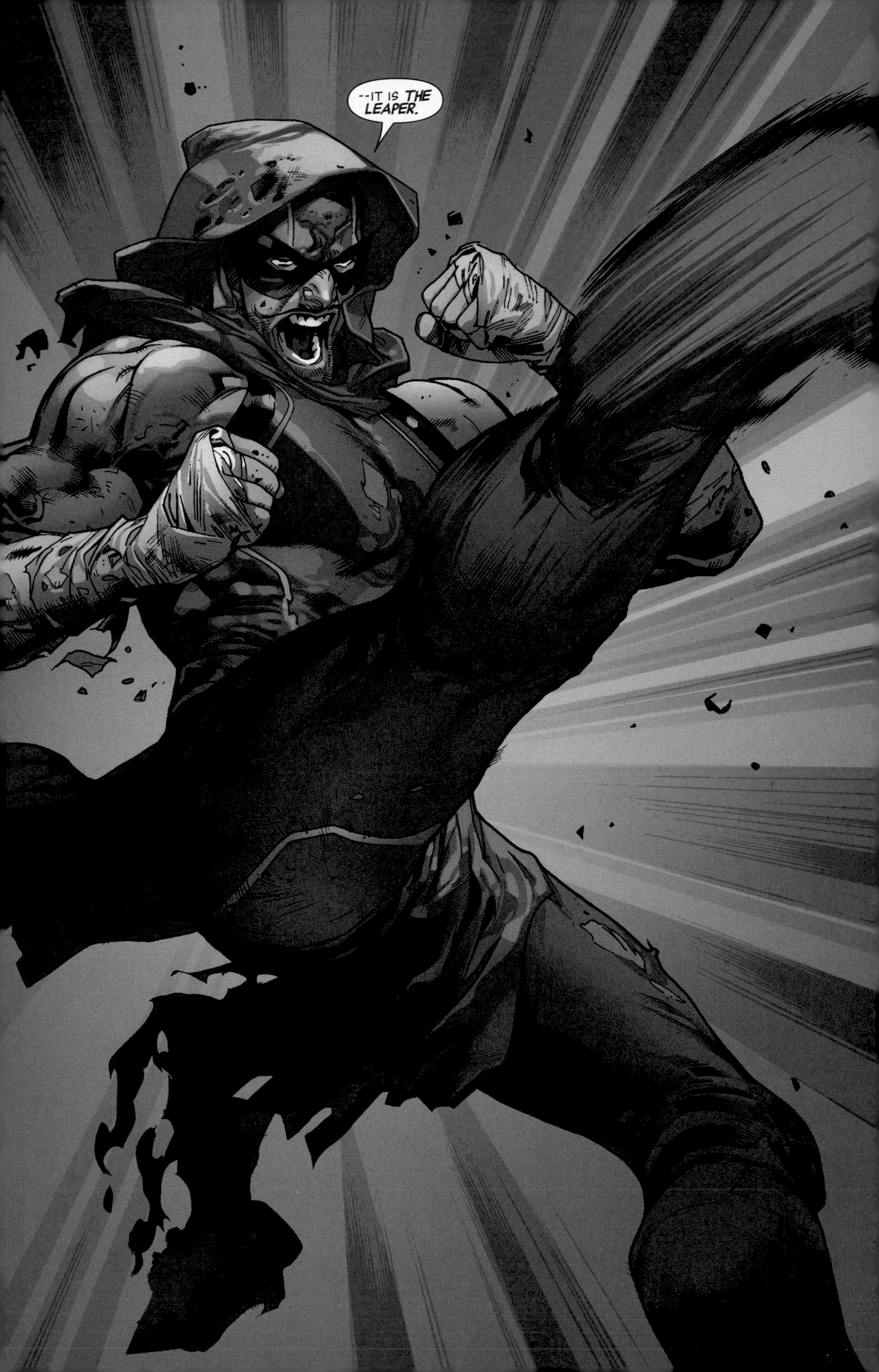
--IT IS THE LEAPER.

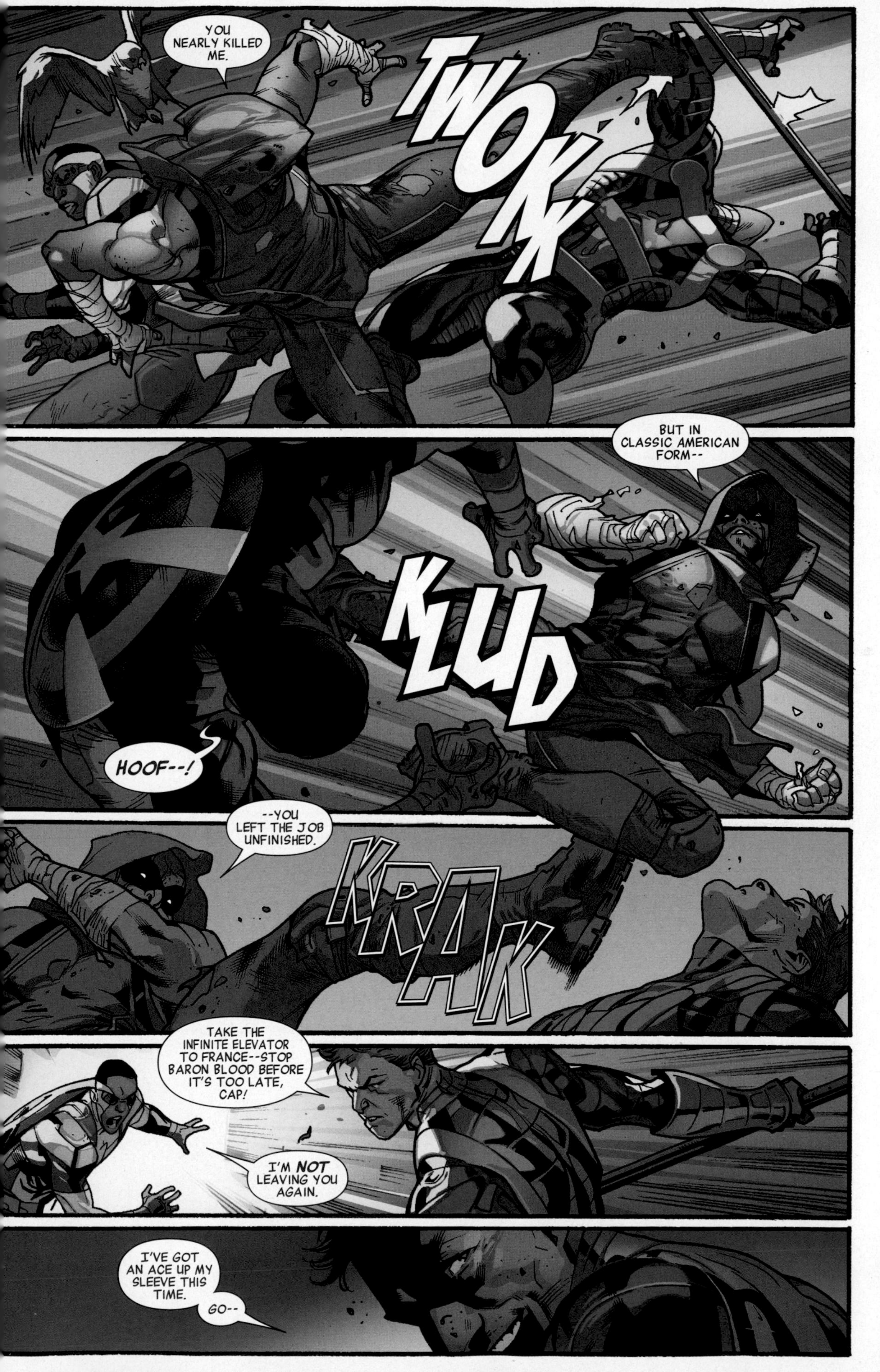
YOU NEARLY KILLED ME.
TWOKK
BUT IN CLASSIC AMERICAN FORM--
KLUD
HOOF--!
--YOU LEFT THE JOB UNFINISHED.
KRAK
TAKE THE INFINITE ELEVATOR TO FRANCE--STOP BARON BLOOD BEFORE IT'S TOO LATE, CAP!
I'M NOT LEAVING YOU AGAIN.
I'VE GOT AN ACE UP MY SLEEVE THIS TIME.
GO--

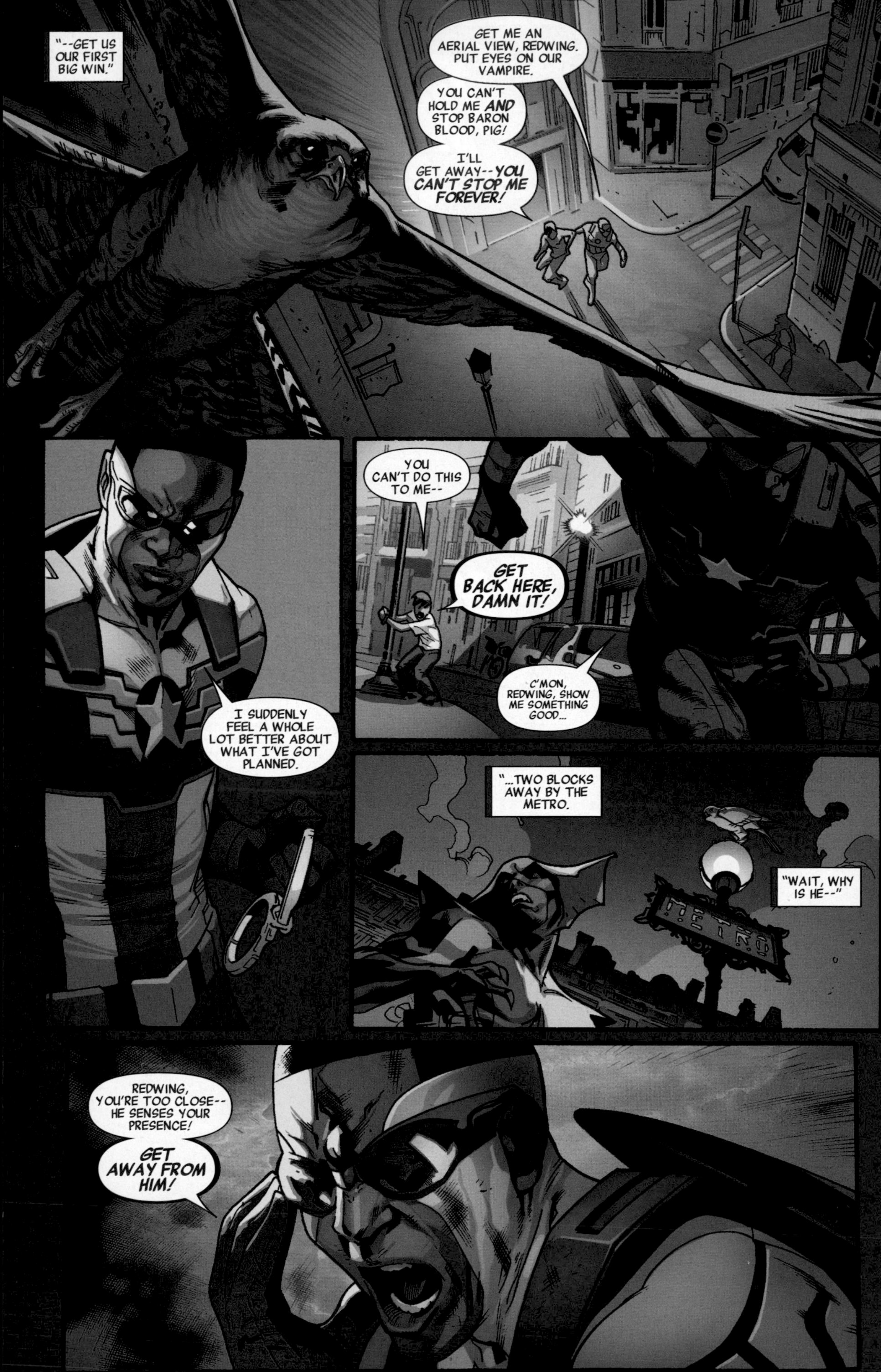
"--GET US OUR FIRST BIG WIN."
GET ME AN AERIAL VIEW, REDWING. PUT EYES ON OUR VAMPIRE.
YOU CAN'T HOLD ME AND STOP BARON BLOOD, PIG!
I'LL GET AWAY--YOU CAN'T STOP ME FOREVER!
I SUDDENLY FEEL A WHOLE LOT BETTER ABOUT WHAT I'VE GOT PLANNED.
YOU CAN'T DO THIS TO ME--
GET BACK HERE, DAMN IT!
C'MON, REDWING, SHOW ME SOMETHING GOOD...
"...TWO BLOCKS AWAY BY THE METRO.
"WAIT, WHY IS HE--"
REDWING, YOU'RE TOO CLOSE--HE SENSES YOUR PRESENCE!
GET AWAY FROM HIM!

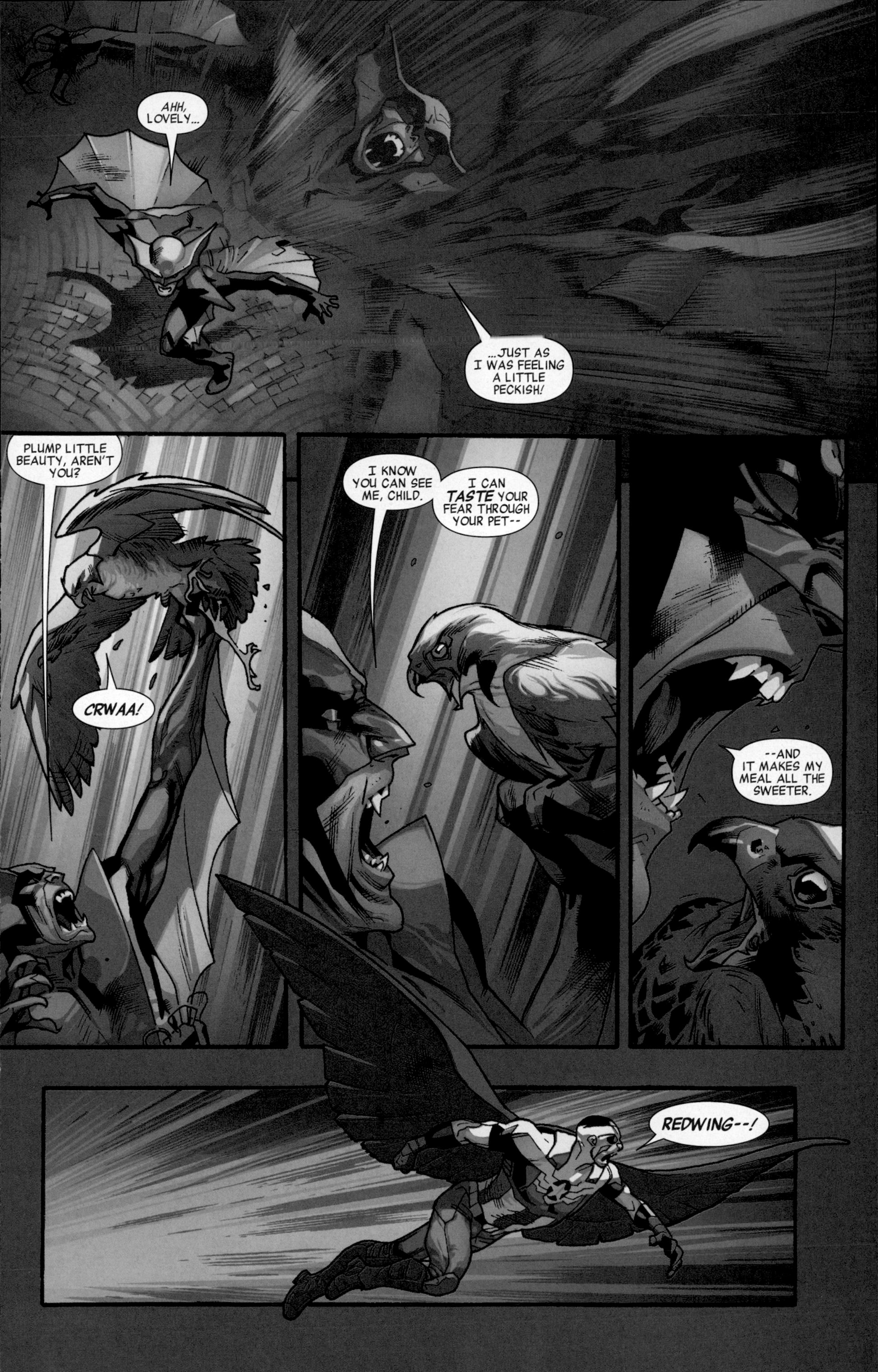
AHH, LOVELY...
...JUST AS I WAS FEELING A LITTLE PECKISH!
PLUMP LITTLE BEAUTY, AREN'T YOU?
CRWAA!
I KNOW YOU CAN SEE ME, CHILD.
I CAN TASTE YOUR FEAR THROUGH YOUR PET--
--AND IT MAKES MY MEAL ALL THE SWEETER.
REDWING--!

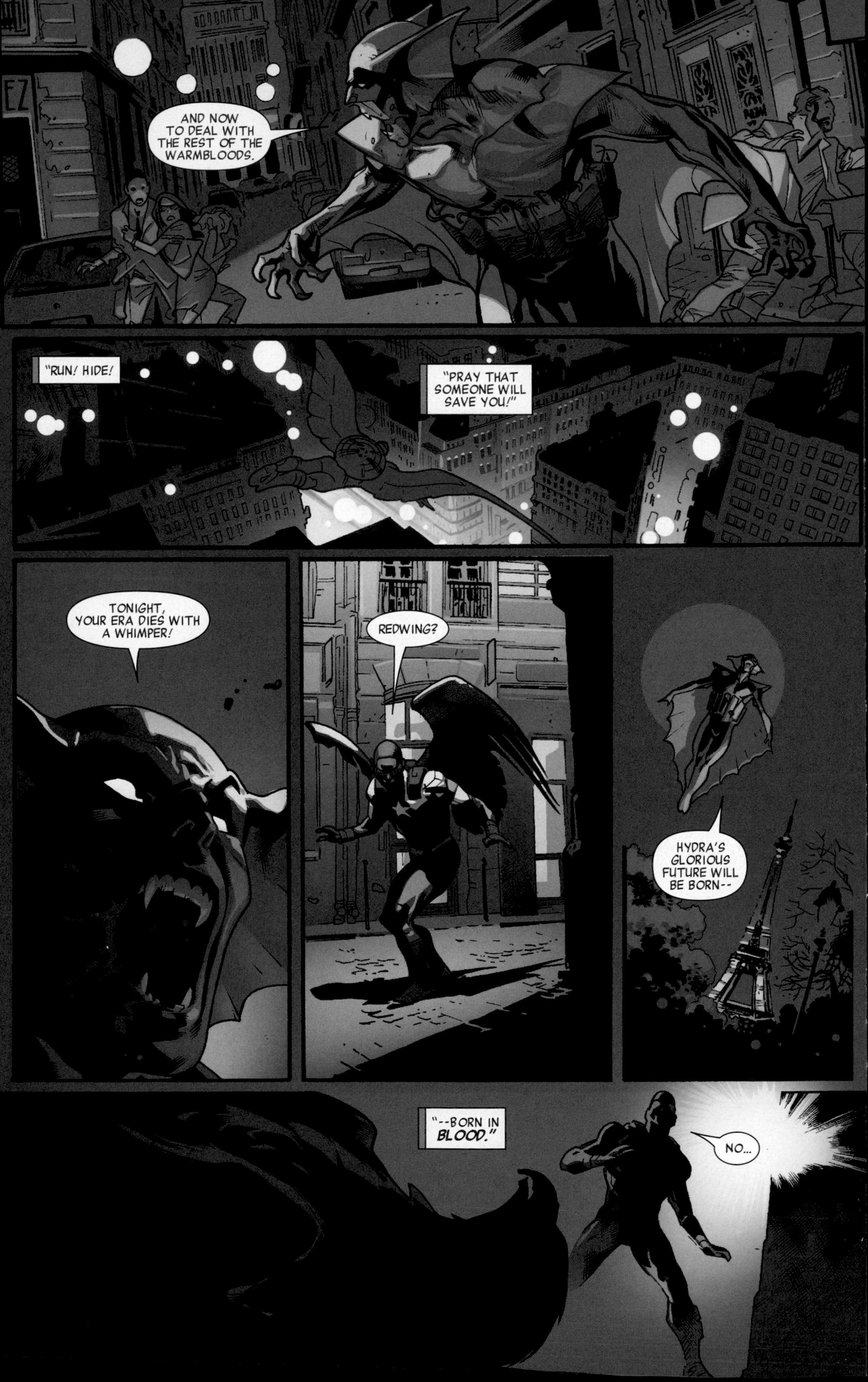
AND NOW TO DEAL WITH THE REST OF THE WARMBLOODS.
"RUN! HIDE!
"PRAY THAT SOMEONE WILL SAVE YOU!"
TONIGHT, YOUR ERA DIES WITH A WHIMPER!
REDWING?
HYDRA'S GLORIOUS FUTURE WILL BE BORN--
"--BORN IN BLOOD."
NO...

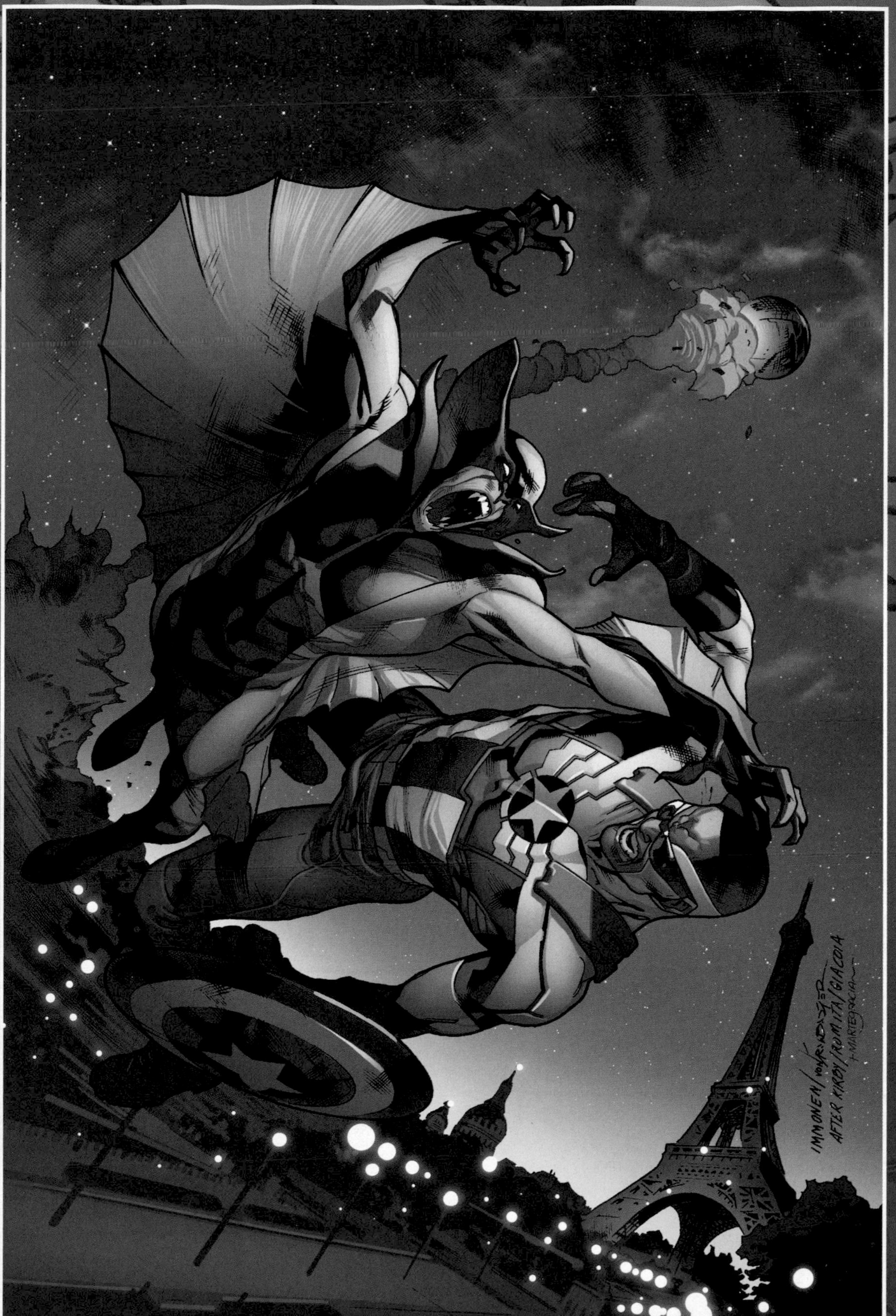

SIX

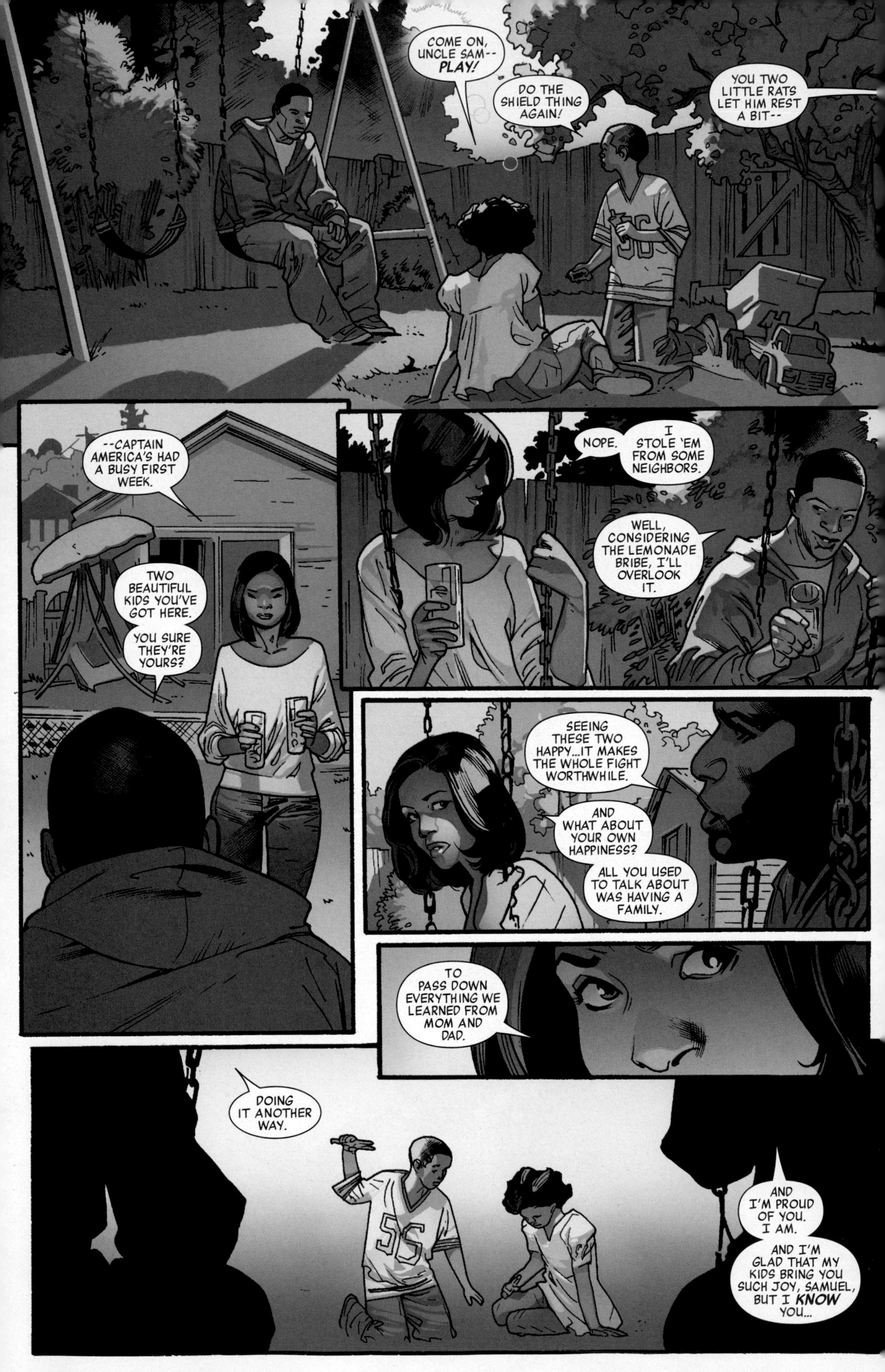
COME ON, UNCLE SAM-- PLAY!
DO THE SHIELD THING AGAIN!
YOU TWO LITTLE RATS LET HIM REST A BIT--
--CAPTAIN AMERICA'S HAD A BUSY FIRST WEEK.
TWO BEAUTIFUL KIDS YOU'VE GOT HERE.
YOU SURE THEY'RE YOURS?
NOPE.
I STOLE 'EM FROM SOME NEIGHBORS.
WELL, CONSIDERING THE LEMONADE BRIBE, I'LL OVERLOOK IT.
SEEING THESE TWO HAPPY...IT MAKES THE WHOLE FIGHT WORTHWHILE.
AND WHAT ABOUT YOUR OWN HAPPINESS?
ALL YOU USED TO TALK ABOUT WAS HAVING A FAMILY.
TO PASS DOWN EVERYTHING WE LEARNED FROM MOM AND DAD.
DOING IT ANOTHER WAY.
AND I'M PROUD OF YOU. I AM.
AND I'M GLAD THAT MY KIDS BRING YOU SUCH JOY, SAMUEL, BUT I KNOW YOU...

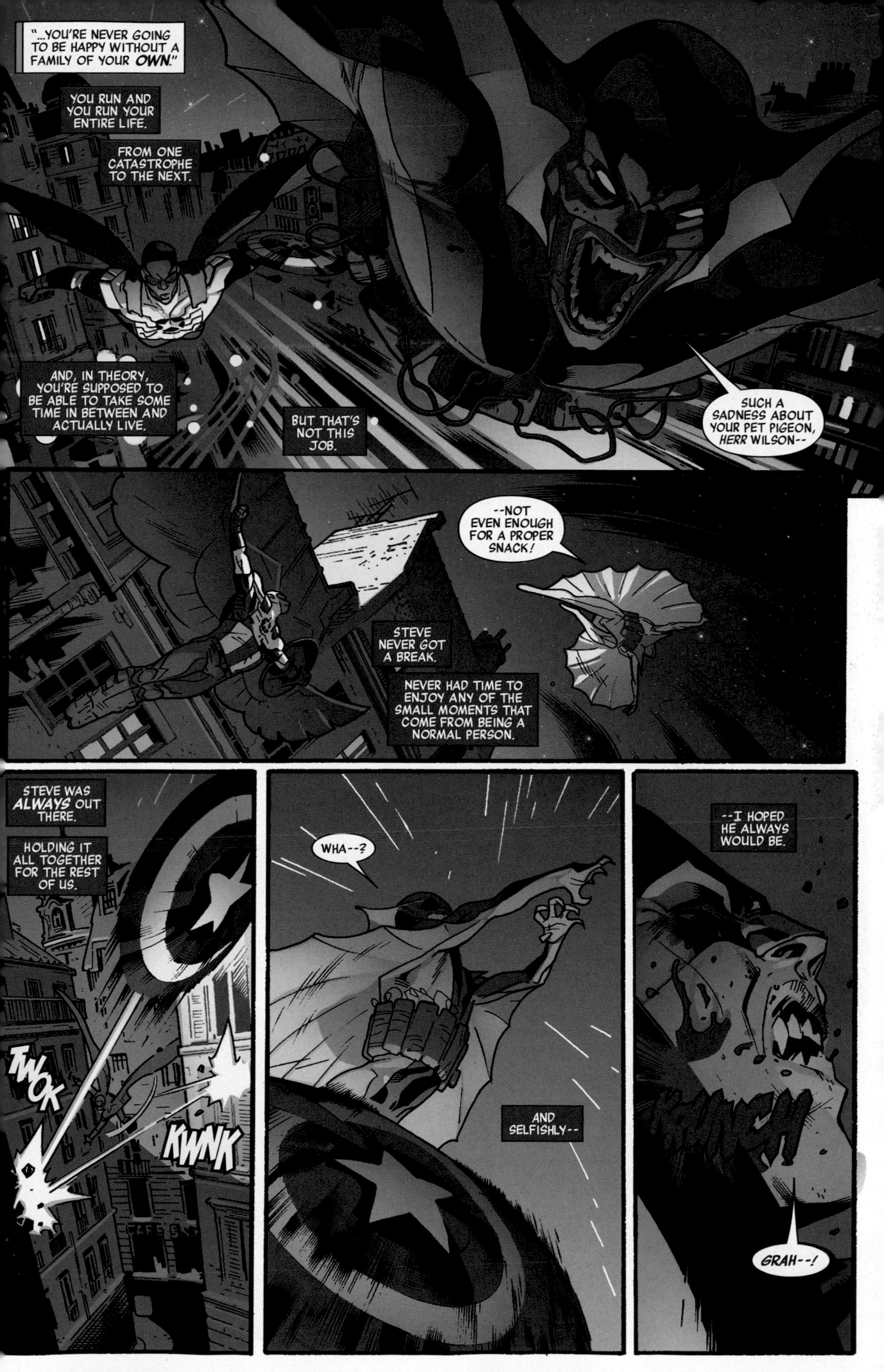
"...YOU'RE NEVER GOING TO BE HAPPY WITHOUT A FAMILY OF YOUR *OWN*."
YOU RUN AND YOU RUN YOUR ENTIRE LIFE.
FROM ONE CATASTROPHE TO THE NEXT.
AND, IN THEORY, YOU'RE SUPPOSED TO BE ABLE TO TAKE SOME TIME IN BETWEEN AND ACTUALLY LIVE.
BUT THAT'S NOT THIS JOB.
SUCH A SADNESS ABOUT YOUR PET PIGEON, *HERR* WILSON--
--NOT EVEN ENOUGH FOR A PROPER SNACK!
STEVE NEVER GOT A BREAK.
NEVER HAD TIME TO ENJOY ANY OF THE SMALL MOMENTS THAT COME FROM BEING A NORMAL PERSON.
STEVE WAS *ALWAYS* OUT THERE.
HOLDING IT ALL TOGETHER FOR THE REST OF US.
TWOK
KWNK
WHA--?
AND SELFISHLY--
--I HOPED HE ALWAYS WOULD BE.
GRAH--!

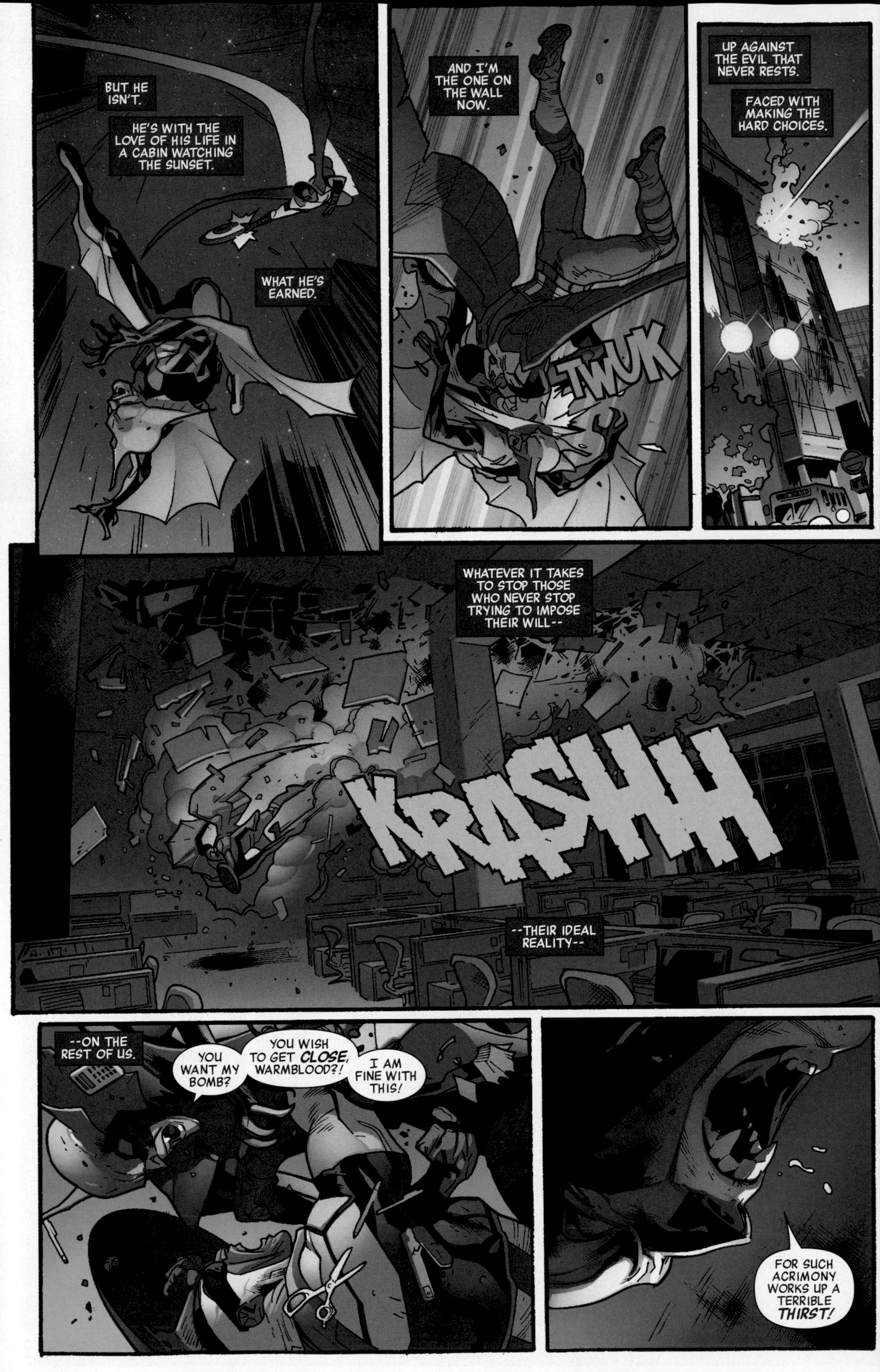
BUT HE ISN'T.
HE'S WITH THE LOVE OF HIS LIFE IN A CABIN WATCHING THE SUNSET.
WHAT HE'S EARNED.
AND I'M THE ONE ON THE WALL NOW.
TWUK
UP AGAINST THE EVIL THAT NEVER RESTS.
FACED WITH MAKING THE HARD CHOICES.
WHATEVER IT TAKES TO STOP THOSE WHO NEVER STOP TRYING TO IMPOSE THEIR WILL--
KRASHH
--THEIR IDEAL REALITY--
--ON THE REST OF US.
YOU WANT MY BOMB?
YOU WISH TO GET CLOSE, WARMBLOOD?!
I AM FINE WITH THIS!
FOR SUCH ACRIMONY WORKS UP A TERRIBLE THIRST!

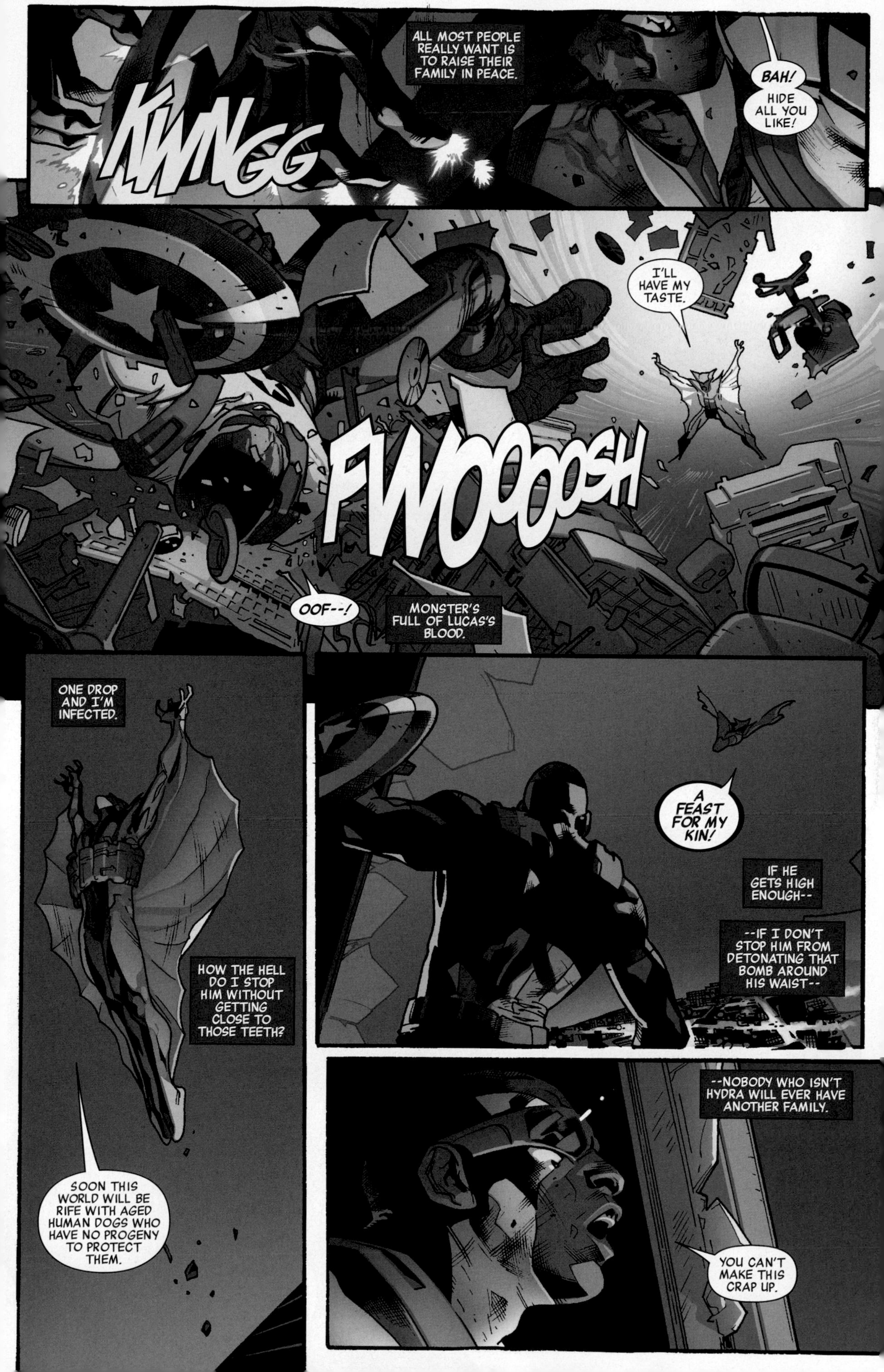
ALL MOST PEOPLE REALLY WANT IS TO RAISE THEIR FAMILY IN PEACE.
KWNGG
BAH! HIDE ALL YOU LIKE!
I'LL HAVE MY TASTE.
FWOOOOSH
OOF--!
MONSTER'S FULL OF LUCAS'S BLOOD.
ONE DROP AND I'M INFECTED.
HOW THE HELL DO I STOP HIM WITHOUT GETTING CLOSE TO THOSE TEETH?
SOON THIS WORLD WILL BE RIFE WITH AGED HUMAN DOGS WHO HAVE NO PROGENY TO PROTECT THEM.
A FEAST FOR MY KIN!
IF HE GETS HIGH ENOUGH--
--IF I DON'T STOP HIM FROM DETONATING THAT BOMB AROUND HIS WAIST--
--NOBODY WHO ISN'T HYDRA WILL EVER HAVE ANOTHER FAMILY.
YOU CAN'T MAKE THIS CRAP UP.

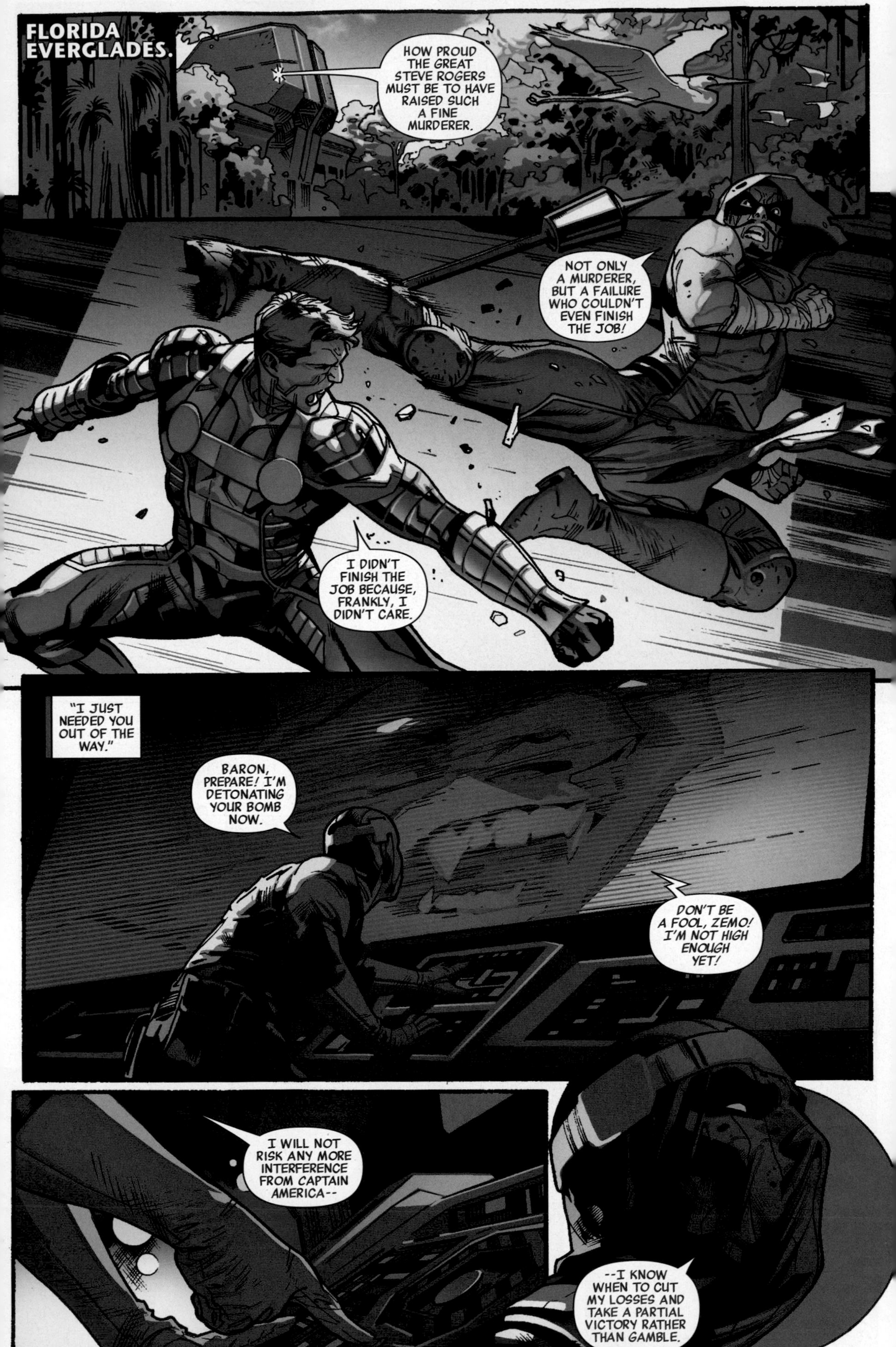
FLORIDA EVERGLADES.
HOW PROUD THE GREAT STEVE ROGERS MUST BE TO HAVE RAISED SUCH A FINE MURDERER.
NOT ONLY A MURDERER, BUT A FAILURE WHO COULDN'T EVEN FINISH THE JOB!
I DIDN'T FINISH THE JOB BECAUSE, FRANKLY, I DIDN'T CARE.
"I JUST NEEDED YOU OUT OF THE WAY."
BARON, PREPARE! I'M DETONATING YOUR BOMB NOW.
DON'T BE A FOOL, ZEMO! I'M NOT HIGH ENOUGH YET!
I WILL NOT RISK ANY MORE INTERFERENCE FROM CAPTAIN AMERICA--
--I KNOW WHEN TO CUT MY LOSSES AND TAKE A PARTIAL VICTORY RATHER THAN GAMBLE.

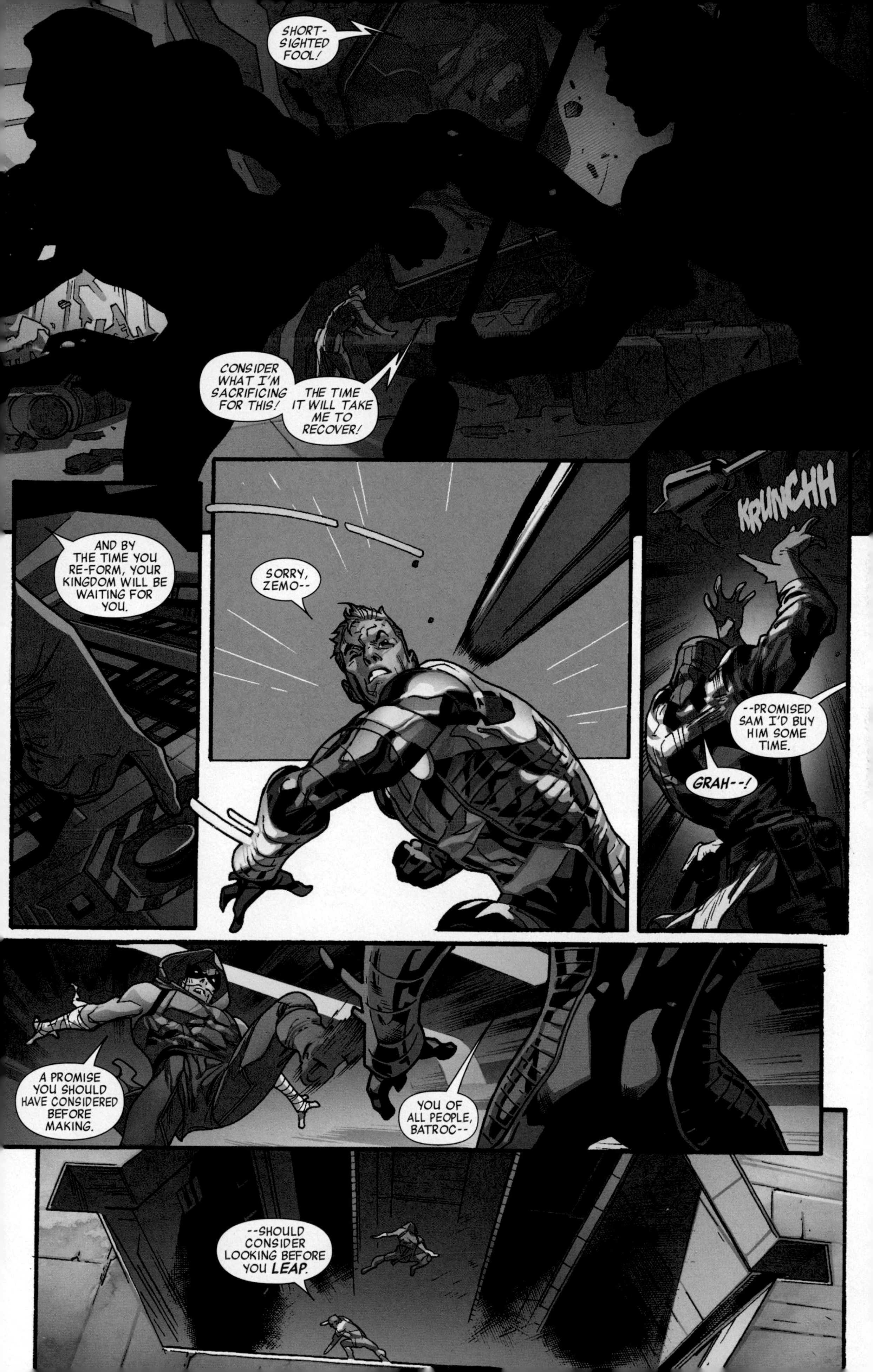
SHORT-SIGHTED FOOL!
CONSIDER WHAT I'M SACRIFICING FOR THIS!
THE TIME IT WILL TAKE ME TO RECOVER!
AND BY THE TIME YOU RE-FORM, YOUR KINGDOM WILL BE WAITING FOR YOU.
SORRY, ZEMO--
KRUNCHH
--PROMISED SAM I'D BUY HIM SOME TIME.
GRAH--!
A PROMISE YOU SHOULD HAVE CONSIDERED BEFORE MAKING.
YOU OF ALL PEOPLE, BATROC--
--SHOULD CONSIDER LOOKING BEFORE YOU LEAP.

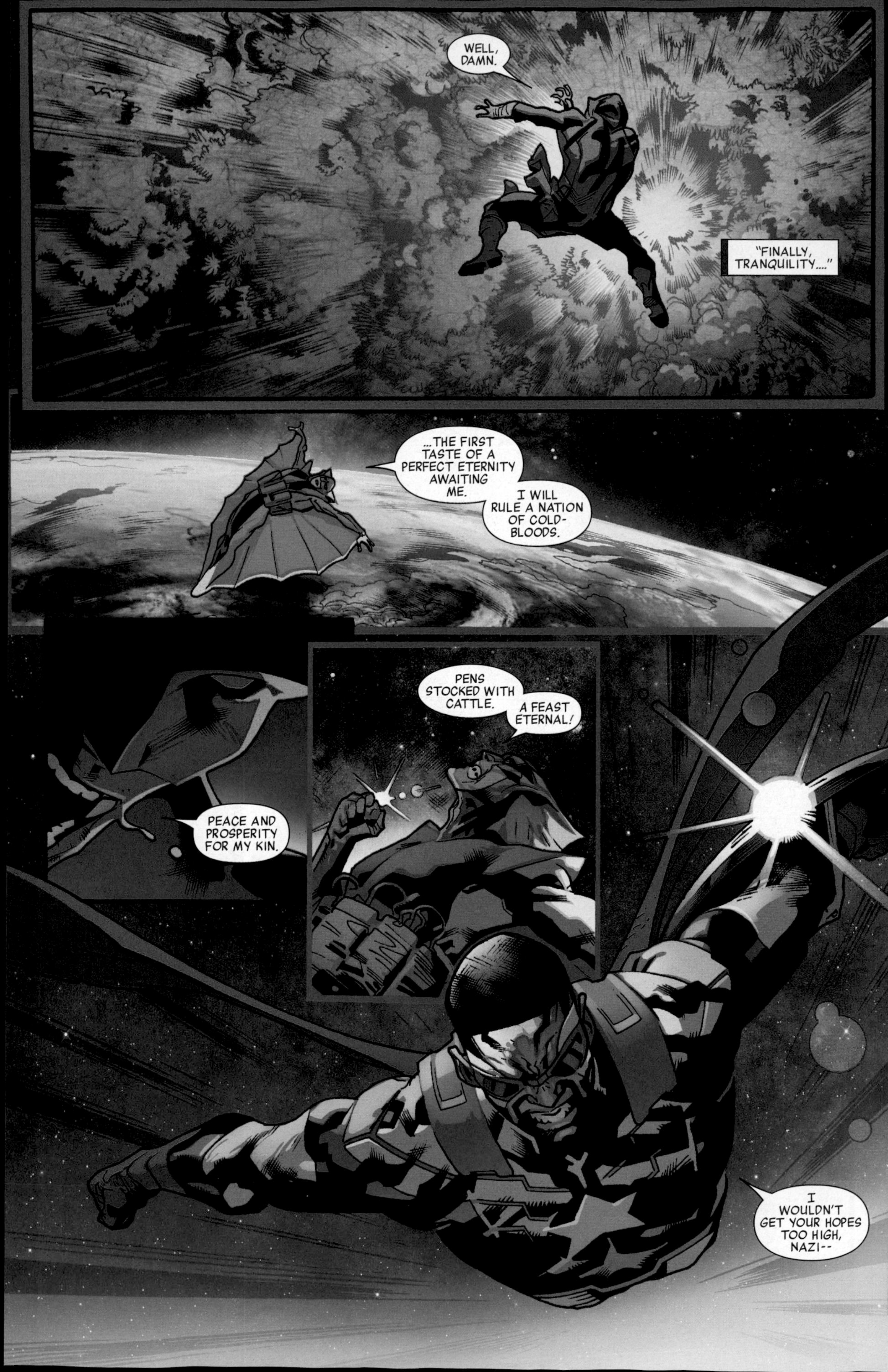
WELL, DAMN.
"FINALLY, TRANQUILITY...."
...THE FIRST TASTE OF A PERFECT ETERNITY AWAITING ME.
I WILL RULE A NATION OF COLD-BLOODS.
PEACE AND PROSPERITY FOR MY KIN.
PENS STOCKED WITH CATTLE.
A FEAST ETERNAL!
I WOULDN'T GET YOUR HOPES TOO HIGH, NAZI--

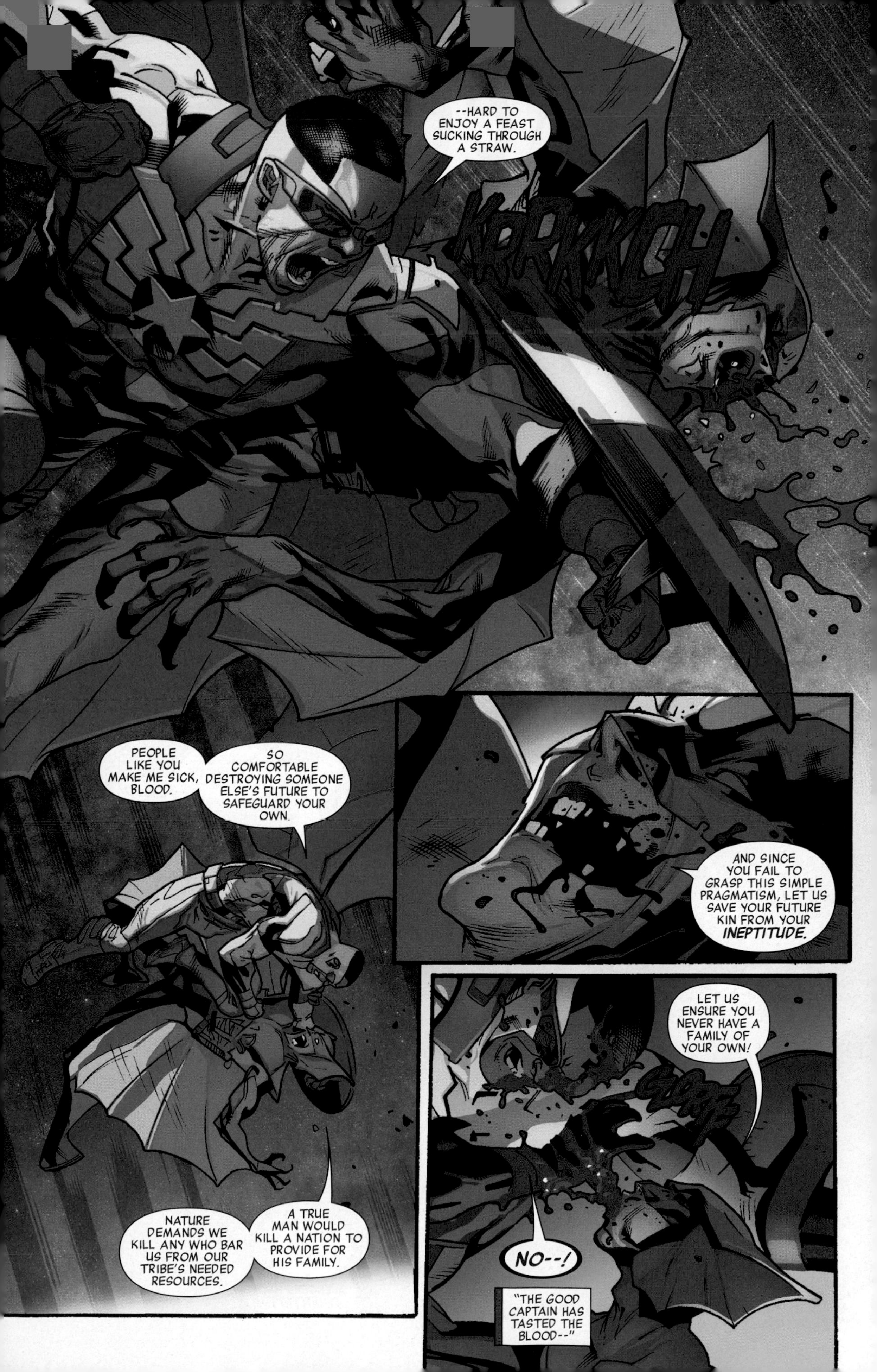
--HARD TO ENJOY A FEAST SUCKING THROUGH A STRAW.
PEOPLE LIKE YOU MAKE ME SICK, BLOOD.
SO COMFORTABLE DESTROYING SOMEONE ELSE'S FUTURE TO SAFEGUARD YOUR OWN.
NATURE DEMANDS WE KILL ANY WHO BAR US FROM OUR TRIBE'S NEEDED RESOURCES.
A TRUE MAN WOULD KILL A NATION TO PROVIDE FOR HIS FAMILY.
AND SINCE YOU FAIL TO GRASP THIS SIMPLE PRAGMATISM, LET US SAVE YOUR FUTURE KIN FROM YOUR *INEPTITUDE.*
LET US ENSURE YOU NEVER HAVE A FAMILY OF YOUR OWN!
NO--!
"THE GOOD CAPTAIN HAS TASTED THE BLOOD--"

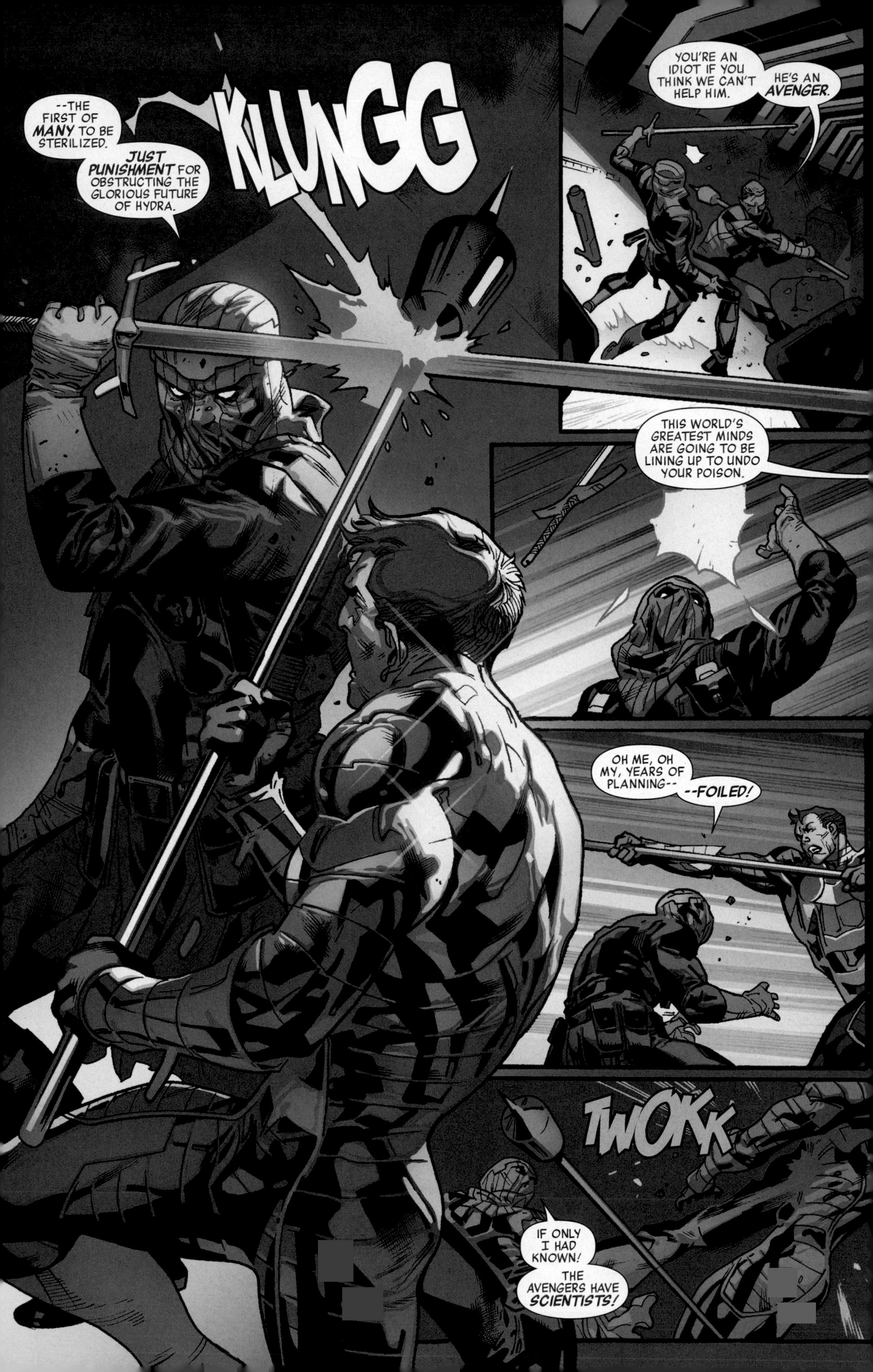
--THE FIRST OF MANY TO BE STERILIZED.
JUST PUNISHMENT FOR OBSTRUCTING THE GLORIOUS FUTURE OF HYDRA.
KLUNGG
YOU'RE AN IDIOT IF YOU THINK WE CAN'T HELP HIM.
HE'S AN AVENGER.
THIS WORLD'S GREATEST MINDS ARE GOING TO BE LINING UP TO UNDO YOUR POISON.
OH ME, OH MY, YEARS OF PLANNING--
--FOILED!
TWOKK
IF ONLY I HAD KNOWN!
THE AVENGERS HAVE SCIENTISTS!

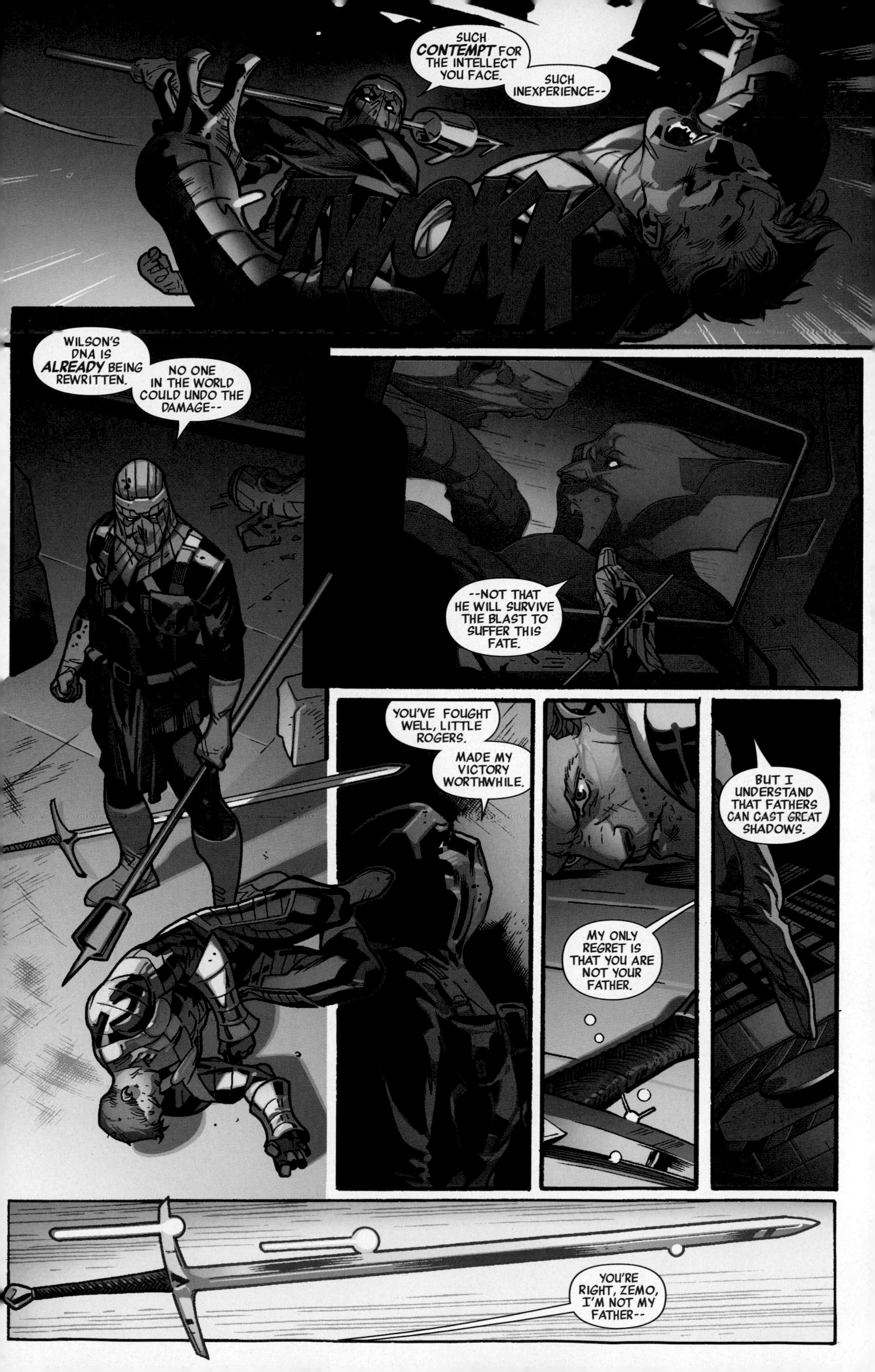
SUCH CONTEMPT FOR THE INTELLECT YOU FACE.
SUCH INEXPERIENCE--
TWOKK
WILSON'S DNA IS ALREADY BEING REWRITTEN.
NO ONE IN THE WORLD COULD UNDO THE DAMAGE--
--NOT THAT HE WILL SURVIVE THE BLAST TO SUFFER THIS FATE.
YOU'VE FOUGHT WELL, LITTLE ROGERS.
MADE MY VICTORY WORTHWHILE.
MY ONLY REGRET IS THAT YOU ARE NOT YOUR FATHER.
BUT I UNDERSTAND THAT FATHERS CAN CAST GREAT SHADOWS.
YOU'RE RIGHT, ZEMO, I'M NOT MY FATHER--

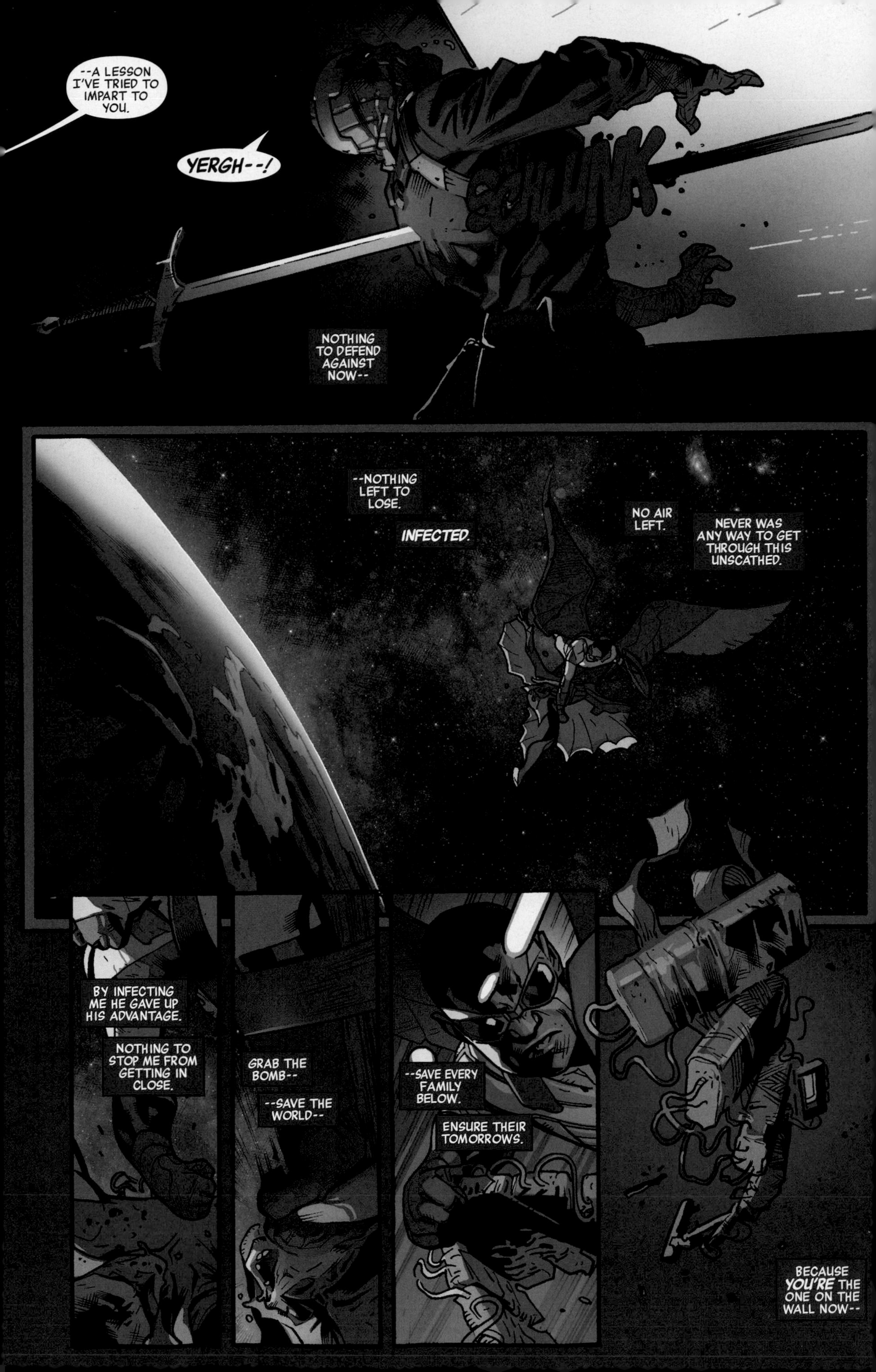
--A LESSON I'VE TRIED TO IMPART TO YOU.
YERGH--!
SCHLUNK
NOTHING TO DEFEND AGAINST NOW--
--NOTHING LEFT TO LOSE.
INFECTED.
NO AIR LEFT.
NEVER WAS ANY WAY TO GET THROUGH THIS UNSCATHED.
BY INFECTING ME HE GAVE UP HIS ADVANTAGE.
NOTHING TO STOP ME FROM GETTING IN CLOSE.
GRAB THE BOMB--
--SAVE THE WORLD--
--SAVE EVERY FAMILY BELOW.
ENSURE THEIR TOMORROWS.
BECAUSE *YOU'RE* THE ONE ON THE WALL NOW--

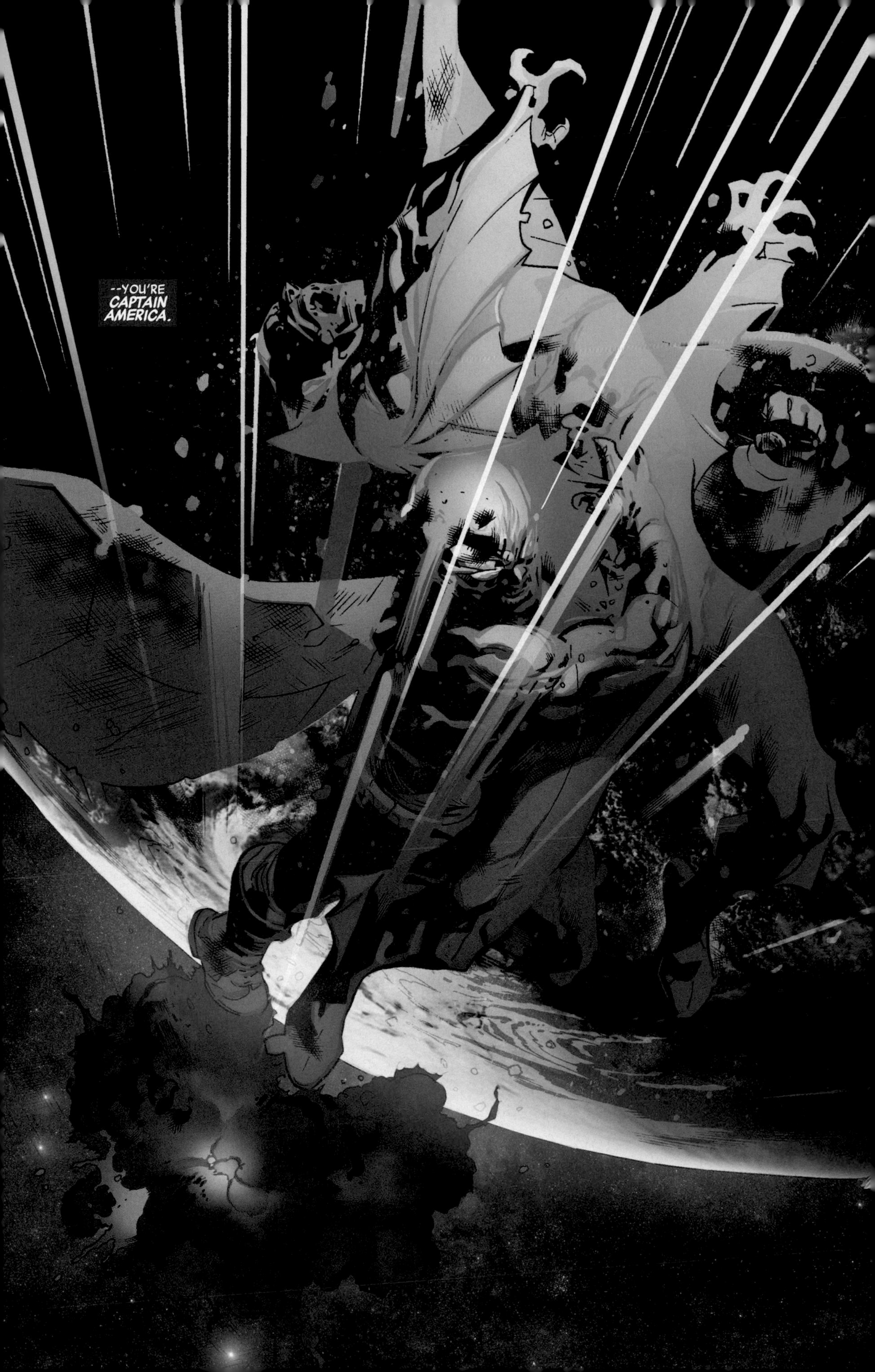
--YOU'RE CAPTAIN AMERICA.

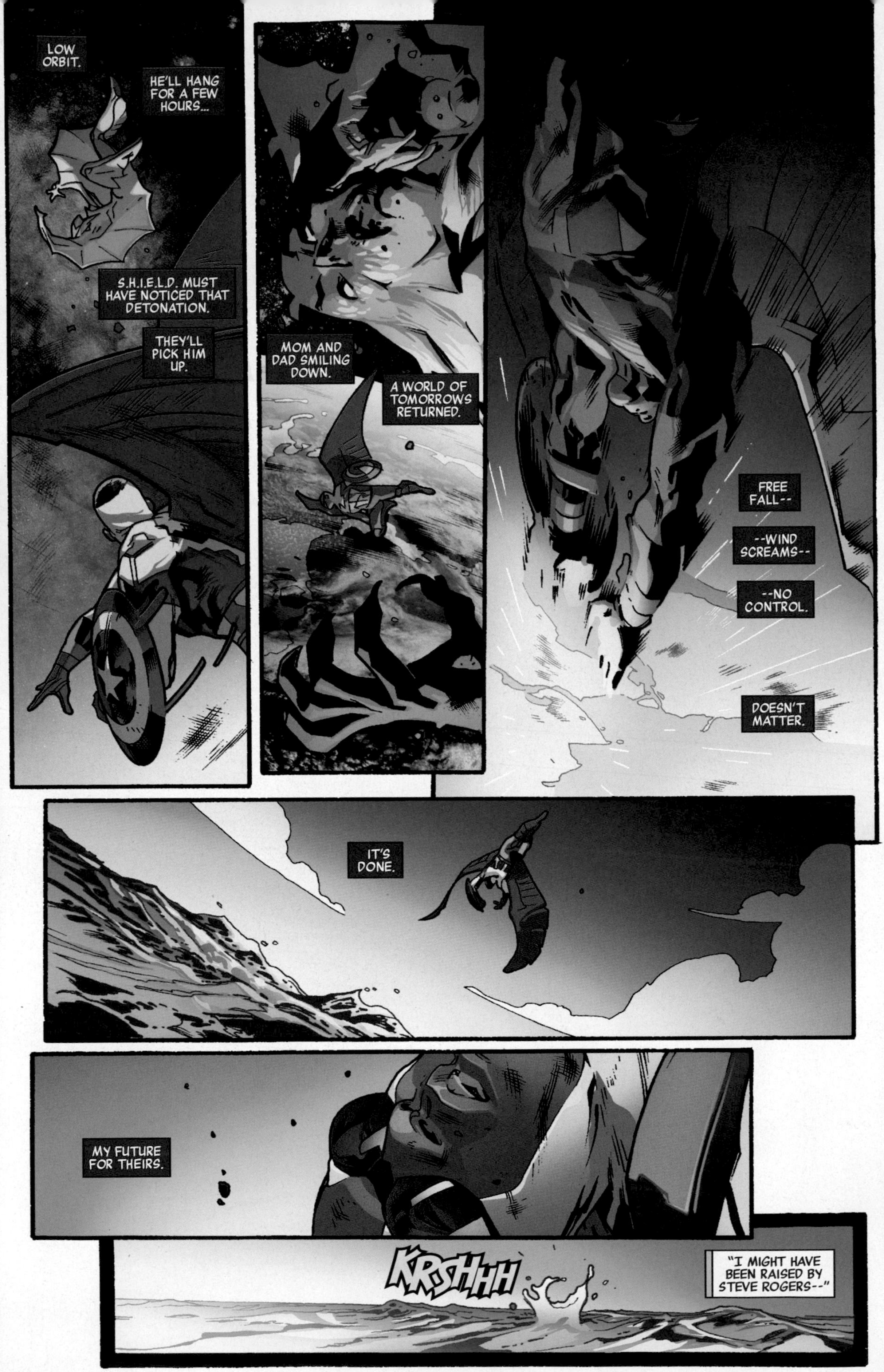
LOW ORBIT.
HE'LL HANG FOR A FEW HOURS...
S.H.I.E.L.D. MUST HAVE NOTICED THAT DETONATION.
THEY'LL PICK HIM UP.
MOM AND DAD SMILING DOWN.
A WORLD OF TOMORROWS RETURNED.
FREE FALL--
--WIND SCREAMS--
--NO CONTROL.
DOESN'T MATTER.
IT'S DONE.
MY FUTURE FOR THEIRS.
KRSHHH
"I MIGHT HAVE BEEN RAISED BY STEVE ROGERS--"

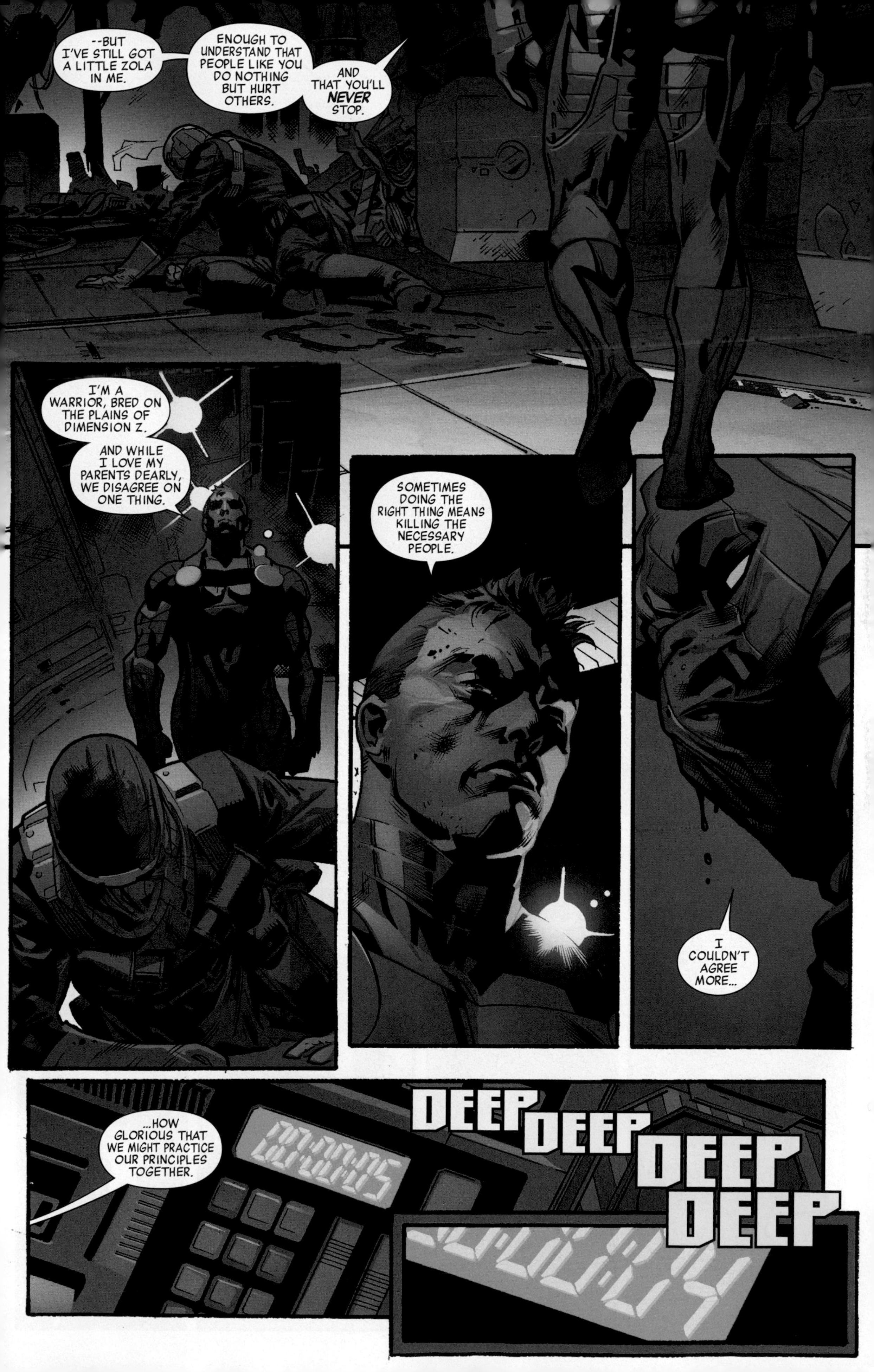
--BUT I'VE STILL GOT A LITTLE ZOLA IN ME.
ENOUGH TO UNDERSTAND THAT PEOPLE LIKE YOU DO NOTHING BUT HURT OTHERS.
AND THAT YOU'LL ***NEVER*** STOP.
I'M A WARRIOR, BRED ON THE PLAINS OF DIMENSION Z.
AND WHILE I LOVE MY PARENTS DEARLY, WE DISAGREE ON ONE THING.
SOMETIMES DOING THE RIGHT THING MEANS KILLING THE NECESSARY PEOPLE.
I COULDN'T AGREE MORE...
...HOW GLORIOUS THAT WE MIGHT PRACTICE OUR PRINCIPLES TOGETHER.
DEEP DEEP DEEP DEEP

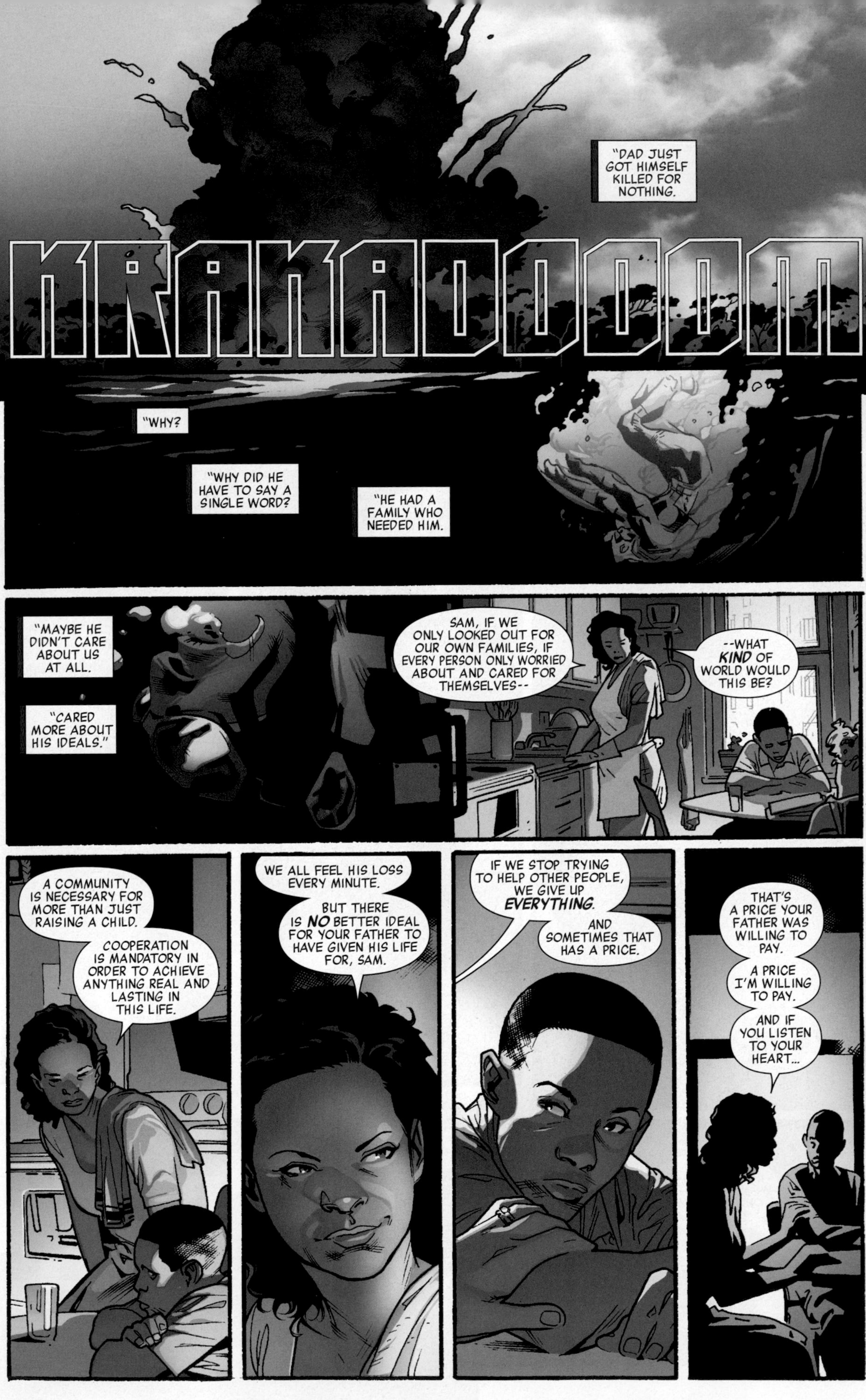
"DAD JUST GOT HIMSELF KILLED FOR NOTHING.
KRAKADOOOM
"WHY?
"WHY DID HE HAVE TO SAY A SINGLE WORD?
"HE HAD A FAMILY WHO NEEDED HIM.
"MAYBE HE DIDN'T CARE ABOUT US AT ALL.
"CARED MORE ABOUT HIS IDEALS."
SAM, IF WE ONLY LOOKED OUT FOR OUR OWN FAMILIES, IF EVERY PERSON ONLY WORRIED ABOUT AND CARED FOR THEMSELVES--
--WHAT KIND OF WORLD WOULD THIS BE?
A COMMUNITY IS NECESSARY FOR MORE THAN JUST RAISING A CHILD.
COOPERATION IS MANDATORY IN ORDER TO ACHIEVE ANYTHING REAL AND LASTING IN THIS LIFE.
WE ALL FEEL HIS LOSS EVERY MINUTE.
BUT THERE IS NO BETTER IDEAL FOR YOUR FATHER TO HAVE GIVEN HIS LIFE FOR, SAM.
IF WE STOP TRYING TO HELP OTHER PEOPLE, WE GIVE UP EVERYTHING.
AND SOMETIMES THAT HAS A PRICE.
THAT'S A PRICE YOUR FATHER WAS WILLING TO PAY.
A PRICE I'M WILLING TO PAY.
AND IF YOU LISTEN TO YOUR HEART...

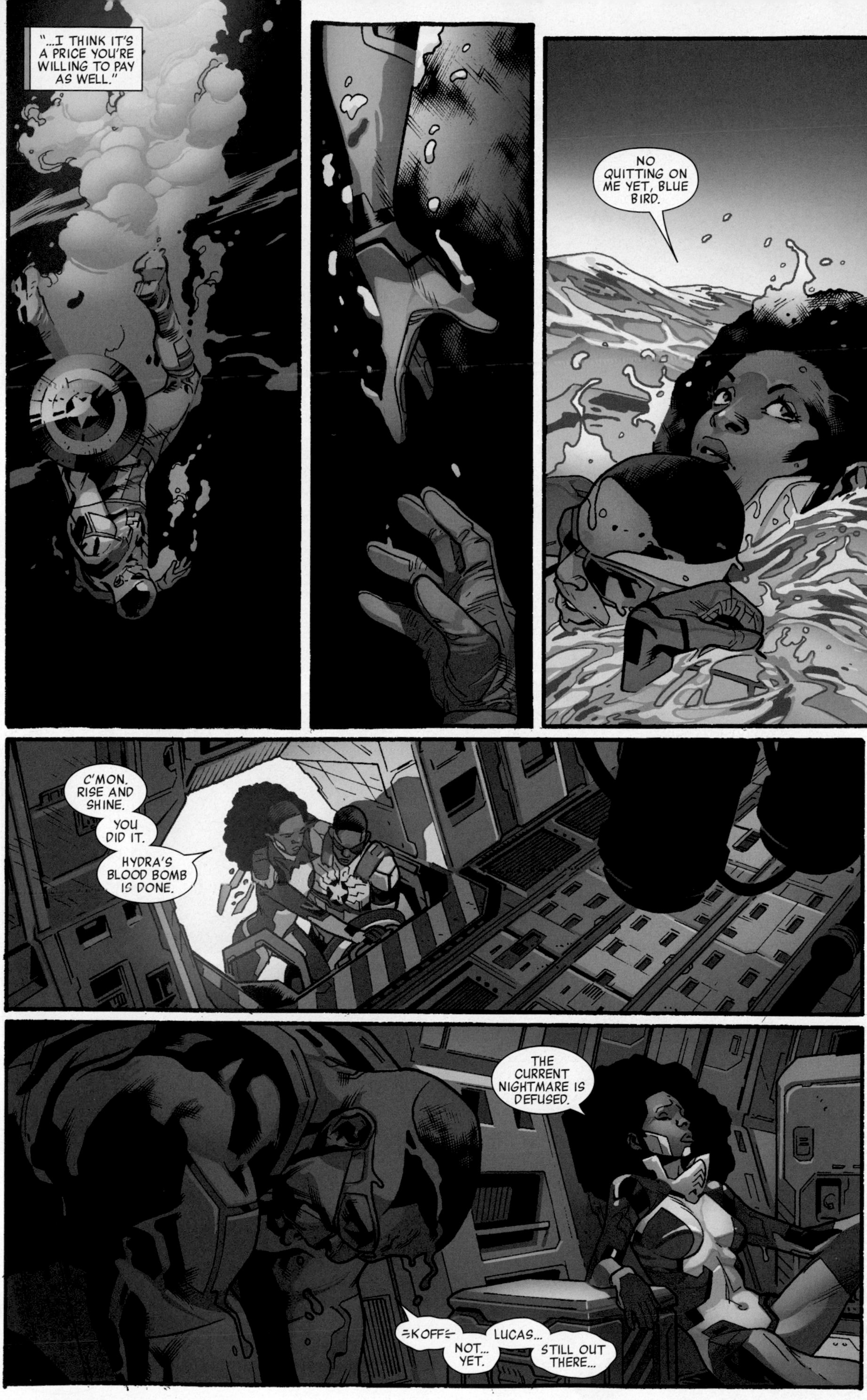
"...I THINK IT'S A PRICE YOU'RE WILLING TO PAY AS WELL."
NO QUITTING ON ME YET, BLUE BIRD.
C'MON. RISE AND SHINE.
YOU DID IT.
HYDRA'S BLOOD BOMB IS DONE.
THE CURRENT NIGHTMARE IS DEFUSED.
=KOFF=
NOT... YET.
LUCAS...
STILL OUT THERE...

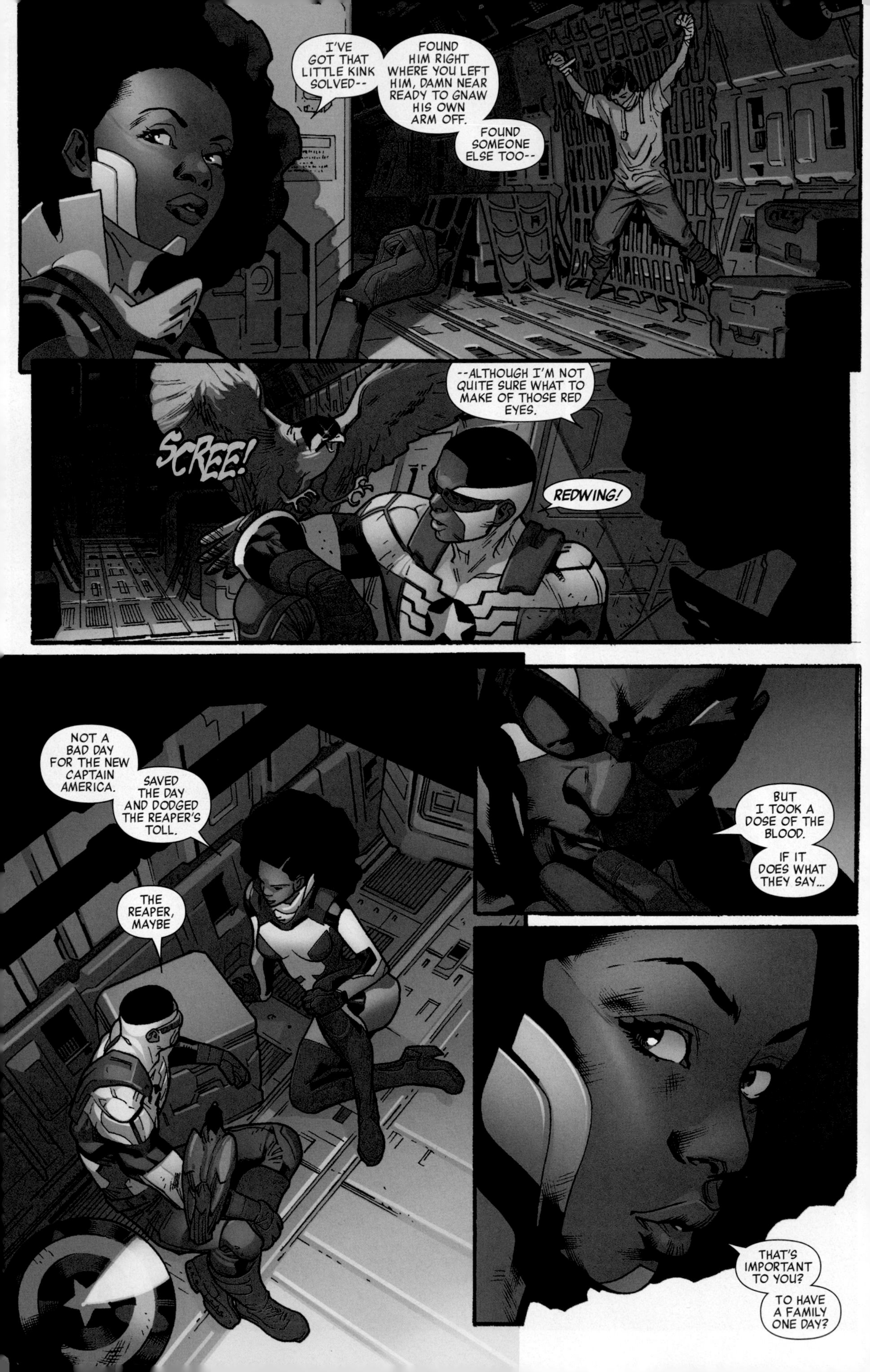
I'VE GOT THAT LITTLE KINK SOLVED--
FOUND HIM RIGHT WHERE YOU LEFT HIM, DAMN NEAR READY TO GNAW HIS OWN ARM OFF.
FOUND SOMEONE ELSE TOO--
--ALTHOUGH I'M NOT QUITE SURE WHAT TO MAKE OF THOSE RED EYES.
SCREE!
REDWING!
NOT A BAD DAY FOR THE NEW CAPTAIN AMERICA.
SAVED THE DAY AND DODGED THE REAPER'S TOLL.
THE REAPER, MAYBE
BUT I TOOK A DOSE OF THE BLOOD.
IF IT DOES WHAT THEY SAY...
THAT'S IMPORTANT TO YOU?
TO HAVE A FAMILY ONE DAY?

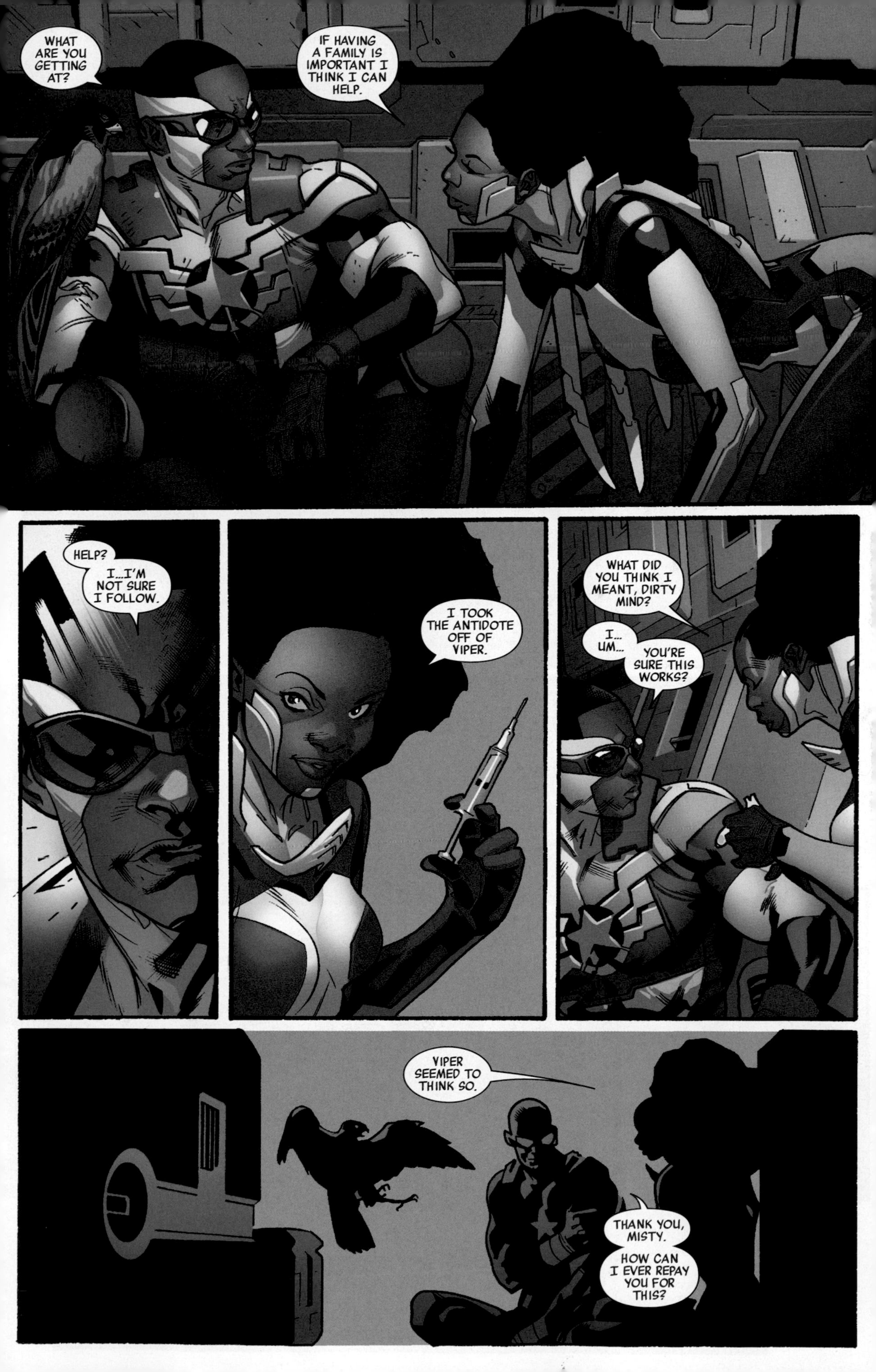
WHAT ARE YOU GETTING AT?
IF HAVING A FAMILY IS IMPORTANT I THINK I CAN HELP.
HELP?
I...I'M NOT SURE I FOLLOW.
I TOOK THE ANTIDOTE OFF OF VIPER.
WHAT DID YOU THINK I MEANT, DIRTY MIND?
I... UM...
YOU'RE SURE THIS WORKS?
VIPER SEEMED TO THINK SO.
THANK YOU, MISTY.
HOW CAN I EVER REPAY YOU FOR THIS?

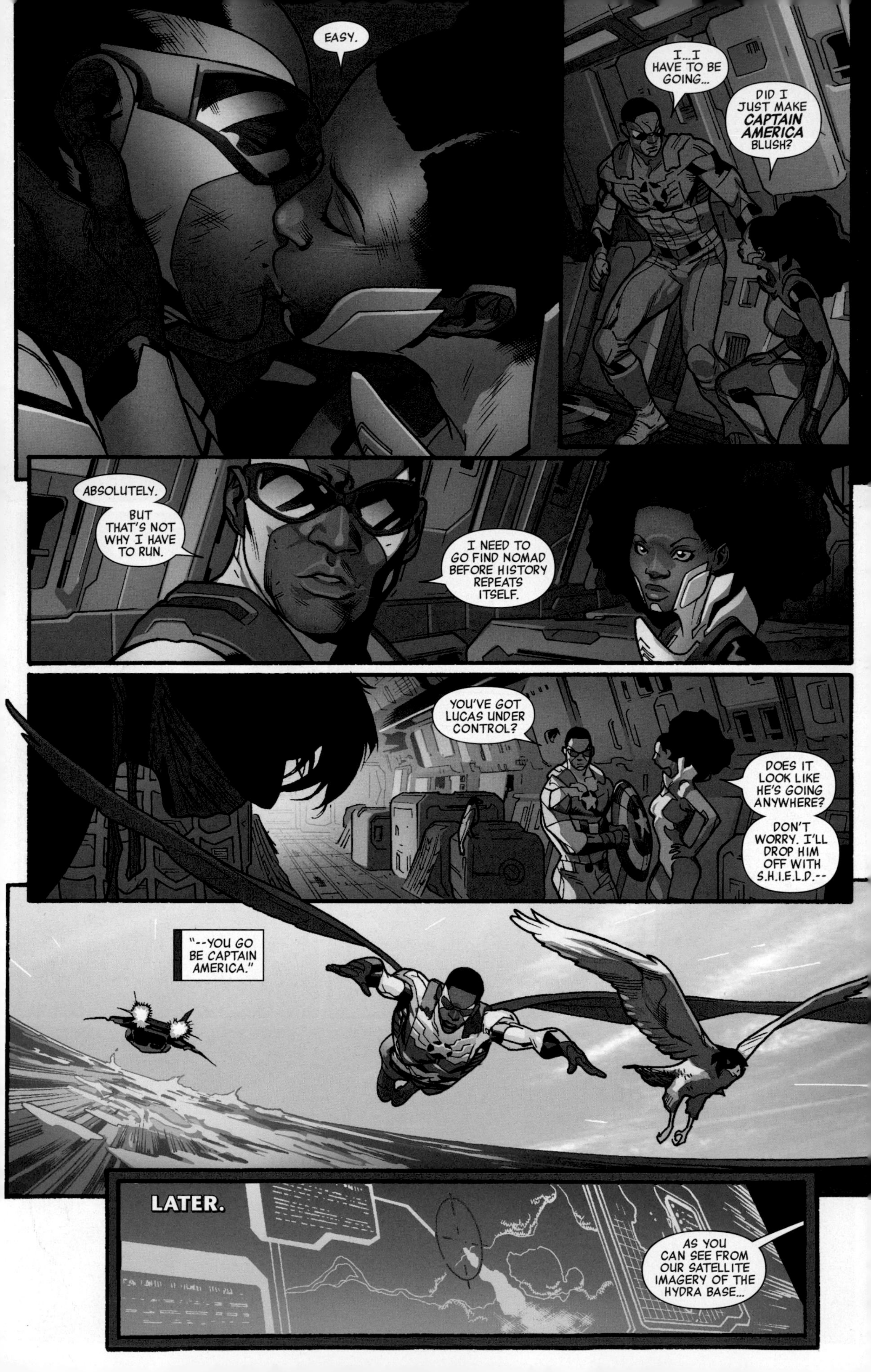
EASY.
I...I HAVE TO BE GOING...
DID I JUST MAKE *CAPTAIN AMERICA* BLUSH?
ABSOLUTELY.
BUT THAT'S NOT WHY I HAVE TO RUN.
I NEED TO GO FIND NOMAD BEFORE HISTORY REPEATS ITSELF.
YOU'VE GOT LUCAS UNDER CONTROL?
DOES IT LOOK LIKE HE'S GOING ANYWHERE?
DON'T WORRY. I'LL DROP HIM OFF WITH S.H.I.E.L.D.--
"--YOU GO BE CAPTAIN AMERICA."
LATER.
AS YOU CAN SEE FROM OUR SATELLITE IMAGERY OF THE HYDRA BASE...

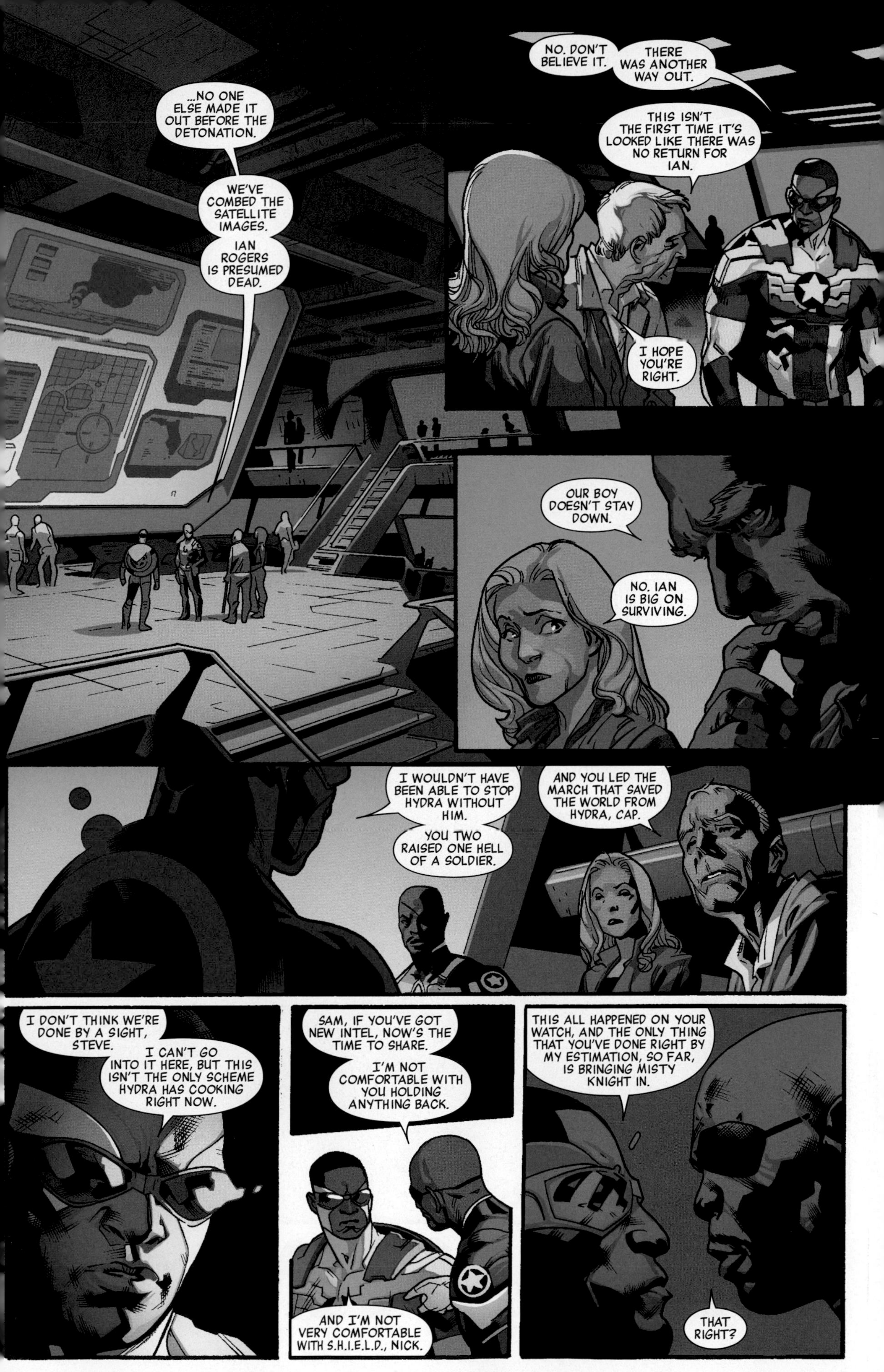
...NO ONE ELSE MADE IT OUT BEFORE THE DETONATION.
WE'VE COMBED THE SATELLITE IMAGES.
IAN ROGERS IS PRESUMED DEAD.
NO. DON'T BELIEVE IT.
THERE WAS ANOTHER WAY OUT.
THIS ISN'T THE FIRST TIME IT'S LOOKED LIKE THERE WAS NO RETURN FOR IAN.
I HOPE YOU'RE RIGHT.
OUR BOY DOESN'T STAY DOWN.
NO. IAN IS BIG ON SURVIVING.
I WOULDN'T HAVE BEEN ABLE TO STOP HYDRA WITHOUT HIM.
YOU TWO RAISED ONE HELL OF A SOLDIER.
AND YOU LED THE MARCH THAT SAVED THE WORLD FROM HYDRA, CAP.
I DON'T THINK WE'RE DONE BY A SIGHT, STEVE.
I CAN'T GO INTO IT HERE, BUT THIS ISN'T THE ONLY SCHEME HYDRA HAS COOKING RIGHT NOW.
SAM, IF YOU'VE GOT NEW INTEL, NOW'S THE TIME TO SHARE.
I'M NOT COMFORTABLE WITH YOU HOLDING ANYTHING BACK.
AND I'M NOT VERY COMFORTABLE WITH S.H.I.E.L.D., NICK.
THIS ALL HAPPENED ON YOUR WATCH, AND THE ONLY THING THAT YOU'VE DONE RIGHT BY MY ESTIMATION, SO FAR, IS BRINGING MISTY KNIGHT IN.
THAT RIGHT?

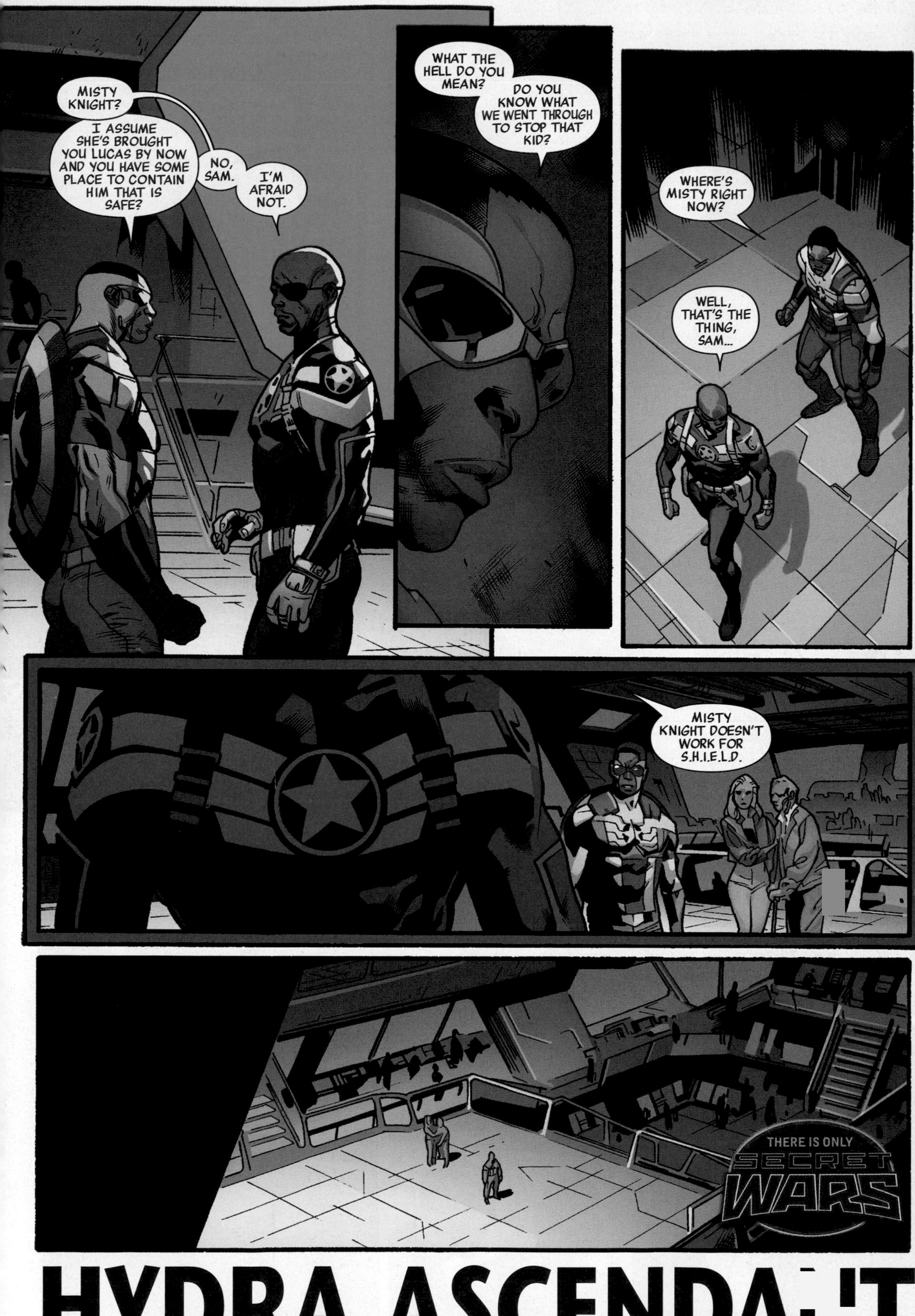
MISTY KNIGHT?
I ASSUME SHE'S BROUGHT YOU LUCAS BY NOW AND YOU HAVE SOME PLACE TO CONTAIN HIM THAT IS SAFE?
NO, SAM.
I'M AFRAID NOT.
WHAT THE HELL DO YOU MEAN?
DO YOU KNOW WHAT WE WENT THROUGH TO STOP THAT KID?
WHERE'S MISTY RIGHT NOW?
WELL, THAT'S THE THING, SAM...
MISTY KNIGHT DOESN'T WORK FOR S.H.I.E.L.D.
THERE IS ONLY
SECRET
WARS

HYDRA ASCENDANT

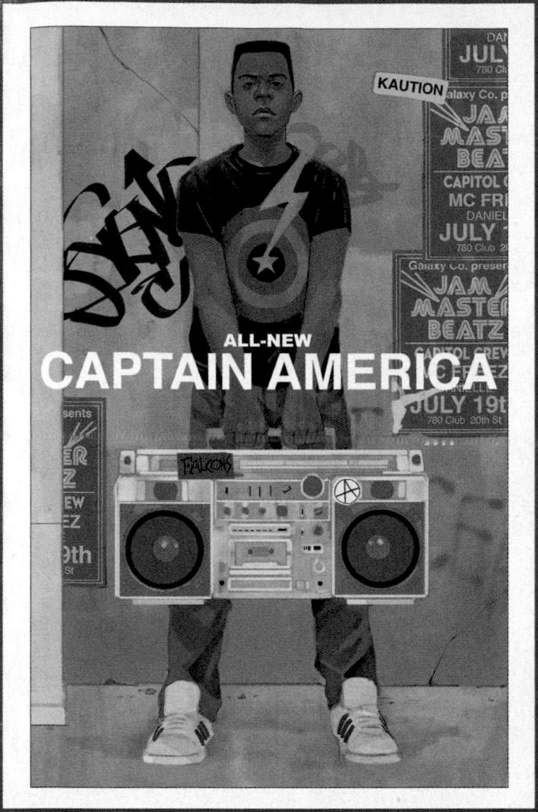
KAUTION
ALL-NEW
CAPTAIN AMERICA

#4 VARIANT BY PHIL NOTO

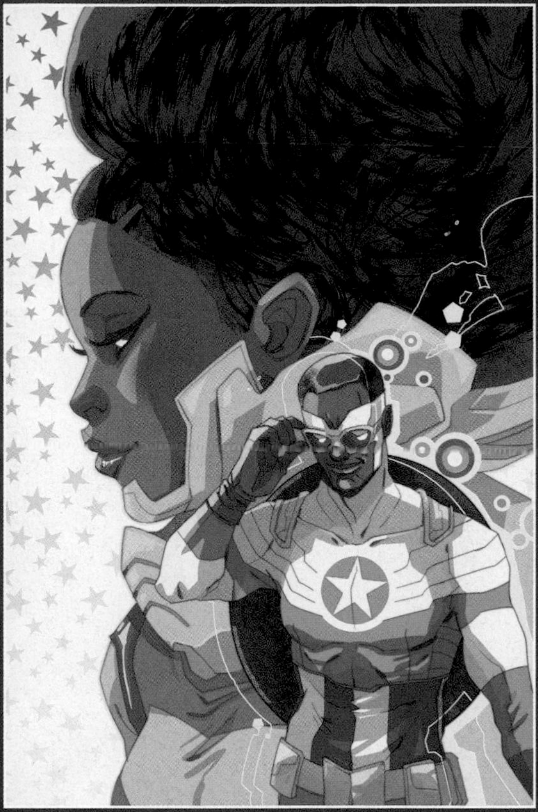

#5 VARIANT BY CHLOE POILLERAT

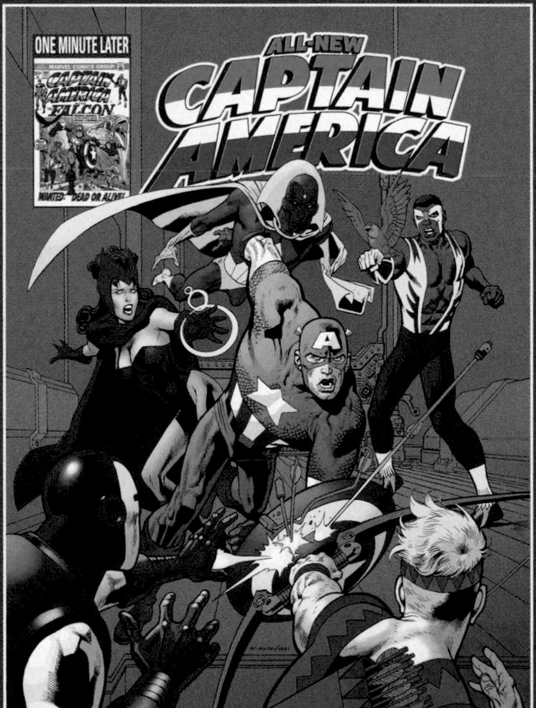
ONE MINUTE LATER
ALL-NEW
CAPTAIN AMERICA

#6 ONE MINUTE LATER VARIANT
BY KEVIN NOWLAN

TO REDEEM YOUR CODE FOR A FREE DIGITAL COPY:

1. GO TO MARVEL.COM/REDEEM. OFFER EXPIRES ON 6/24/17.
2. FOLLOW THE ON-SCREEN INSTRUCTIONS TO REDEEM YOUR DIGITAL COPY.
3. LAUNCH THE MARVEL COMICS APP TO READ YOUR COMIC NOW!
4. YOUR DIGITAL COPY WILL BE FOUND UNDER THE *MY COMICS* TAB.
5. READ & ENJOY!

YOUR FREE DIGITAL COPY WILL BE AVAILABLE ON:

MARVEL COMICS APP FOR APPLE® iOS DEVICES

MARVEL COMICS APP FOR ANDROID™ DEVICES

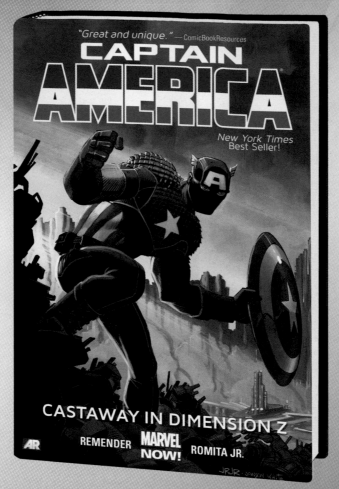

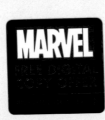